Taiwan Straits

Global Flashpoints
A series on Foreign Policy
and International Security Issues

In contributions to Global Flashpoints, authors trace the origins, structural character, and policy responses to international challenges. Contributors explain in simple and clear language the causes behind the symptoms of regional tensions that can erupt into open hostilities at any moment. Policy recommendations consider not only American interests, but those of friendly, neutral and even opposing actors on the international stage in an effort to broaden readers' comprehension of the interconnectedness of policy responses at the global level.

Titles in the Series

Somali Piracy and Terrorism in the Horn of Africa, by Christopher L. Daniels, 2012
South China Sea: Energy and Security Conflicts, by Christopher L. Daniels, 2014
Taiwan Straits: China, Taiwan, and the Role of the U.S. Navy, by Bruce A. Elleman, 2015

Taiwan Straits

*Crisis in Asia and
the Role of the U.S. Navy*

Bruce A. Elleman

ROWMAN & LITTLEFIELD
Lanham • Boulder • New York • London

Published by Rowman & Littlefield
A wholly owned subsidiary of The Rowman & Littlefield Publishing Group, Inc.
4501 Forbes Boulevard, Suite 200, Lanham, Maryland 20706
www.rowman.com

Unit A, Whitacre Mews, 26-34 Stannary Street, London SE11 4AB

Copyright © 2015 by Bruce A. Elleman

All rights reserved. No part of this book may be reproduced in any form or by any electronic or mechanical means, including information storage and retrieval systems, without written permission from the publisher, except by a reviewer who may quote passages in a review.

British Library Cataloguing in Publication Information Available

Library of Congress Cataloging-in-Publication Data

Elleman, Bruce A., 1959–
 Taiwan Straits : crisis in Asia and the role of the U.S. Navy / Bruce A. Elleman. pages cm. — (Global flashpoints)
 Includes bibliographical references and index.
 ISBN 978-0-8108-8889-0 (hardcover : alk. paper) — ISBN 978-0-8108-8890-6 (ebook)
 1. United States—Foreign relations—China. 2. China—Foreign relations—United States. 3. United States—Foreign relations—Taiwan. 4. Taiwan—Foreign relations--United States. 5. China—Foreign relations—Taiwan. 6. Taiwan—Foreign relations—China. 7. Taiwan Strait—Strategic aspects. 8. United States. Navy. Fleet, 7th. I. Title.
 E183.8.C5E45 2015
 327.73051—dc23
 2014033640

∞ ™ The paper used in this publication meets the minimum requirements of American National Standard for Information Sciences Permanence of Paper for Printed Library Materials, ANSI/NISO Z39.48-1992.

Printed in the United States of America

Contents

Maps, Figure, and Photos	vii
Acknowledgments	ix
Introduction: The Taiwan Strait	xi

1	The Historical Origins of the "Two China" Problem	1
2	The Two Chinas, the Offshore Islands, and the Korean War	13
3	The U.S. Seventh Fleet and the Taiwan Patrol Force	29
4	Debates on the U.S.–China Policy	47
5	The First Taiwan Strait Crisis, 1954 to 1955	59
6	American Military and Financial Support for the Nationalists	75
7	The Second Taiwan Strait Crisis, 1958	89
8	The Third Taiwan Strait Crisis and Sino–American Rapprochement	103
9	PRC Economic Development, Tiananmen, and the Fourth Taiwan Strait Crisis, 1995 to 1996	119
10	Beijing–Taipei Cross-Strait Tensions and Cooperation	135

Conclusion: The Taiwan Strait Challenge	149
Further Reading	163
Time Line of Major Events in the Taiwan Strait	167
U.S.–ROC Mutual Defense Treaty, 2 December 1954 (Ratified 3 March 1955; terminated by the United States in 1980)	173
The U.S. Congress Formosa Resolution (1955)	177
Shanghai Communiqué, February 28, 1972	179
Joint Communiqué on the Establishment of Diplomatic Relations between the People's Republic of China and the United States of America, December 16, 1978	185
Taiwan Relations Act, April 10, 1979	187
Joint Communiqué of the United States of America and the People's Republic of China, August 17, 1982	199
Anti-Secession Law adopted by NPC, March 14, 2005	203

Cross-Straits Economic Cooperation Framework Agreement,
    June 29, 2010   207
Acronyms   215
Bibliography   219
Index   227
About the Author   237

Maps, Figure, and Photos

Fig. 2.1	Nationalist Blockade of the Yangzi River.	18
Fig. 2.2	Taiwan's "Critical Sea Areas."	22
Fig. 2.3	Nationalist-Controlled Offshore Islands.	24
Fig. 3.1	Taiwan Patrol Force. Organizational Matrix.	33
Fig. 3.2	Typical Air Reconnaissance Mission over the Taiwan Strait.	38
Fig. 5.1	Chief of Naval Operations Admiral Arleigh A. Burke Is Greeted by Generalissimo Chiang Kai-shek in a 1955 Visit to Taiwan.	69
Fig. 6.1	USN Equipment and Training Helped the Nationalists Resupply Jinmen Island.	78
Fig. 7.1	U.S. Navy's Jinmen Convoy Operations.	95
Fig. 8.1	Missile Testing Zones North of Taiwan.	107
Fig. 8.2	Crew of *Hissem* Assisting Damaged Chinese Fishing Boat.	110
Fig. 9.1	Location of PRC Missile Tests from 1995 to 1996.	131
Fig. 10.1	1927 Nationalist Map with "Former Borders" Outer Black Line.	145

Acknowledgments

I thank those who shared their insights and expertise, including James Barber, Lyle Bien, Bob Chamberlin, Doug Hatfield, Jay Pryor, Paul Romanski, Michael Westmoreland, and James P. Wisecup. At the NWC, I benefited from the support of John B. Hattendorf, Robert Rubel, and Mary Ann Peters. In the NWC Security Office, Lenny Coleman and Sandra Blogette helped me obtain clearances to use materials at the National Archives, where I was assisted by Alan Lipton, Don Mcilwain, and Paula Ayres.

At the Naval Historical Center (now Naval History and Heritage Command), John Hodges gave me access to the U.S. Navy archives and John Greco located biographies, while Edward J. Marolda and Jeff Barlow helped me locate essential documents. At the U.S. Army Center of Military History, Mason Schaefer and Frank Shirer assisted my research. At the Air Force History Division, John Q. Smith patiently answered all my questions. At the Marine Corps History Division, Annette Amerman was very helpful, as were Rachel Kingcade and Lindsay Kleinow in the U.S. Marine Corps Research Library. Professor Andrew Lambert, King's College, provided advice on the UK National Archives, Kew Garden, and on the British Library. Ben Primer helped me use the John Foster Dulles Papers at the Seeley G. Mudd Manuscript Library, Princeton University.

I also owe a considerable debt to Alice Juda, Wayne Rowe, Robin Lima, and Bob Schnare for assistance at the NWC Library. At the NWC Press, I thank Cary Lord and Pelham Boyer. I am especially indebted to Andrew Marshall of the Office of Net Assessment for his ongoing support for this and other China-related projects. All American and British sources with a classification designation have been declassified in accordance with standard procedures in those countries.

In particular, I thank John B. Hattendorf, Edward J. Marolda, and S. C. M. Paine for reading and commenting on the entire manuscript. And a big thanks to Andrew Yoder and Bennett Graff at Rowman & Littlefield for producing this book. All mistakes, however, remain mine and mine alone.

The thoughts and opinions expressed in this publication are those of the author and are not necessarily those of the U.S. government, the U.S. Navy Department, or the Naval War College.

Introduction

The Taiwan Strait

There were valid historical reasons why the Nationalists decided to retreat to Taiwan in 1949 and, more than sixty-five years later, are still thriving there. During the seventeenth century, Zheng Chenggong (Cheng Ch'eng-kung), known in the West as Koxinga, made Taiwan his base when attempting to defeat the invading Manchus from North China. Koxinga used a number of small offshore islands—including Jinmen (formerly Quemoy) Island—as stepping stones to cross the Taiwan Strait. Beginning in 1661, he based his forces on the Penghu (Pescadores) Islands to conduct naval operations to expel the Dutch colonizers from Taiwan. In 1683, Qing forces also retook control of the island by using various offshore islands to defeat the Ming loyalists.

Taiwan has been fought over many times, including in the seventeenth century by Ming loyalists, in the eighteenth century when the Manchus put down local rebellions, and during the 1880s Sino–French War. As a result of the first Sino–Japanese War (1894–1895), China ceded Taiwan to Japan in perpetuity in the 1895 Treaty of Shimonoseki. Japan maintained control over Taiwan for fifty years, until Japan's surrender in 1945, at which point—according to the terms of the Cairo and Potsdam agreements—Taiwan was returned to China, in this case meaning the internationally recognized government of Chiang Kai-shek and his Nationalist Party.

Facing military defeat at the hands of his Chinese Communist opponents, Chiang and his advisors officially moved the government to Taiwan on 8 December 1949, the eighth anniversary (Tokyo time) of the Japanese attack on Pearl Harbor; this date symbolized Chiang's view that his fight with Soviet-backed communism was a direct continuation of his former battle with Japanese invaders. Tacit acknowledgment by Washington of this interpretation occurred a year later, when the U.S. government adopted a full strategic embargo of the People's Republic of China on 8 December 1950.

* * *

The geography of China's southeastern coastline is highly conducive to maritime activities, so having a large navy is essential to providing security. Steep mountains run mainly southeastward to the sea, before disappearing under the water. Interspersed with bays and coves are thousands of offshore islands. Zhejiang Province alone has over 1,800 islands off its coast, while Fujian Province has almost 600 and Guangdong Province approximately 550, making about 3,000 islands total, or three-quarters of all the islands along China's entire coastline. Many are too small to support settlements, while others, such as the sixty-square mile island of Jinmen, had over sixty thousand people living there in the 1950s, and it is now closer to eighty-five thousand, while the Mazu Islands have about ten thousand inhabitants.

Even though this area of China has long supported naval activity, the waters between the mainland and Taiwan are treacherous. The weather in the Taiwan Strait is highly unpredictable. The water north of Taiwan is usually quite cold, chilled by the icy Oyashio current from the Sea of Okhotsk. Meanwhile, the waters in the South China Sea tend to be balmy. Ocean currents from the islands of Micronesia split after hitting the Philippines into two branches, one southward and one that flows northward and splits into the Tsushima and Kuroshio currents. Seasonal monsoons tend to move northeast in winter and to the southwest in summer. The northeast monsoon is the more powerful of the two. Winds are at their strongest during the five months from October through February; sea currents can run southwest with an average speed of ten to fifteen miles a day to as much as sixty miles a day in the Taiwan Strait. By contrast, the southwest monsoon is weaker and more variable, usually lasting from June to August, during which time the air currents drift north and northeast at the rate of thirty miles a day.

Superimposed upon the monsoon are frequent storms. Ocean hurricanes are known as typhoons in Asia. These usually originate in the Pacific Ocean east of the Philippines, blow westward and northwestward over Luzon, and hit Taiwan from the southeast. Sailing during typhoons can be very dangerous, and fully two-thirds of China's typhoon shelters are located along the southeastern coast, along the coast of Taiwan, or in the Penghu Islands. Typhoons usually occur intermittently from June to October but are most violent in July and August, when winds can reach 145 miles an hour.

The general seaward flow of the winds favored outbound voyages from China and so have traditionally encouraged maritime voyages from the continent to Taiwan. However, the unexpected arrival of typhoons—known in Japan as kamikaze winds—has acted as a strong deterrent to naval invasions from the continent, as best shown by the destruction of not one, but two, Mongol fleets attacking Japan during the thirteenth century. This makes control of strategically located offshore islands a prerequisite for invasion; in a similar manner, control by Taiwan over these same offshore islands can protect against invasion from the mainland.

Since 1949 there have been numerous crises over the Taiwan Strait, and this book will discuss four of them: (1) 1954–1955, (2) 1958, (3) 1962, and (4) 1995–1996. In all four, it was the U.S. military, and in particular the U.S. Navy, that intervened in support of Taiwan, thereby undermining any chance that a People's Liberation Army (PLA) invasion from the mainland could be successful. With a military solution unlikely, diplomacy has more recently come to the fore, and as of February 2014 the two sides have held ten rounds of talks and signed twenty-one separate agreements, all of them intended to strengthen cross-strait relations. Still, cross-strait tensions have been high in the past, and there is no guarantee they will not ramp up again in the future. This makes the Taiwan Strait one of the most hazardous regions in the world today.

ONE

The Historical Origins of the "Two China" Problem

Although originally settled by Polynesians, Taiwan has a long history of succoring rebels from Mainland China, including during the early Qing dynasty from 1644–1683, when Ming rebels fled there to continue their fight against the Manchu invaders. Following their defeat on the mainland in 1949, the Nationalist government also retreated to Taiwan, which became the last bastion of the Republic of China (ROC). This military standoff has now continued unsettled for sixty-five years.

Although the Nationalist Chinese Navy was comparatively large in 1949, and the waters surrounding Taiwan acted as a moat protecting the island from invasion, to many it seemed almost certain that the People's Republic of China (PRC) would attack and take Taiwan, perhaps as early as the summer of 1950. The U.S. government made it clear that it had washed its hands of the Nationalists. This changed after the beginning of the Korean War on June 25, 1950, however, which seemed to be the first step in a general advance of communism throughout Asia. The possibility of a PRC invasion of Taiwan was countered on June 27, 1950, when President Harry S. Truman ordered the Seventh Fleet to "neutralize" the Taiwan Strait.

Faced with constant U.S. Navy patrols up and down the strait—which, if attacked, would have triggered the intervention of the Seventh Fleet—Mao Zedong at first postponed, and eventually cancelled altogether, the PLA's planned invasion of Taiwan. This left the two opposing Chinas facing each other across the Taiwan Strait, one espousing communism and the other a Chinese hybrid, albeit gradually strengthening over time, of Western-style democracy. While this split was similar politically to the post–World War II division of Germany into East and West, or of Korea into North and South, Taiwan's relatively small size compared to the mainland gives the appearance of David fighting Goliath. For this reason, profound differences between the PRC's centralized economy and the ROC's capitalist model had a much greater impact over time on the cross-strait balance of power.

THE DUTCH OCCUPATION AND MING INVASION

According to DNA analysis, the original inhabitants of Taiwan were related to the Polynesians living primarily farther to the south. After the Dutch occupied the East Indies (Indonesia), they moved northward to establish a base on the island of Taiwan, which had earlier been named Formosa—or "beautiful island"—by the Portuguese. In 1624, the Dutch built a fort, Zeelandia, in Anping (modern-day Tainan) in central Taiwan. They urged Chinese merchants and traders from the mainland to immigrate to Taiwan. From this strategically located base the Dutch dominated much of the coastal trade in southeast China. Perhaps because of their small size, the Dutch became early proponents of free trade, a position Britain later adopted, and their global bases allowed them to exert much greater economic clout than the tiny size of the Netherlands would normally have allowed.

Far to the north, Manchu invaders had been trying for many years to invade central China. This was in line with the long-accepted "dynastic cycle," where one ruling family-based autocracy could be defeated militarily and replaced by another. The Manchus declared that their dynasty was called the Qing. Following the collapse of the Ming dynasty in 1644, mixed Han-Mongol-Manchu military forces under Manchu control invaded northern China and slowly moved the extent of the Qing empire southward. In reaction, a group of Ming loyalists led by Zheng Chenggong (1624–1662), known in the West as Koxinga,[1] decided to retreat to Taiwan, which had, at this point, been under Dutch control for thirty-five years, since 1624.

Lacking a modern navy, offshore islands in the Taiwan Strait played a particularly important role. In April 1661, Koxinga's 25,000–man force moved from Jinmen Island to the Penghu Islands to Taiwan, based on an explicit strategy: *Clear away a thorny path to drive out the Dutch barbarians*. Koxinga's forces surrounded the Dutch stronghold at Anping. After a nine-month siege, the fortress capitulated in February of 1662. Koxinga obtained control over the island in return for allowing the Dutch to leave Taiwan unharmed; the remaining Dutch forces retreated to Batavia, their colony in the East Indies. Zheng's successful strategy used the Penghus as stepping stones. Ever since, the offshore islands in the Taiwan Strait have remained strategically important for both the defense and invasion of Taiwan.

The Ming loyalists retained control over Taiwan for another two decades, through 1683. Although the Ming loyalists opposed the central government in Beijing, which normally would make them appear to be antigovernment, because Koxinga was opposing a Manchu—not Han—dynasty, he has avoided condemnation in modern Chinese histories for being antigovernment or unpatriotic. Koxinga is instead lauded for kicking out the Dutch and is variously described by contemporary PRC sources as a "patriotic general," a "Chinese national hero," and a military leader who "commanded landing operations to expel the Dutch colonizers and recover Taiwan."[2]

Koxinga followed his military success over the Dutch by establishing an opposition government in Tainan and basing his troops on Taiwan. He also supported a massive program of Han Chinese emigration from the mainland; many of today's native Taiwanese can trace their family lines back to this exodus, just as many mainland-born Taiwanese came to the island in 1949. In just a few years, over one hundred thousand Chinese emigrated, mainly from Fujian Province. Over time, they gradually pushed the indigenous peoples into the foothills of Taiwan's central mountain range, formed their own distinctive culture, and spoke the southern Fujian Min dialect, also known today as Taiwanese.

Although Koxinga intended to continue his anti-Manchu offensive from Taiwan, hoping to overthrow the Manchus and revive Ming rule, he died soon afterward in 1662. Koxinga's successors held out against the Qing another twenty years, but Taiwan finally fell to a Qing fleet in 1683, fifty-nine years after it had been lost to the Dutch. The number sixty in Chinese thinking is considered highly important, since this represents a full cycle according to the zodiac: to have surpassed this number might have added legitimacy to the anti-Qing movement.[3] After it was reincorporated into China, Taiwan was made a prefecture of Fujian Province. It did not become a province of China until 1885.

The Han Chinese who had moved to Taiwan were not content with Manchu rule and repeatedly tried to rebel during the eighteenth century. Qing naval forces successfully intervened in Taiwan to put down one of these rebellions spanning 1787 and 1788. The Manchus, not known for their maritime prowess, staged an amphibious landing to eliminate local unrest. Although the Qing dynasty retained control over Taiwan, the island remained a remote backwater with little economic or strategic significance down through the nineteenth century. Taiwan did not become particularly prosperous until after the Japanese colonized it from 1895 to 1945; neither was it strategically significant until the Nationalist arrival on the island in 1949 overlapped with the advent of modern navies, the growth of global trade, and the Cold War.

TAIWAN AS A CONTINENTAL BACKWATER

In the late seventeenth and early eighteenth centuries, China's strategic focus remained mainly continental, not maritime. Government funding for continental campaigns against rebellions in Xinjiang and Mongolia diverted scarce tax money away from the coast, which might have otherwise been spent to develop a more modern navy. Prior to the outbreak of the first Opium War in 1839, these continental threats were considered more dangerous to the survival of the Chinese empire than any conceivable foreign maritime threat. Imperial Russia, in particular, was eager to expand into Mongolia and Xinjiang.

China's military composition did not support a strong naval force. After 1644, the Qing segregated the military by race, with eight banners each of Manchu, Han, and Mongol troops. Regular infantry and navy were composed mainly of Han Chinese, who were assigned to minor garrisons along China's lengthy coastline and throughout southern China, far from Beijing. By contrast, the Manchu banners were spread throughout China, with especially large garrisons of Manchu cavalry located in sensitive frontier regions in the north and in major cities along the Yangzi River to protect the Grand Canal carrying much needed grain from south to north. Regional navies were purposefully left weak; many naval officers were assigned to their posts because of academic success in the Imperial exams rather than because they held any real knowledge of military or naval affairs.[4]

By the end of the eighteenth century, when European merchants first began arriving in force in southern China, the number of reliable bannermen loyal to the Qing court was estimated at a quarter of a million men, while Han Chinese troops numbered about six hundred sixty thousand.[5] Since so few of China's top troops were assigned to coastal areas, the Qing navy was not particularly proficient. This meant that, in terms of organization, force distribution, and the comparative backwardness of their weaponry and ships, the Han Chinese navy could not compete effectively with their Western counterparts.

China put severe restrictions on foreign trade, which could only be conducted in the southern city of Guangzhou (Canton), the capital of Guangdong province. These policies undermined maritime trade with the West. Prior to the first Opium War (1839–1842), the Qing navy focused its attention mainly on China's immediate neighbors, especially Japan and Vietnam, the only two Asian countries that had successfully repelled Chinese naval forces in the past. When under attack, the Chinese navy had traditionally halted maritime invaders by blocking harbors with log booms and chains strung from a row of floating junks. The Chinese could also stop a naval foe by utilizing various offshore islands, many of them outfitted with impregnable—at least, by premodern standards—fortresses armed with cannons. China also made use of embargoes. As a last resort, foreign trade in Canton could be halted by the Chinese government, and Beijing could simply wait until the attackers gradually weakened and dispersed; after the foreign threat was gone, normal trade could then be resumed.

Prior to the nineteenth century, any conceivable maritime threat remained largely regional and so could be managed by a small, Han-dominated naval force, which depended mainly on defensive strategies, such as trade embargoes. Qing coastal-defense strategies included three key elements: (1) keeping maritime threats at arm's length, as opposed to fighting continental enemies in wars of extermination, (2) garrisoning less-dependable Han Chinese divisions in the south and southeast to protect the coast, as opposed to assigning loyal Manchu bannermen to protect the vulnerable borders and the Grand Canal, and (3) adopting trade restrictions and defensive coastal-defense strategies, rather than utilizing more offensive strategies.

Although extremely effective against regional enemies, these three elements had a negative impact on how Chinese strategic thinkers were to face the newly emerging threat from Europe. After centuries of battling Asian fleets, the Qing navy proved to be particularly ill suited to opposing the arrival of the deep-sea European navies. Exacerbating these strategic limitations was the fact that the comparative backwardness of the Han-dominated Chinese navy was to some degree intentional, since China's Manchu rulers were well aware that any weapon they provided the Han troops might one day be turned against them during a mutiny.[6] Therefore, keeping China's naval forces weak and divided had positive benefits for Manchu rule.

Such domestic security concerns ultimately created the ingredients for an international military disaster during the early nineteenth century, when Chinese naval forces first encountered the West in battle and subsequently lost both the first Opium War and second Opium War (1856–1860). China was forced to open more ports to foreign trade and ceded lands—including the island of Hong Kong not far from Canton—in perpetuity to foreign powers. So far, the many other small islands off the Chinese coastline and the much larger island of Taiwan had been largely ignored by Westerners, but a rapidly westernizing Japan soon set its gaze on these highly strategic islands.

JAPAN FORGES AHEAD OF CHINA

While Chinese leaders were focusing on resisting the West, their contemporaries in Japan were focusing on using Western methods in order to counter Western power. Unlike the Chinese, Japanese officials proved willing to adapt Western institutions. One of Japan's first actions was to reform its military. This, in turn, allowed for naval expansion both to the north, to take Hokkaido and the Kurile Islands, and to the south, to make its claim to the Ryukyu Islands, including Okinawa at the far north and the Senkakus (Diaoyu Islands in Chinese) to the south. Later, the Japanese empire would expand even further to include Taiwan. Much of Japan's southern maritime expansion would come at China's expense, and certain islands—such as the Diaoyus—are still in dispute today.

Sino–Japanese diplomatic relations were opened on July 24, 1871, in accordance with Western norms of juridical equality. Many Chinese conservatives opposed signing a treaty with Japan, however, because they regarded that state to be a tributary, not an equal. The treaty mandated trade at the various treaty ports, mutual consular jurisdiction, mediation to help the other against a hostile third party, and recognition of the territorial possessions of the other. Japan and China did not agree on which country held sovereignty over the Ryukyu Islands (Liuqiu Islands in Chinese), which had paid tribute to both.

China had already ceded the island of Hong Kong to Britain and Macao to Portugal. It had also lost control over large but ill-defined Siberian and central Asian territories to Russia. Japanese claims to the Ryukyu Islands for the first time put one tributary at risk of being taken over by another. The Japanese referred to a group of over seventy islands stretching for more than eight hundred miles as the Nansei Island Chain. Since the beginning of the Ming dynasty these islands had paid tribute to China and had been registered as tributaries since 1372. Beginning in 1609, however, the Satsuma fief in Japan had dominated these islands politically but had allowed the Ryukyu Islands to continue sending tribute missions to Beijing to avoid disrupting trade with China. A massacre of fifty-four shipwrecked Ryukyu sailors by Taiwanese aborigines became the pretext for Japan to claim the island chain. The Japanese government immediately protested to China on behalf of the sailors and their families. The Qing court responded that the murders were an internal matter, since both the Ryukyu Islands and Taiwan were Chinese.

When Beijing refused to take action against the Taiwanese aborigines, which it acknowledged were living in a province of China but stressed this area had never before been under Beijing's administrative control, the Japanese launched a punitive expedition against Taiwan. In 1874, the Japanese expedition occupied the northern coast of Taiwan. Beijing threatened to send its own ships but lacked an adequately modern naval force to respond. Chinese land forces were preoccupied at the exact same time putting down the Panthay, Donggan, and Xinjiang Muslim rebellions far inland. As a result, China agreed to open diplomatic negotiations with Japan to resolve the dispute.

The Chinese and Japanese negotiators disagreed whether or not Japan's naval expedition had broken the nonaggression provisions of the Sino–Japanese treaty of 1871. The Japanese negotiator argued that China's lack of administrative control over the Taiwanese aborigines meant that there was no violation of the nonaggression clauses. The Chinese negotiators acquiesced to this interpretation and did not condemn Japan's action. When China agreed to pay a 500,000 tael (US$750,000) indemnity both to cover the cost of Japan's expedition and to compensate the murdered Ryukyu sailors' families, Japanese sovereignty was implied. The last Ryukyu tribute mission traveled to China in 1875, while in 1879 Japan ousted the royal family, annexed the islands, and officially incorporated them into Okinawa Prefecture.

China's inability to protect its national security was no longer confined to the Western countries but now also included Japan. Funds that China might otherwise have spent on the acquisition of warships had instead been spent suppressing the Muslim Rebellion in Xinjiang and diplomatically resolving the Ili Crisis with Russia. The Qing viceroy of Zhili Province, Li Hongzhang, led a group of progressive Qing officials to push for building a proposed forty-eight-ship navy, arguing that Beijing was most vulnerable mainly from the coast, not from the western borderlands. But because of the constant Russian threat in Xinjiang, the Qing continued to allocate most of China's limited military funds to frontier defense. Naval expenditures were largely wasted on incompatible equipment divided among uncoordinated commands.

FOREIGN THREATS TO CHINA'S TRIBUTARIES

China soon faced other European challenges on its southern periphery, where most of its neighbors paid tribute to Beijing. In particular, French efforts to dominate its tributary state of Annam (north and central Vietnam) were considered to be particularly dangerous. The Chinese government hoped to use its recently modernized navy to force the French government to back down, but France had an even better state-of-the-art navy, capable of efficiently deploying troops in the Vietnam theater, and more than capable of countering the Chinese naval fleets. The French even took Taiwan hostage to force China to come to terms. The Sino–French War in Vietnam (1884–1885) would eventually lead to China's loss of a second tributary state—Vietnam.

Vietnam had intermittently fallen under Chinese control as early as the reign of Han Wudi (140–87 b.c.) and as late as the Tang dynasty (a.d. 618–907), after which it gained its hard-fought independence. During the Qing period, Vietnam sent tributary missions to China. But beginning in the seventeenth century, Western influence in Vietnam increased with the arrival of the Jesuits. In 1859, antimissionary riots gave the French an excuse to send troops, which transformed Vietnam's three southernmost provinces into a French colony in 1862. In 1874, France completed the task of turning Vietnam into a protectorate when it obtained rights to navigate the Red River in northern Vietnam. This agreement not only confirmed French control over Vietnam's foreign affairs but also French domination over foreign trade with northern Vietnam. By 1880, the French had built forts along the Red River and had stationed troops as far north as Hanoi and Haiphong.

Faced with this growing threat, the government of Vietnam called on China for assistance. Despite French opposition, Vietnam sent tributary missions to Beijing in 1877 and 1881. As the suzerain power, Qing dynasty could not ignore the request of a tributary to send troops, particularly after the loss of the Ryukyu Islands to Japan. Therefore, China intervened in 1883, stationing its forces close to the Sino–Vietnam border. The Chinese troops were more numerous than their French counterparts, but their training remained inferior. In August 1884, the French expanded the war in Vietnam to Taiwan, blockading the island and bombarding the forts at Keelung, at its northern extremity. But a larger Chinese force under the former commander of the Anhui army forced the French to withdraw from the island.

On August 23, 1884, a French fleet of eight ships destroyed a Chinese regional fleet in port at Fuzhou Harbor. The French then proceeded to blockade the Nanyang Fleet on the Yangzi River, cutting the flow of tribute grain up the Grand Canal to the capital. When on August 26, 1884, the Qing court officially declared war on France, the French made a second—this time successful—attempt to take Taiwan while maintaining the blockade of the Yangzi River fleet. Like the Japanese before them, French control over Taiwan was limited to the northern coast, but it gave enormous leverage over the sea-lanes passing nearby through the Taiwan Strait. This French strategy put huge pressure on China to negotiate peace.

Facing defeat, China called off the fighting on April 4, 1885, in order to negotiate a settlement with the French minister in China. The agreement, concluded on June 9, 1885, recognized all former French treaties with Vietnam, transforming it into a French protectorate. The peace settlement also entailed the opening of five treaty ports along China's southern border. In return, the French agreed to evacuate Taiwan and the Penghu Islands, and China paid no indemnity. The Qing responded to the crisis by formally integrating Taiwan into the Chinese administrative system, making it a province in 1885. A decade later, however, China would lose the island province—apparently permanently—to Japan.

CHINA LOSES TAIWAN IN THE SINO–JAPANESE WAR

During the first Sino–Japanese War (1894–1895), Japan and China fought mainly in Korea and Manchuria, but near the end of the war Japan continued southward to take Taiwan and the Penghu Islands. This potentially cut off the sea-lanes running through the Taiwan Strait. A pincer movement on Beijing from Manchuria and Shandong was then sufficient to bring the Qing dynasty to the bargaining table. The Qing Dynasty had to choose between settling the war on Japanese terms or risking rebellion by its own Han subjects. Li Hongzhang's military strategy had been to avoid war if possible and, after it broke out, to secure foreign mediation to broker a peace on Chinese terms. But as with France ten years before, this strategy proved insufficient against states that had profited from the Industrial Revolution.

Japan's victory reversed the long-standing balance of power in Asia, unseating China as the dominant regional power. The war went badly for China, and negotiating peace arguably went even worse. Rather than negotiating seriously with Japan, the Chinese government sent two lower-level sets of delegates to Tokyo; both attempts were rejected. Had China appointed high-ranking and properly credentialed representatives for either of the earlier two peace missions, it might have retained Taiwan and the Penghu Islands, because the Japanese took these only in the final days of the war. In other words, China's failure to take peace negotiations seriously came at a very high price, and it lost these strategic islands to Japan as a result.

The separation of Taiwan and the Penghu Islands from the mainland has effectively hemmed in Chinese naval ambitions. Through 1945, the geographic arc composed of the Japanese archipelago, the Ryukyu Islands, the Senkakus, Penghus, and Taiwan continued to frustrate China's ambitions to project power from its coastline. Some Chinese commentators even point to this first island chain (the second island chain is much farther out from the Chinese coast and includes the American-held island of Guam) as "blockading" China's free access to the Pacific Ocean.

The Qing court finally became desperate to achieve a peace settlement. Li Hongzhang and Prime Minister Ito Hirobumi signed the Treaty of Shimonoseki on April 17, 1895. The main points of the peace treaty included (1) recognition of Korean independence, (2) a two hundred million tael indemnity, (3) the permanent cession of Taiwan, the Penghu Islands, and the Liaodong Peninsula (the transfer of Liaodong was later reversed by the triple intervention of Russia, France, and Germany), (4) the opening of four additional treaty ports, and (5) the right of foreigners to open factories, manufacturing plants, and other industrial enterprises, thereby opening up China to direct foreign investment, making possible rapid industrialization, particularly in the treaty ports.

The Treaty of Shimonoseki marked the epochal reversal in the Far Eastern balance of power. Japanese control of Taiwan and the Penghu Islands marked the beginnings of the Japanese Empire that would later challenge China in the second Sino–Japanese War (1937–1945). Japanese colonization of Taiwan also marked a sharp divergence between Taiwanese and Chinese history, since Japan implemented a Meiji-style reform program for Taiwan, which the Taiwanese people generally profited from. The Taiwanese economy rapidly developed under Japanese management. When Taiwan was returned to China in 1945, it quickly became one of the most developed provinces in China.

CONCLUSIONS

Taiwan was invaded and separated from China many times, in particular by the Dutch, the Ming loyalists, the French, and finally the Japanese. But it was the Sino–Japanese War of 1894 and 1895 that marked what appeared to be the "permanent" cession of Taiwan. This event was in many ways the origin of the two-China problem today. Henceforth, Taiwanese development would diverge radically from that of the Chinese mainland, creating a unique mix of Japanese industry and administration with Taiwanese work ethic and culture. After the Nationalists fled to Taiwan in 1949, they led the island nation on a new path that included both modern industry and—eventually—the creation of a true democratic government.

While it appeared certain that the PRC might try to invade and retake Taiwan, the United States decided to protect it from invasion when the Korean War broke out the next year. As of June 1950, the U.S. Navy's Seventh Fleet began patrolling the Taiwan Strait, neutralizing it so that neither side could attack and spread the war from Korea further south. The U.S. Navy's Taiwan Patrol Force was active from the summer of 1950 until 1979 and arguably continued sporadically even after that date. At twenty-nine years in duration, the Taiwan Patrol Force was one of the most successful naval operations in modern history, since—as the most obvious symbol of American power—it ensured that frictions over the Taiwan Strait did not escalate into full-blown war.[7]

U.S. Navy ships acted both as a buffer between the two antagonists and also as a trip wire in case of aggression, which happened twice in the 1950s, during the first (1954–1955) and second (1958) Taiwan Strait crises, and once again in a third (1962) crisis, at which point additional U.S. Navy vessels were called in to assist. Even after the Taiwan Patrol Force was terminated in 1979, it continued in spirit, as shown by a fourth (1995–1996) Taiwan Strait crisis. The U.S. Seventh Fleet's constabulary role continues largely unchanged to this day, as U.S. Navy vessels stand ready to intercede in the PRC's military, economic, and political relations with her maritime neighbor across the Taiwan strait.

NOTES

1. This transliteration comes from his Ming title, "Lord of the Imperial Surname," which in the Chinese Wade-Giles transliteration system reads as "Kuo Hsing Yeh."

2. Yang Zhiben 杨志本, ed., 中国海军百科全书 [*China Navy Encyclopedia*], vol. 2 (Beijing: 海潮出版社 [Sea Tide Press], 1998), 1,912–14.

3. Taiwan was separated from China between 1624 and 1683, or for fifty-nine years, while during the late nineteenth century, Taiwan was ceded to Japan after the Sino–Japanese War of 1894–1895 but was reclaimed again in 1945 after only fifty years. Currently, Taiwan has been separated from the PRC for just over sixty-five years.

4. Frank A. Kierman Jr. and John K. Fairbank, eds., *Chinese Ways in Warfare* (Harvard, MA: Harvard University Press, 1974).

5. Ralph L. Powell, *The Rise of Chinese Military Power, 1895–1912* (Princeton, NJ: Princeton University Press, 1955), 8–13.

6. See Christopher Bell and Bruce A. Elleman, eds., *Naval Mutinies of the Twentieth Century: An International Perspective* (London: Frank Cass, 2003).

7. For more on the Taiwan Patrol Force, see the February 24, 2003, report by Edward J. Marolda, "Invasion Patrol: The Seventh Fleet in Chinese Waters," Naval History and Heritage Command, accessed December 13, 2010, http://www.history.navy.mil/colloquia/cch3c.htm. The report was originally published as Edward J. Marolda, *A New Equation: Chinese Intervention into the Korean War; Proceedings of the Colloquium on Contemporary History* (Washington, DC: Naval Historical Center, 1991). Some materials appeared earlier in Edward J. Marolda, "The U.S. Navy and the Chinese Civil War, 1945–1952," PhD diss., The George Washington University, 1990.

TWO

The Two Chinas, the Offshore Islands, and the Korean War

By early 1950, the two Chinas—the People's Republic of China (PRC) on the mainland and the Republic of China (ROC) on Taiwan—faced each other across the Taiwan Strait. By June of 1950, the Taiwan Patrol Force was created. It eventually became the U.S. Navy's most robust buffer patrol in its two-century-plus history, as well as one of the longest naval operations of any type in world history. From 1950 to 1979, and arguably until the mid-1990s and sporadically even to the present day, the U.S. Navy (USN) has sent ships to patrol the Taiwan Strait separating the PRC from the ROC. Given the Cold War context from 1950 to 1979, a PRC–ROC conflict in the Taiwan Strait might easily have spread to include the USSR and the United States.

The most important goal of this USN operation was to ensure that neither side attacked across the Taiwan Strait. While it is often assumed that the U.S. government's focus was just on the PRC, in fact there were equally valid concerns that it could be the Nationalists that might invade across the Taiwan Strait and accidentally spark a new world war; this USN operation, therefore, was—at least initially—also intended to operate as a neutral buffer separating both sides of the Taiwan Strait.

A second important function of the Taiwan Patrol Force beginning in late 1950 was to help enforce a trade embargo on strategic goods against the PRC. On December 23, 1950, the U.S. secretary of Commerce announced that "effectively immediately no vessel or aircraft registered under the laws of the United States shall enter Chinese Communist Port or any other place under control of Chinese Communists." In effect, "No cargoes shall be transported to such ports."[1] This U.S. embargo was focused exclusively against the PRC. In line with this decision, USN vessels often secretly cooperated with ships from the Nationalist Navy to enforce the strategic embargo. Finally, when not engaged in patrol duties, USN personnel participated in training of the Nationalist Navy and morale-building exercises on Taiwan. To set the stage, this chapter will examine the creation of the "two Chinas" conflict, the strategic importance of the Taiwan Strait and the offshore islands, the beginning of the Korean War, and the contribution of these factors to the establishment of the Taiwan Patrol Force.

THE TWO CHINAS

The division of China into a Taiwan-based Republic of China and the mainland-based People's Republic of China was a direct outcome of World War II and the Chinese Civil War. During World War II, the U.S. government encouraged the Nationalists and Communists to form a coalition government. In December 1945, right after the end of the war, President Harry S. Truman even appointed General George C. Marshall as a special envoy to China to negotiate a cease-fire between the Nationalists and the Communists. Truman also urged the peaceful reunification of China under the auspices of a joint Political Consultative Conference.

Following Japan's surrender, the internationally recognized government of China was under the control of the Nationalist Party, led by Chiang Kai-shek. By late 1945, the United States had equipped thirty-nine Nationalist army divisions, and during August 1946 the U.S. government sold the Nationalists approximately $900 million worth of war surplus for a mere $175 million. This war surplus included ships, trucks, airplanes, and communications equipment. The Nationalists had both an air force and a navy, while the Communists had neither.

Communist forces were concentrated in North China and in Manchuria, while the Nationalists held China's central provinces. When Soviet troops began to withdraw in mid-March 1946, the Communists quickly filled the political vacuum in the northeast. By May 1946, the Communists controlled the northern two-thirds of Manchuria. Meanwhile, growing economic problems in the Nationalist-controlled areas began to erode Chiang's political legitimacy. Inflation quickly spiraled out of control: between September 1945 and February 1947, wholesale prices in Shanghai alone increased thirty-fold, which destroyed many small businesses and hindered China's economic recovery.

The civil war in China intensified during 1946. By early 1947, the Marshall Mission had ended in failure. On January 29, 1947, the United States notified Chiang Kai-shek's government in Nanjing that it would stop its efforts to negotiate a peaceful end to the Chinese Civil War. As Nationalist rule imploded, the Communists orchestrated an increasingly effective campaign to rally popular support. For example, on May 4, 1946, the Communists announced a land-redistribution program in their areas. During the summer of 1947 they held a National Land Conference to draft a land-reform law confiscating landlord property. This reform proved to be very popular among the rural peasantry.

The Communists began to win on the battlefield as well. Massive defections weakened the Nationalist Army. By contrast, the People's Liberation Army (PLA) experienced enormous growth, from an estimated half a million in mid-1945 to 1.3 million in mid-1946, 2 million in mid-1947 to 2.8 million by mid-1948, and as many as 4 million by early 1949.[2] During September of 1947, the Communists were able to shift to the offensive in Manchuria. They pushed the retreating Nationalist troops into a small triangle, bounded by the cities of Jinzhou, Changchun, and Mukden. Millions surrendered. By the summer of 1948, the PLA had cleared most of the Nationalist troops from northeast China.

Following their victory in the north, Communist forces spread south into China proper. During the Huaihai Campaign, one of the largest battles of the Chinese Civil War involving well over one million combatants, Communist forces moved into Jiangsu and Anhui provinces. On December 15, 1948, after sixty-three days of fighting, the Communists took Xuzhou, opening the road south to the Yangzi River and to the Nationalist capital at Nanjing.[3] Although they lost North China, the Nationalists retained their traditional power base in South China. Many foreign commentators assumed that China would now be divided into a North and South, with the Yangzi River acting as the new boundary.

This new division of China along the Yangzi River did not last. On February 25, 1949, the Nationalist flagship, *Chongqing*, mutinied and defected to the Communist side. It became a potent symbol of the waning Nationalist mandate to rule. By the end of April 1949, much of the rest of the Nationalist fleet guarding the Yangzi River also defected.[4] On April 20, 1949, Communist forces crossed the Yangzi River, overrunning Nanjing three days later. Thereafter, the PLA quickly consolidated control over all of mainland China, taking Shanghai and Wuhan in May, Xi'an and Changsha in August, Guangzhou in October, and the Nationalist wartime capital of Chongqing in November 1949.

The PLA's rapid advance forced the remaining Nationalist units to retreat to Taiwan to continue their anti-Communist struggle. This followed in line with the Ming retreat during the seventeenth century, also in response to a northern invasion. After relocating his government to Taipei, Chiang Kai-shek claimed that the ROC remained the legitimate government of all of China. Meanwhile, in late September of 1949, Mao Zedong assembled a new Political Consultative Conference, which elected him chairman of the central government, and once again made Beijing the capital. On October 1, 1949, Mao officially proclaimed the creation of the People's Republic of China.

While the Nationalists were forced to retreat, they were not defeated. Instead, Chiang shifted from a land-based offensive to a naval offensive, by supporting a blockade strategy against the PRC. Although the Nationalist Navy was comparatively large, it was retained mainly for the defense of Taiwan. To conduct their blockade against the PRC, the Nationalists fortified a number of offshore islands not far from China's coast. Later, the USN provided military assistance—especially aircraft—that made air patrols of the blockade possible. The Nationalist blockade lasted from 1949 to 1958.

THE NATIONALIST BLOCKADE STRATEGY

The Nationalist Army was defeated, but they still had a large navy. As World War II was ending, the U.S. Congress passed Public Law 512, providing for the transfer of as many as 271 surplus naval vessels to China.[5] The United States eventually donated to China approximately 130 ships of various classes, including six 1,300-ton destroyer escorts, plus a number of Landing Ship, Tank, and Landing Ship Medium.[6] Britain also gave China nine small ships and a light cruiser, HMS *Aurora*, which was renamed *Chongqing* after the Nationalist wartime capital.[7] Finally, China was supposed to acquire one-quarter of the thirty destroyers and sixty-seven escort vessels confiscated from Japan at the end of the war.[8] According to one estimate, an additional forty demilitarized Japanese warships were given to China.[9] Taken together, the Nationalists controlled a total of 824 vessels of various types, including a handful of modern ships, like the British cruiser *Chongqing*, and numerous small patrol boats.

By 1947, the Nationalist Navy had grown to almost forty thousand men, and near the end of 1948 it had reached 40,859. This included 2,452 line officers, 5,221 staff corps officers, and 389 marine corps officers, for a total of 8,062 officers. The enlisted personnel included 19,252 regular navy, 3,554 marines, and then 9,991 noncombatants.[10] Chinese students trained in England during the war brought back a corvette, *Petunia*, while later groups returned with one destroyer escort and eight torpedo boats. In November of 1946, six hundred Chinese went to England, where two hundred were trained to bring back two submarines and the rest to man *Chongqing*. During 1945, one thousand Chinese arrived in Miami to undergo training. Later, forty-nine officers were enrolled at Swarthmore College, Philadelphia, to study naval science, and of these twenty-five were later sent to the U.S. Naval Academy in Annapolis and twenty-four to the Massachusetts Institute of Technology for advanced training.[11]

With their navy both equipped and manned, in 1947 the Nationalists adopted a naval blockade to halt Soviet shipments to the Chinese Communists in Manchuria via Port Arthur (now Lüshun) and Dalian.[12] Because Manchuria's ports were already closed to most foreign shippers, the blockade of Lüshun and Dalian elicited no complaint from the other foreign powers. Beginning on June 18, 1949, however, the Nationalists announced that any Chinese port not under their control would be closed to trade as of midnight on June 25. The majority of China's territorial waters would be closed to foreign vessels from a point just north of the Min River to the mouth of the Liao River. In practical terms, this included China's coastline just north of Taiwan all the way to Beijing. Major Chinese ports to be closed included Qinhuangdao, Tianjin, Shanghai, Ningbo, and Wenzhou.

A July 1949 report by the UK Admiralty's Intelligence Division was optimistic about the Nationalist blockade. After comparing the Communists' thirty warships to the Nationalists' thirty-two and analyzing refueling and rearmament, this admiralty study concluded that retaining the Miao Islands in the north allowed the Nationalists to blockade most of the ports on the Bo Hai Gulf and provided them with a 50 percent cover of Qingdao.[13] However, other British reports warned that, while the Nationalists could effectively close the major ports, they could not control junk traffic.[14] But the Commander-in-Chief Far Eastern Squadron Afloat argued on July 18, 1949, that the blockade was effective and was delaying the Communists and so might help bring about a political solution to China's problems. Therefore, he recommended, holding firm, saying, "I am strongly averse in present circumstances to breaking the blockade which Nationalists appear to be operating very reasonably."[15]

There was also American backing for the Nationalist blockade. During July of 1949, the U.S. minister to China, John Leighton Stuart, supported the blockade as part of an American "stew in their own juices" strategy toward a Communist-run China. This was based on the belief that the Marxist-Leninist ideology was inappropriate for China. The best possible policy would be to allow the Soviet Union to "demonstrate, if they could, that they were able to give a Communist China the assistance she will need." Once Beijing realized that Moscow could not finance China's development alone, then "China would have to turn to us again and we might then be able to come back on terms which would suit us."[16]

As the Nationalists retreated from their northern bases, the focus of the naval blockade necessarily moved farther and farther southward. For example, a British map shows that the blockade cut access to the Yangzi River during 1949 and 1950 (see figure 2.1). For the U.S. government, the fear of a complete Communist victory eventually outweighed other considerations. On December 24, 1949, Washington warned American ship owners that their operating licenses could be revoked if they attempted to run the Shanghai blockade.[17] According to one U.S. assessment, the Nationalist Navy's approximately eighty ocean-going vessels could maintain a reasonably effective blockade of China's major ports from Shanghai southward to Fujian Province.[18]

In addition to enforcing the blockade, during 1949 the Nationalist Navy also helped transport Chiang Kai-shek's government-in-exile to

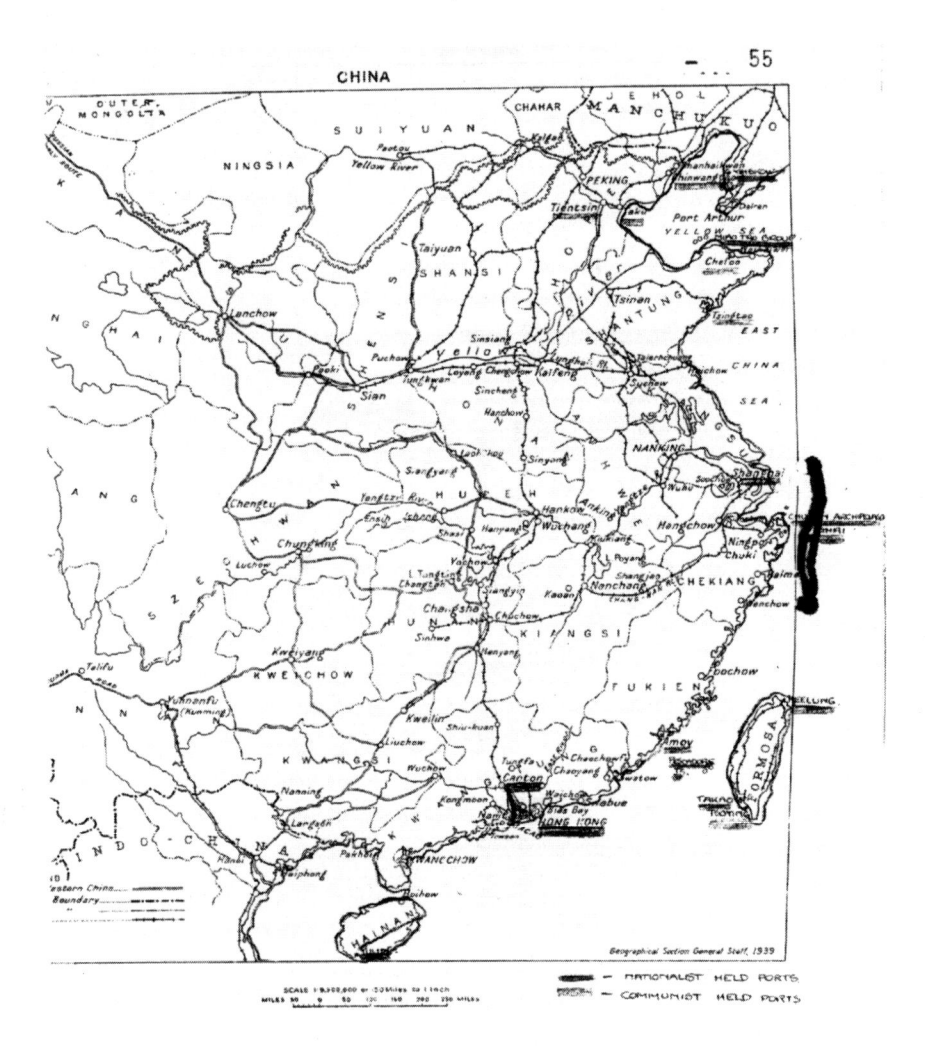

Figure 2.1. Nationalist Blockade of the Yangzi River. Source: UK National Archives

Taiwan. The Nationalist retreat to Taiwan was a major maritime undertaking, during which the Nationalist Navy and other ships impressed into service transported approximately two million civilians and soldiers to Taiwan.[19] More importantly, the Nationalist Navy helped fortify and protect a large number of offshore islands that were to become the first barrier defending Taiwan from an expected PRC invasion. These military and political developments faced off the two competing Chinas across the Taiwan Strait, which made this roughly 81-mile-wide stretch of water strategically important.

THE STRATEGIC IMPORTANCE OF THE TAIWAN STRAIT

Given the Cold War context in the late 1940s, which had already seen the division of Germany into a communist East and democratic West, the division of China was not as surprising as the dividing line itself, which ran along the Taiwan Strait. China's split largely fit within the framework of the Cold War, and later both Korea and Vietnam would be split into a communist North and a nominally democratic South. Whereas these other divided states were somewhat similar in territory and populations, the small size of the Nationalist island stronghold was greatly overshadowed by the enormous geographic dimensions and population of the PRC. To many outside observers, it seemed that the PRC could overwhelm Taiwan at will. But the maritime security provided by the eighty-one-mile-wide Taiwan Strait must not be overlooked. In fact, it was four times wider than the much smaller English Channel, which is only twenty-one miles at its narrowest point. Yet the English Channel had proven itself to be an effective moat against Napoleon, Imperial Germany, and the Nazis. The Taiwan Strait would prove to be an equally important barrier protecting the Nationalists from attack.

The Taiwan Strait is an important strategic region, since it lies along the primary north–south sea-lane in East Asia. Japanese, Korean, and northern and central Chinese produce and luxury goods flowing primarily from north to south must transit this strait to reach Southeast Asia, just as goods and raw materials flowing from south to north must also travel through this region. The Taiwan Strait has long been a choke point. Whichever country dominated both sides of the strait could close these waters to international shipping. Such an action would force commercial vessels to take the longer and more exposed route far to the east of Taiwan.

Taiwan is part of a chain of islands running from the Aleutians through Hokkaido to the Japanese main islands, and then on through Okinawa and Taiwan to the Philippines. These islands would play an important role in any north–south invasion. Communist control over Taiwan would also put both Japan and the Philippines at risk. U.S. Navy planners during World War II, for example, were keenly aware that Japan's successful invasion of the Philippines had been launched from Taiwan. Assuming Taiwan fell to the Chinese Communists, therefore, the PLA could use it as a base from which to invade other islands in the chain, as well as to interfere with international shipping.

For these reasons, keeping Taiwan out of Communist hands was vital to Western powers.[20] In 1955, Australian prime minister Menzies put it succinctly. "From the point of view of Australia and, indeed, Malaya," he said, "it would be fatal to have an enemy installed in the island chain so that by a process of island hopping Indonesia might be reached and Malaya and Australia to that extent exposed to serious damage either in the rear or on the flank."[21] A year later, Foreign Minister Shigemitsu told the U.S. ambassador in Tokyo that "Japan would consider the fall of Taiwan to the Communists as a threat to its interests and therefore supports the U.S. policy of preventing such an eventuality."[22] Finally, in 1958 British Foreign Secretary Selwyn Lloyd reaffirmed that the United Kingdom and United States shared the view that there was a "Communist menace in the Far East" and that the "containing line" had to be drawn to include Japan, South Korea, Okinawa, Taiwan, Hong Kong, South Vietnam, and Malaya.[23]

Due mainly to the strategic location of Taiwan, therefore, it was not in the interest of the United States or her allies to see it fall to Communism. It was this geographic divide between continental China and Taiwan that helped to precipitate the "two Chinas" problem. More importantly, it is the protection afforded by the Taiwan Strait that has allowed this political division to continue to the present day. Additional protection for Taiwan was provided by Nationalist domination of a large number of offshore islands, some of them right off the PRC's coast. It would be these offshore islands, not Taiwan proper, that would be at the heart of two Taiwan Strait crises during the 1950s and one in the early 1960s.

PRC PLANS TO USE OFFSHORE ISLANDS TO INVADE TAIWAN

After their retreat from the mainland in 1949, the Nationalist government in Taiwan continued to support a naval blockade of the PRC. Although Taiwan's share of the former Chinese Navy was large, most of these ships were needed to defend the island's security. Therefore, it was often Nationalist guerrillas, located on offshore islands along China's southeastern coastline, who carried out the naval blockade against the PRC. Later, the U.S. government provided Taiwan with additional ships and even jet aircraft to help enforce the blockade.

During the summer and fall of 1949, Nationalist forces fiercely defended their hold over numerous offshore islands. The Nationalists initially kept one regiment of marines on the Miao Islands north of Shandong Peninsula to blockade the Bo Hai Gulf and the northern ports, while they fortified Zhoushan and the Saddle islands to blockade the Yangzi River. Meanwhile, the Dachen, Matsu (Mazu), Penghu, and Jinmen islands near Taiwan, the Lema and Wan Shan islands near Guangzhou, and Hainan Island, less than twenty miles off China's southern coast, blockaded about two-thirds of China's coastline. The Nationalists allied with guerrilla groups located on many of these islands, who earned their living by preying on passing ships. As the U.S. Navy's Office of Naval Intelligence (ONI) reported, the Nationalists did not try very hard to suppress these guerrilla attacks, since it would "undoubtedly lose them the guerrilla support in the coastal islands."[24]

The tide in the Chinese Civil War began to shift back toward the Nationalists during the fall of 1949. A Communist attack on the Nationalist-held base on Jinmen Island was bitterly opposed by Nationalist troops, and the PLA failed to take the island during October 1949. However, the southern city of Guangzhou soon fell to Communist forces, and the loss of a number of strategic islands in the north effectively narrowed the blockade to central and southern China. As early as October 1949, Admiral Sa Zhenbing, a former commander of the Chinese Navy during the Qing dynasty, concluded that the blockade would probably not last long.[25] In 1950, in spite of naval and air inferiority, Communist forces succeeded in overwhelming the Nationalist base on Hainan Island from February to May, the Zhoushan Archipelago during May, and Tatan Island as late as July.

By that summer, therefore, the Nationalists had lost their crucial island bases in the Bo Hai Gulf, off the mouth of the Yangzi River, and on Hainan Island. These losses cut the Nationalist blockade area by over half. The Communists' mass attack on Hainan, only twenty miles from the mainland, could not be so easily replicated against Taiwan, however, which was over eighty miles from shore. Traditionally, offshore islands had acted as forward supporting bases during invasion of Taiwan. Thus, continued Nationalist control of the offshore islands in the Taiwan Strait was considered crucial to deterring the Communists from launching an invasion of Taiwan.

By the spring of 1950, the Communist forces seemed to be getting ready to invade. The PLA concentrated thousands of junks in the port cities along the Taiwan Strait in preparation for a massive amphibious invasion.[26] According to one USN estimate, the Communists could assemble seven thousand ships and two hundred aircraft to transport two hundred thousand troops across the Strait.[27] This made continued Nationalist control over a number of strategic offshore islands even more important. After a 1954 visit to Taiwan, former Commander of the Seventh Fleet Admiral Charles M. Cooke Jr. drew a map highlighting Taiwan's most "critical sea areas" (see figure 2.2).

The key to the PLA's success in Hainan had been numerous fleets of small boats crossing the Qiongzhou Strait simultaneously, mainly at night. PRC forces overwhelmed the Nationalist air and surface units and their relatively small island garrisons. As one USN report concluded, "The tremendous losses in men and boats sustained by the Communists attested to their stubborn determination to remove this threat to their security and their economy."[28] The PLA was successful in taking Hainan Island in large part because it was so close to the Chinese mainland. But these tactics would be of little use against Taiwan, where distances were on average six times greater.[29] In fact, for the PRC to invade Taiwan would require a major naval effort on its part, including the gathering of

Figure 2.2. Taiwan's "Critical Sea Areas." Source: Naval History and Heritage Command Archives

hundreds, perhaps thousands, of ships and the training of tens of thousands of troops.

To foil just such an invasion, the Nationalists retained control over the large island bases of Jinmen and Mazu, right off the coast of Fujian Province, and the Penghu Islands in the Taiwan Strait halfway between the mainland and Taiwan. ROC control over offshore islands allowed the Nationalist Navy to interdict any PRC cross-strait maritime invasion (see figure 2.3). Nationalist naval dominance in the Taiwan Strait meant that they retained the capability to carry out an offensive policy, including capturing cargoes destined for Chinese ports, using the offshore islands to mount raids against the Chinese mainland, and procuring valuable intelligence on mainland areas. According to one ONI report, the naval blockade allowed for the Nationalist interception of Communist armed junks, and so led to "numerous junk battles."[30]

Control over about twenty-five of the larger offshore islands was to remain extremely contentious throughout the 1950s. On July 30, 1953, the USN report "Security of Offshore Islands Presently Held by the Nationalist Government of the Republic of China" divided twenty of these into three categories. In category 1 were four offshore islands off Fuzhou, including Mazu, and four islands off Xiamen, including Jinmen, which could be used to counter a Communist invasion of Taiwan. Retaining these eight islands was militarily desirable. Category 2 including two islands in the Dachen group that were not crucial for defending Taiwan and the Penghu Islands. Category 3 included ten smaller offshore islands, which defended the ten islands in categories 2 and 3.[31]

As for the other offshore islands under Nationalist domination, USN planners concluded they were simply not considered worth the effort necessary to defend against a determined PLA attack. Still, as one USN report was quick to point out, none of the offshore islands could be called essential to the defense of Taiwan and the Penghus in the sense of being "absolutely necessary" militarily. Their importance to the Nationalists was mainly for psychological warfare as well as for "pre-invasion operations, commando raiding, intelligence gathering, maritime resistance development, sabotage, escape, and evasion."[32]

After the PLA retook the northernmost and southernmost offshore islands held by the Nationalists during spring 1950, their offensive stopped. To take the remaining Nationalist-controlled islands would have required more advanced naval technology, such as amphibious landing craft. This was beyond the People's Liberation Army Navy's capabilities in the early 1950s. Instead, the Communist army and naval forces could retake the offshore islands either with massive force or by-passing the islands entirely and making a strike directly for Taiwan. Preparations for such an invasion would be hard to hide, especially from air reconnaissance.

Given this historical background, and granting Taiwan's strategic importance to both sides in the evolving Cold War, China's southeastern coastline was especially tense during the early 1950s. Both Communist and Nationalist forces fiercely defended their positions on numerous offshore islands, in the hopes of changing the strategic balance. Although "for the United States," according to Secretary of State John Foster Dulles, "the offshore islands were of no intrinsic importance except in the context of an attack on Formosa," they could be used as "stepping stones for such an attack."[33] Losing additional islands to the Communists might also undermine Nationalist morale—plus open up the Truman and Eisenhower administrations to accusations of retreating before Communist aggression. It was for these reasons that the U.S. government felt obliged to support Chiang Kai-shek's efforts to retain a number of offshore islands.

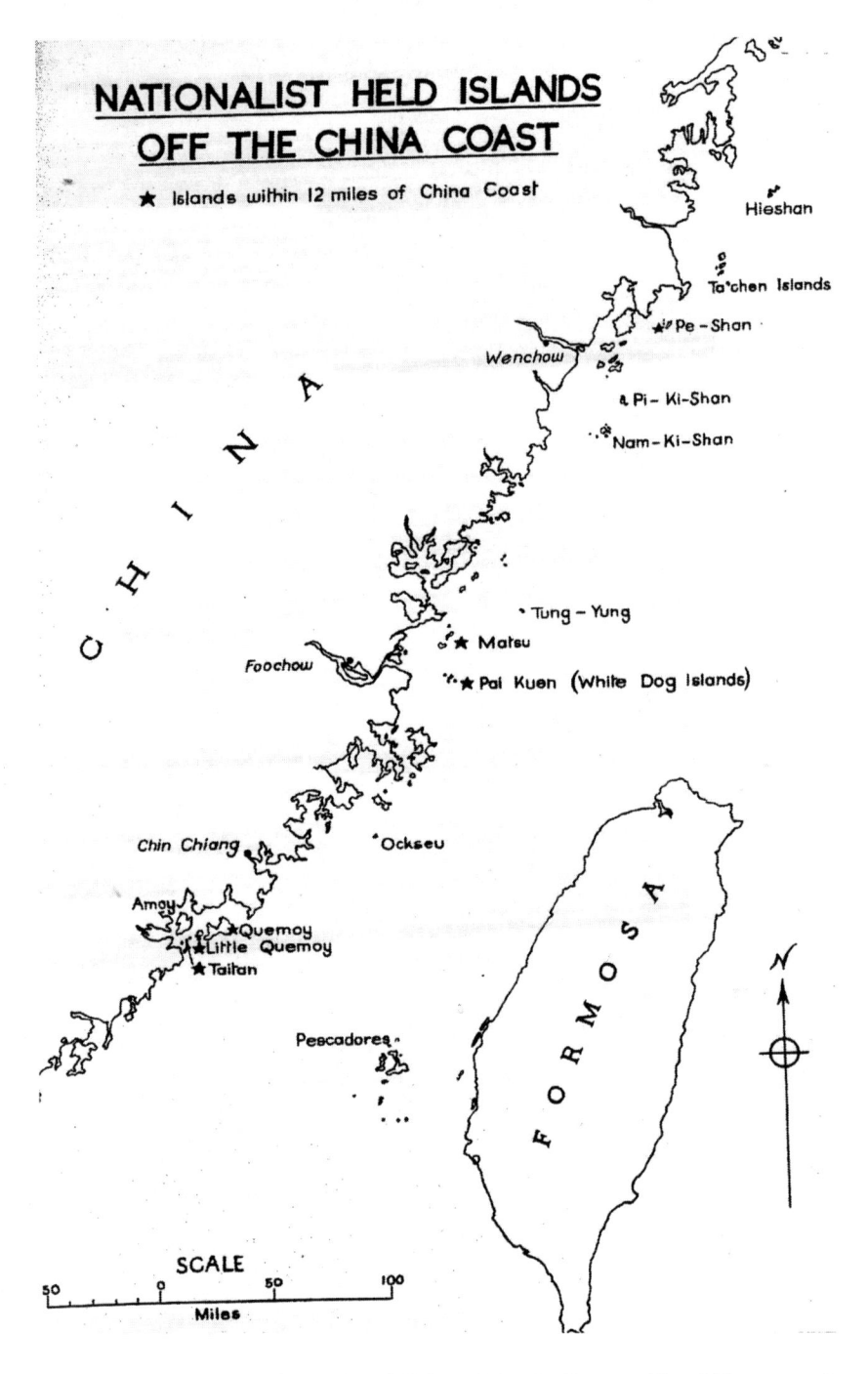

Figure 2.3. Nationalist-Controlled Offshore Islands. Source: Naval History and Heritage Command Archives.

CONCLUSIONS

By the spring of 1950, the two Chinas were poised facing each other across the Taiwan Strait. To many it appeared that the PLA would quickly replicate its success in Hainan by organizing a mass attack against Taiwan. Due to the Truman administration's disillusionment with exiled Nationalist Chiang Kai-shek and his government, it seemed highly unlikely that the United States would risk a wider war with the USSR by intervening openly on the side of Taiwan. Meanwhile, Great Britain's official recognition of the PRC government on January 6, 1950, also precluded British intervention. If a spring or summer cross-strait attack had gone forward in 1950, then Taiwan might have become part of the PRC during that year.

Any possibility of a PRC attack against Taiwan was effectively countered, however, by the beginning of the Korean War on June 25, 1950. Two days later, on June 27, President Truman ordered the Seventh Fleet to neutralize the Taiwan Strait. The very next day, the destroyer USS *Brush* (DD 745) pulled into Keelung, Taiwan. This was the first U.S. Navy ship to visit Taiwan since Truman had adopted a hands-off policy in January of 1950.[34] One day later, the aircraft carrier USS *Valley Forge* (CV 45), escorted by two destroyer divisions, two submarines, and several logistic ships, steamed past Taiwan in a show of force.[35]

The United Nations (UN) immediately condemned North Korea's attack, and UN forces began to flow into South Korea. Suddenly, Taiwan's continued existence became both militarily and politically important, since the war in Korea could always spread to include a naval invasion of Taiwan. Should the PRC succeed in taking Taiwan, it could cut off a major sea line of communication (SLOC) bringing UN troops and supplies to the Korean theater. To help prevent this, a U.S. Navy contingent initially operated out of Keelung, and later also at Kaohsiung, Taiwan. Due to the U.S. military intervention and the presence of USN ships, airplanes, and submarines to neutralize the Taiwan Strait, the planned PRC invasion of Taiwan was postponed to the following year and was eventually canceled altogether. In fact, the Taiwan Patrol Force would be instrumental in maintaining the peace in East Asia during the next three decades of the Cold War.[36]

NOTES

1. "U.S. Special Warning Number 19," U.S. Secretary of Commerce, December 23, 1950, the National Archives, Ministry of Justice, United Kingdom (hereafter TNA/UK), Foreign Office Files (hereafter FO) 371/92272.

2. Bruce A. Elleman and S. C. M. Paine, *Modern China: Continuity and Change, 1644 to the Present* (Upper Saddle River, NJ: Prentice-Hall, 2010), 343–44.

3. Bruce A. Elleman, "Huai-Hai," in *The Seventy Great Battles of All Time*, ed. Jeremy Black, 279–81 (London: Thames and Hudson, 2005).

4. Bruce A. Elleman, "The *Chongqing* Mutiny and the Chinese Civil War, 1949," in *Naval Mutinies of the Twentieth Century: An International Perspective*, ed. Christopher Bell and Bruce A. Elleman, 232–45 (London: Frank Cass, 2003).

5. U.S. Office of Naval Intelligence, "The Chinese Navy, Past and Present," *ONI Review* (January 1947): 21–29.

6. U.S. Office of Naval Intelligence, "The Chinese Nationalist Navy," *ONI Review* (January 1955): 29–34.

7. U.S. Office of Naval Intelligence, "The Chinese Navy, Past and Present," 21–29.

8. U.S. Office of Naval Intelligence, "Intelligence Briefs: Japan," *ONI Review* (October 1946): 47.

9. U.S. Office of Naval Intelligence, "The Chinese Nationalist Navy," 29–34.

10. U.S. Office of Naval Intelligence, "Intelligence Briefs: China," *ONI Review* (January 1949): 39.

11. U.S. Office of Naval Intelligence, "The Chinese Navy, Past and Present," 21–29.

12. Bruce A. Elleman, "The Nationalists' Blockade of the PRC, 1949–58," in *Naval Blockades and Seapower: Strategies and Counter-strategies, 1805–2005*, ed. Bruce A. Elleman and S. C. M. Paine, 133–44 (London: Routledge Press, 2006).

13. "Appreciation of the Ability of the Chinese Nationalist Navy to Effect a Blockade of Communist Territorial Waters (Secret)," Intelligence Division, Naval Staff, Admiralty, July 9, 1949, TNA/UK, FO 371 75902.

14. "C.O.I.S. to the Admiralty (Secret)," July 2, 1949, TNA/UK, FO 371 75900.

15. "C. in C. F.E.S. Afloat to the Admiralty (Secret)," July 18, 1949, TNA/UK, FO 371/75903.

16. "British Consulate-General, Canton, to Political Adviser, Hong Kong (Confidential)," July 25, 1949, TNA/UK, FO 371/75810-75815.

17. "The Illegal Blockade," *China Weekly Review*, December 31, 1949.

18. "Study on the Problems Involved in Military Aid to China," in *Foreign Relations of the United States* (hereafter *FRUS*), vol. 9, *The Far East: China, 1949*, ed. (Washington, DC: United States Government Printing Office, 1974), 563.

19. Jeffrey Hays, "Communists Take Over China," Facts and Details (last updated August 2013), http://factsanddetails.com/china/cat2/sub6/item74.html.

20. "Meeting of Prime Ministers: The Strategic Importance of Formosa; Memorandum by the United Kingdom Chiefs of Staff (Top Secret)," signed by Fraser, P. S. Slessor, and W. J. Slim, January 6, 1951, TNA/UK, PREM 8/1408.

21. "Formosa and Off-Shore Islands, Note by the Prime Minister of Australia (Secret)," meeting of Commonwealth Prime Ministers, February 8, 1955, TNA/UK, PREM 11/867.

22. John Foster Dulles Papers, Princeton University, Reel 212/213, December 2, 1956, 94413.

23. "Letter from Selwyn Lloyd to John Foster Dulles (Top Secret)," September 11, 1958, TNA/UK, CAB 21/3272.

24. U.S. Office of Naval Intelligence, "The Southeast China Coast Today," *ONI Review* (February 1953): 51–60.

25. "Central People's Government Formed; KMT Seizes U.S. Ships," *China Weekly Review*, October 8, 1949.

26. He Di, "The Last Campaign to Unify China," in *Chinese Warfighting: The PLA Experience since 1949*, ed. Mark A. Ryan, David M. Finkelstein, and Michael A. McDevitt, 73–90 (Armonk, NY: M. E. Sharpe Publishers, 2003).

27. Edward J. Marolda, "Hostilities along the China Coast during the Korean War," in *New Interpretations in Naval History*, ed. Robert W. Love Jr., Laurie Bogle, Brian VanDeMark, and Maochun Yu, 352 (Annapolis, MD: Naval Institute Press, 2001).

28. U.S. Office of Naval Intelligence, "The Southeast China Coast Today," 51–60.

29. David Muller, *China as a Maritime Power* (Boulder, CO: Westview Press, 1983), 16.

30. U.S. Office of Naval Intelligence, "The Southeast China Coast Today," 51–60.

31. Appendix to "Security of the Offshore Islands Presently Held by the Nationalist Government of the Republic of China," memorandum from Chief of Naval Operations, Admiral Robert B. Carney, to Joint Chiefs of Staff (top secret), July 30, 1953, Strategic Plans Division, Naval History and Heritage Command Archives (hereafter NHHC), Washington, DC, box 289.

32. Ibid.

33. Telegram from UK Embassy, Washington, DC, to Foreign Office (secret), February 9, 1955, TNA/UK, PREM 11/867.

34. Edward J. Marolda, "The U.S. Navy and the Chinese Civil War, 1945–1952," PhD diss., The George Washington University, 1990, 156.

35. Edward J. Marolda, "Invasion Patrol: The Seventh Fleet in Chinese Waters," Naval History and Heritage Command (accessed December 13, 2010), http://www.history.navy.mil/colloquia/cch3c.htm.

36. George W. Anderson, *Reminiscences of Admiral George W. Anderson, Jr., U.S. Navy (Retired)*, Oral History 42 (Annapolis, MD: U.S. Naval Institute, 1983), 5.

THREE
The U.S. Seventh Fleet and the Taiwan Patrol Force

The Taiwan Patrol Force was created immediately on the outbreak of the Korean War, when it was as yet unclear whether the PRC might use the chaos and confusion surrounding the conflict in Korea to stage an invasion of Taiwan. Whereas in late 1949 and early 1950, the U.S. government's backing of the Nationalists on Taiwan had waned, immediately following the beginning of the Korean War the Nationalists gained active U.S. Navy support. In particular, the arrival of the Seventh Fleet in the Taiwan Strait provided Taiwan security from a PRC attack. By contrast, the PRC condemned the neutralization policy as aggressive and demanded the immediate withdrawal of the Seventh Fleet.[1]

From 1950 through the 1960s and until the late 1970s, the USN maintained a near-continuous buffer patrol of ships and aircraft between the PRC and the Nationalists on Taiwan. This was mainly intended to prevent the Communists from invading across the Taiwan Strait. From 1950 to 1953, the Taiwan Patrol Force also prevented the Nationalists from launching an invasion of mainland China that might accidentally trigger a new world war. But this did not mean the Nationalist blockade of the PRC ended in 1950. In fact, the U.S. Navy actively assisted the Nationalists in trying to prevent the movement of specific goods into the PRC. This policy was largely in line with a U.S.–sponsored strategic-goods embargo, adopted in January 1950, which listed a large number of goods into restricted Coordinating Committee for Multilateral Export Controls (COCOM) I, II, and III categories. This U.S. embargo lasted in varying degrees of intensity for twenty-one years, through June 1971.

Since the Taiwan Patrol Force was a trip wire for bringing in larger ships, including aircraft carriers, at any one time the number of USN ships in the Taiwan Strait could be quite small. While published maps illustrating the patrol usually placed a silhouette of an aircraft carrier in the Taiwan Strait, in reality the Taiwan Patrol Force was normally carried out by one or two smaller USN ships, including beginning in late July 1950 by the U.S. light cruiser *Juneau* (CL 119) and in early August 1950 the destroyer USS *Maddox* (DD 731). If these ships were attacked, they could then call in the larger and more powerful aircraft carriers to assist.[2]

ESTABLISHING THE TAIWAN PATROL FORCE

The U.S. government's policy on Taiwan was extremely controversial during early 1950. Some U.S. groups had written off Chiang Kai-shek's regime completely, while others, including the U.S. Navy, advocated continued support. During January 1950, however, President Truman stated that the United States did not intend to use its armed forces to interfere in the present situation between the PRC and ROC.[3] His statement implied that the United States would not intervene if the PRC invaded Taiwan. This policy changed, however, when North Korea attacked South Korea on June 25, 1950. Even before this crucial event, General Douglas MacArthur had given Secretary of Defense Louis Johnson a memorandum arguing that Taiwan should not be allowed to fall to the PRC but should instead be fully protected by the United States.[4]

On June 27, 1950, Truman accepted MacArthur's reasoning and ordered the Seventh Fleet to prevent Communist attacks on Taiwan, as well as to stop all Nationalist attacks on the Chinese mainland. For this reason, it was referred to as a "neutralization" plan.[5] According to the terms of a USN operations order from October 1950, units of the U.S. Seventh Fleet had since June 1950 been stationed in the Taiwan Strait to "prevent an invasion of Formosa Straits area to prevent an invasion of Formosa." But during this early period the U.S. Navy was also stopping any Nationalist invasion, so it was responsible to ensure that Taiwan and the Penghu Islands were not being used by the Nationalists as a base for operations against the PRC.[6]

When he ordered the neutralization of the Taiwan Strait, Truman explained that the occupation of Taiwan by Communist forces would be a direct threat to the security of the Western Pacific, as well as to U.S. forces performing their lawful functions in that area. He declared, "The determination of the future status of Formosa must await the restoration of security in the Pacific, a peace settlement with Japan, or consideration by the United Nations."[7] In other words, it was the United States' intention to put the political problem of Taiwan "on ice."[8]

MacArthur decided it was imperative to visit Taiwan in person to assess the risk of a PRC invasion. He was accompanied by Vice Admiral Arthur Dewey Struble, Commander of the Seventh Fleet, as well as the commander U.S. Naval Forces, Far East. Two days of meetings began with Chiang Kai-shek on July 31, 1950. During MacArthur's visit to Taiwan, the world press speculated on supposed secret agreements between the U.S. government and Chiang Kai-shek. Fearful that the newspaper reports were true, on August 4 Truman wrote to MacArthur, reminding him that "No one other than the President as Commander-in-Chief has the authority to order or authorize preventive action against concentrations on the mainland. The most vital national interest requires that no action of ours precipitate general war or give excuse to others to do so." MacArthur's reassuring reply on August 7, 1950, explained that he had directed sweeps of the Taiwan Strait by the Seventh Fleet, reconnaissance flights over coastal China, and familiarization flights by U.S. aircraft to locate possible refueling airstrips on Taiwan.[9]

It was in this highly charged political climate that the first full-time USN patrol ships arrived on the scene. Clearly, the Taiwan Patrol Force's origins were neither secret nor went unnoticed by the world at large. It is important to emphasize, however, that at this point it was the U.S. Navy's job to neutralize the threat of invasion from each side of the Taiwan Strait so as to ensure that neither side could attack the other and thereby ignite a new global war. Early organizational problems reflect the largely ad hoc nature of the Taiwan Patrol Force's creation.

ORGANIZATION AND CONDUCT OF THE TAIWAN PATROL FORCE

The Taiwan Patrol Force was a direct response to the outbreak of the Korean War. On August 4, 1950, the U.S. Navy's Seventh Fleet established task group 77.3 as the Formosa Patrol. But on August 24, it was renamed the Formosa Strait Force, and the number was changed to task force 72, and later the surface component became 72.1. Rear Admiral Thomas Binford was the first commander of this task force, using the heavy cruiser USS *Saint Paul* (CA 73) as his flagship. The USN ships initially worked out of Keelung, on the northern tip of Taiwan, and later also out of Kaohsiung, on the southwestern corner of the island. The difficult geography and harsh weather that the ships in the Taiwan Patrol Force had to withstand on a normal patrol were usually poor and all too often were horrific. Darkness, rough weather, and heavy seas could make the conduct of the patrol a true nightmare. As one veteran of the patrol later humorously recounted, "the Straits were rougher than a [corn] cob."[10]

Conducting patrols in the Taiwan Strait was a tedious assignment. If four destroyers were assigned to the patrol, then the ships could rotate five days on patrol and five days in port. However, there were often equipment failures or other duties that made this impossible. For example, during one patrol *Cowell* (DD 547) became nonoperational due to an engine problem, *Cushing* (DD 797) was deployed away from the Taiwan Strait for some other essential duty, while USS *Pritchett* (DD 561), the flagship, was away most of the time visiting Subic Bay or Hong Kong. Out of the four destroyers, therefore, only USS *Denny J* was available "to plow up and down the Strait. . . . It carried the most junior ship Captain of all the Seventh Fleet destroyers, which meant it was logical for *Denny J* to bear the brunt of the patrol work. It did not mean we did not grumble. When *Denny J* would then return to Kaohsiung at the end of a patrol we would top off our fuel tanks and take on stores. If we were lucky one of the sections would get liberty until 2300. Then it was back to sea."[11]

During most of the 1950s, the Taiwan Patrol Force was usually carried out by four destroyers, with an embarked Division Commander in the rank of captain as commander, task group (CTG) 72.1 (see figure 3.1). During the 1960s, as the Vietnam War heated up, the destroyers with their five-inch guns were required for shore bombardment duties. As a result, the smaller, 1,700-ton, 150-man crew destroyer radar picket escort ships (DER) were assigned to the patrol, mainly because the DER's three-inch guns were poorly suited for shore bombardment. The command structure was retained unchanged, however, even with the reduced forces.[12]

One of the biggest challenges was weather. Although averaging one hundred miles across, the Taiwan Strait is three times wider in the south than it is in the north. Storms tend to enter from the south and get more and more constricted as the strait narrows. One USN document referred to the Taiwan Strait as a "giant venturi," in which fluid velocity was forced to increase while passing through the constricted area.[13] During one storm, a USN ship making eight knots forward was found to be actually moving one knot backward. The ship was rolling so violently that it took on green water down the aft stack.[14] These conditions made patrolling the Taiwan Strait grueling and at times absolutely dangerous. The swells were particularly bad at either end of the north-to-south run, when the ship needed to turn around and head back in the opposite direction. According to one account, turning the ship was the most dangerous operation. "When we got stuck in the trough (between the swells)," recalls one crew member, "the rolls the ship took were steep, up to forty and sometimes fifty degrees at times. Also, the pitching when heading into the seas was incredible. You could feel the ship pass over a thirty-foot swell, and then you would need to brace yourself for the crash as the ship buried its nose into the next wave."[15] Another sailor remembers the ship taking a sixty-degree roll that threw him completely out of his bunk and injured his ribs when he hit the night-light across the passageway.[16]

A normal patrol might include five to six days at sea followed by an evening in port. Gunnery departments would go to port and starboard watch, with one five-inch gun and one twin three-inch gun manned at all

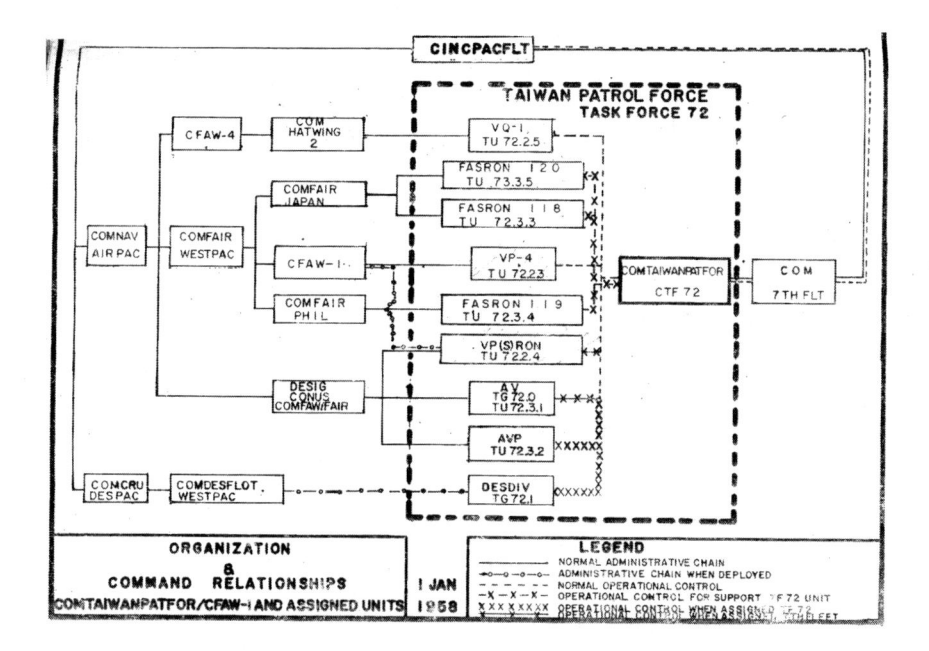

Figure 3.1. Taiwan Patrol Force. Organizational Matrix. Source: Naval History and Heritage Command Archives

times. Often, due to concerns about being attacked, the operations department would run on twenty-four-hour duty, with officers bedding down on cots at their duty stations.[17] Generally a tender or repair ship was anchored in harbor with the destroyers moored next to it. Otherwise the ships were moored in the harbor at a buoy. Depending on weather conditions, this arrangement could, on occasion, be dangerous. "The weather," recalls one crew member, "together with the harbor layouts, often made mooring or getting underway an adventure. In Keelung we had to do a Mediterranean moor, with a line from the stern to a buoy, and port and starboard anchors set on either side of the bow.... The entrance to Kaohsiung harbor is tight, and we had to moor to buoys or alongside USN destroyers already tied up to the buoys. With the frequent strong beam winds that prevailed, it often took all of our available power to handle a safe entrance or exit."[18]

Due to the treacherous nature of the Taiwan Strait, four rules were eventually published to assist new vessels assigned to the Taiwan Patrol Force:

1. When heading upwind, keep the ship's head close enough to dead into the seas to keep the ship level, generally a course within twenty degrees of the seas and wind.
2. Always go slow upwind, making only steerage way if necessary.

3. When heading downwind, adjust the ship's course and speed to keep the seas from coming aboard the fantail and to keep the roll moderate. Generally for a destroyer, a course within forty degrees of dead before the sea and speeds of fifteen knots or more are effective.
4. Turn with full rudder, and assist with the engines. As much as ahead full on the outboard engine and back two-thirds on the inboard engine may be necessary.[19]

The seas were rough, and storms were common. As one veteran recounted, if you arrived in the Taiwan Strait with seasickness, you were cured by the end of your patrol.[20] New ships to the patrol were warned that "the speed and destructiveness of these relatively low seas is a surprise to officers accustomed to the long period waves of open, deep water." During peacetime, ships were ordered to avoid heavy weather or seek shelter, since there was no justification for "loss or damage to a ship by heavy weather" if the mission was not urgent.[21]

PREPARING FOR A PRC INVASION

To most outside observers, the opposing forces facing each other across the Taiwan Strait during the early 1950s may have seemed unevenly matched on the side of the United States and its allies. However, in warfare between forces of radically different technological capabilities—often referred to as *asymmetric warfare*—the advantages are not all on one side. In Korea, for example, low-tech mass armies successfully fought modern armies with higher-technology weaponry. During the early 1950s, the U.S. Navy was particularly concerned that its large, seagoing ships might encounter unexpected troubles fighting the more lightly armed but numerous and highly mobile junk fleets that were at the disposal of Communist China.

One disparaging term used in the Korean conflict was *primitivism*. This described Communist tactics based on mass mobilization. Primitivism also affected the Taiwan Strait theater. Beginning in early 1951, intelligence reports of Chinese troop and junk concentrations in mainland ports indicated the possibility of a PRC invasion. In line with the seasonal monsoons, the best time to invade would be in early spring, when relatively good weather was the norm. A likely PRC invasion fleet, described as a heterogeneous armada, would probably include a few oceangoing vessels, accompanied by a larger number of river steamers, and perhaps a few conventional landing craft, but, by contrast, "Motorized junks and sailing junks will be employed by the thousands."[22]

To make sure that China could not invade Taiwan, the U.S. Navy began a series of exercises to oppose hypothetical mass fleets composed, not of modern ships, but of traditional Chinese junks. During early 1950,

U.S. naval intelligence warned of advanced preparations by the Chinese Communists for an amphibious attack across the Taiwan Strait, appropriately labeled Operation TAIWAN. Walter McConaughy, the U.S. consul general at Shanghai, even reported that the liberation of Taiwan was being trumpeted publicly by Beijing as the nation's paramount mission, and one on which the PRC was staking its reputation and all the resources of the new regime. By late spring in 1950, it was reported that approximately five thousand vessels—including freighters, motorized junks, sampans, and refloated ships that had been sunk in the Yangzi River during World War II—had been gathered and that 30,000 fishermen and other sailors had been drafted to man the ships during their crossing.[23]

Due to the Korean War and the creation of the Taiwan Patrol Force, the long-expected PRC cross-strait invasion never took place. In case of attack, the USN battle plan for Taiwan put a priority on attacking enemy aircraft, submarines, and steamships first and leaving junks for last.[24] Since traditional wooden junks had separate watertight compartments, they were difficult to sink, even when holed below the water line. However, because of their flammable sails, junks would burn easily. One proposed plan to oppose a large number of junks would be to give the Nationalists napalm, which their older propeller-driven planes could then drop on attacking junk fleets.[25]

By mid-February of 1951, rumors of a new invasion buildup began to be reported. In response, Admiral Struble visited Taiwan to prepare an improved and expanded Taiwan defense plan. Late in the month, the commander of naval forces in the Far East (ComNavFE) studied the situation and inaugurated a series of experimental exercises to determine the optimum choice of weapons against a junk fleet. Such fleets presented numerous small targets, which were hard to hit, almost impossible to sink because of their watertight compartments, and whose destruction might prove excessively costly in ammunition expenditure.

The comparatively short distance across the Taiwan Strait appeared to favor the Communist forces: "Planners in the Office of the Chief of Naval Operations estimated that a Communist junk flotilla would be able to transit the strait in one day, at a four- or five-knot speed of advance. For this reason, and because of the multitude of targets presented by a large fleet of junks, they believed a sizeable body of enemy troops might reach the shore of Taiwan without being intercepted. And everyone agreed that if any significant Communist forces landed on the island, the jig was up. Nationalist resistance would collapse. Morale was clearly eroded."[26]

On February 24, 1951, therefore, with the possibility of a spring Taiwan invasion in mind, Rear Admiral Lyman A. Thackrey was ordered to provide some sample junks at Yokosuka for practice purposes. Eight sixty-foot Korean junks were salvaged at Inchon and brought across in the USS *Tortuga* (LSD 26). In addition, they located a sunken six hundred–ton

Chinese junk. Acquiring this ship required overcoming great difficulties, but in time it was refloated, beached at Wolmi Do, and later embarked in *Colonial* (LSD 18) for delivery to Japan.

During March and April of 1951 extensive tests on how to counter a Chinese fleet made up of numerous junks were conducted under the direction of Rear Admiral Edgar A. Cruise, commander of the Hunter-Killer (HUK) Task Group. But his report on ordnance selection was not completed until May 1951. By this time, the PLA buildup in and around the Taiwan Strait had already had the effect of focusing USN resources on this region. In the end, the expected PRC junk fleet did not materialize, and there was never a PRC attack directed against Taiwan. During the next two decades, there was continual U.S. Navy monitoring, primarily by air, to see if the PRC was once again preparing for a cross-strait invasion. Another important mission included constant reconnaissance by air and sea throughout the Taiwan Strait region to make sure that any PLA-organized concentration of junks were discovered early on.

AIR-RECONNAISSANCE MISSIONS IN THE TAIWAN STRAIT

From the very first days of the Taiwan Patrol Force, reconnaissance from the air was a vital part of the patrol mission. On June 29, 1950, Rear Admiral John M. "Peg-Leg" Hoskins, acting commander of the Seventh Fleet, sent twenty-nine fighters and attack planes from *Valley Forge* roaring through the strait to show that the U.S. Navy had arrived.[27] This was the first sign of a long-term U.S. air-reconnaissance mission over the Taiwan Strait. Throughout the duration of the Taiwan Patrol Force, numerous U.S. aircraft patrolled off of the Chinese coast. This proved to be a much-needed addition to the normal Nationalist reconnaissance flights.

Beginning in late July 1950, patrol aircraft began reconnaissance missions in the Taiwan Strait. The Patrol Squadron 28 (VP-28), known as the Hawaiian Warriors, flying P4Y Privateers from Naha, Okinawa, initiated a daily surveillance of the northern strait and along the China coast. In Korea, this unit developed new techniques to repel mass attacks and worked closely with the U.S. Marine Corps to perfect night flare–dropping techniques that proved to be "amazingly effective against the 'human sea' tactics employed by huge masses of attacking North Korean and Chinese Communists troops."[28]

The day after VP-28 started operations, Patrol Squadron 46 (VP-46), with five patrol-bomber mariner (PBM) flying boats began patrolling the strait's southern sector from a base in the Penghu Islands.[29] Called the Grey Knights, VP-46 deployed twice more to the region before hostilities in Korea ended in July of 1953. The Grey Knights conducted antisubmarine warfare patrols, as well as overwater search and reconnaissance.[30] If VP-46 airplanes saw a junk formation heading for Taiwan, they were to use incendiary or hundred-pound bombs from about one thousand to fifteen hundred feet. To attack larger ships, however, they could drop to two hundred feet to conduct masthead-level bombing.[31] Seaplane Patrol Squadron One (VP-1), nicknamed "Fleet's Finest" from the mid-1950s onward, assisted this effort.[32] VP-1, deployed to the Western Pacific under the operational control of Fleet Air Wing-1 (FAW-1), was designated Task Group (TG) 70.6. It began combat operations from Naha AFB, Okinawa, on August 19, 1950, patrolling the sea-lanes in search of enemy resupply vessels.[33]

Throughout 1950 and 1951, one seaplane and one land-based squadron carried out the near-round-the-clock patrols from secure sea anchorages and land bases (see figure 3.2). Flying the patrol could be hazardous, especially in the poor weather conditions that existed in the Taiwan Strait area. Pilots were ordered to remain outside of the PRC's twelve-mile territorial border, but to obtain more useful photographs the aviators sometimes strayed over Chinese territory. For example, in September of 1952, in airspace not too far from Shanghai, a pair of PRC MiG-15s fired repeatedly on a Navy patrol plane but failed to shoot it down.[34]

Over time, the reconnaissance focus shifted from seaplanes to land-based air support. While seaplanes could land on water, which was a plus, they had more corrosion and rough-water problems than land-based planes. With limited funds, Admiral George Anderson determined in 1955 that it was easier to guarantee effective operations out of a squadron of landplanes rather than seaplanes. Without a huge research and development (R & D) investment to improve seaplanes, which clearly was not going to happen, the U.S. Navy knocked up against the seaplane's technological limits. Based on a wide range of considerations, Anderson concluded, "It was really, in my mind, the end of the seaplane operations of the U.S. Navy."[35]

It was fairly common in the early 1950s for U.S. aircraft to fly into Chinese airspace. U.S. reconnaissance planes were shot down over Chinese territory. In 1957, CNO Admiral Arleigh Burke ordered the Seventh Fleet to begin search and rescue (SAR) when a plane was lost just off the Chinese coast. With approval from President Dwight D. Eisenhower, the USN ships conducted operations up to the three-mile limit of China's territory, ignoring China's self-proclaimed twelve-mile limit. Although the pilot and his plane were not found, Burke kept the ships on station longer than necessary. "Let's stay there so that we rub it in just a little bit," Burke said, "We [will] make sure that they recognize that we're mad." Later, in 1973, Burke said, "Now, that's the use of power. Never again did they shoot down one of our planes."[36]

While passive signals intelligence from the air was the wave of the future, it was still extremely risky, especially before long-range equipment had been developed and successfully tested. Over time, special airplanes like the EA-3B Skywarriors and the EA-6B Prowlers led to the

38   Chapter 3

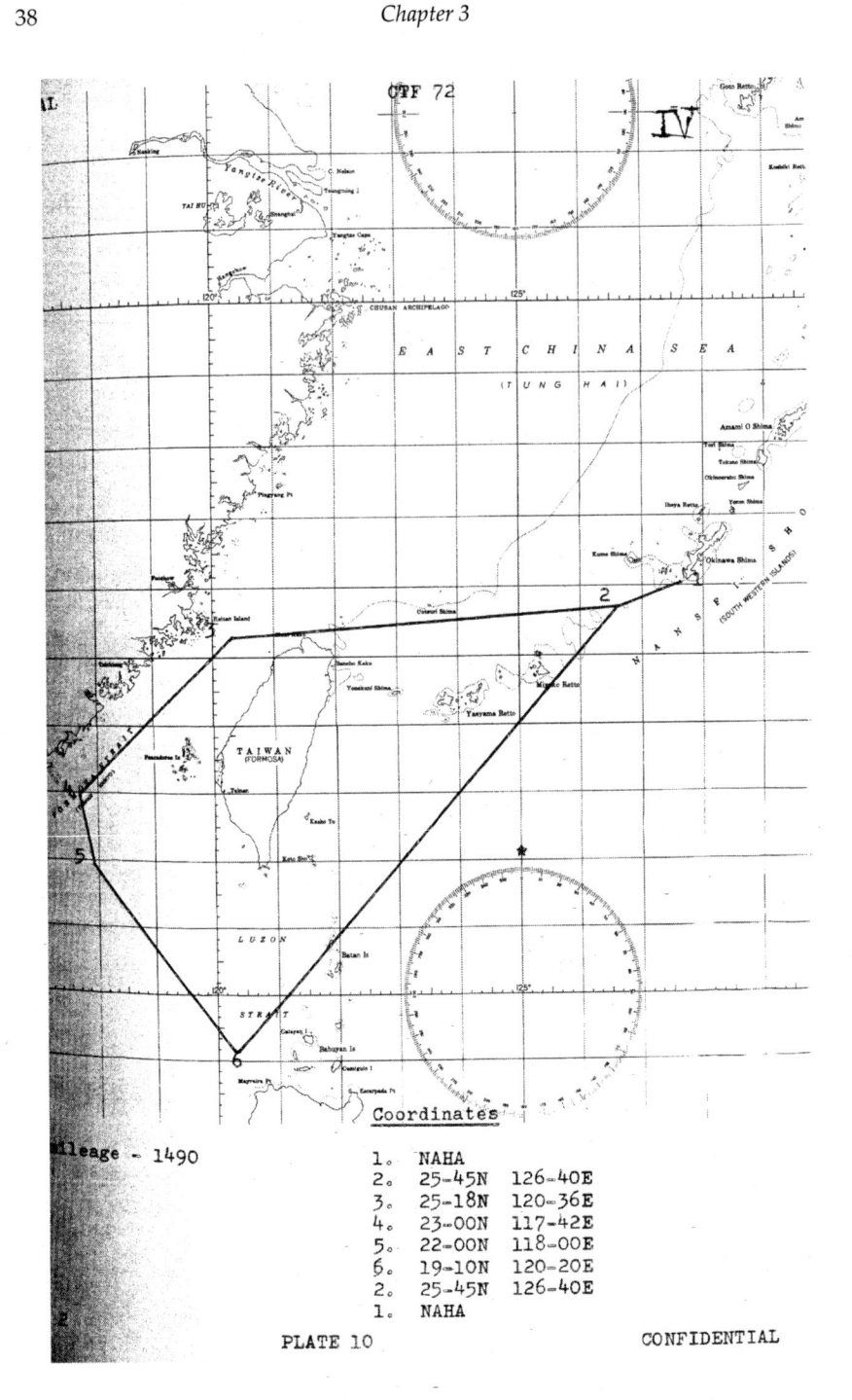

Figure 3.2.   Typical Air Reconnaissance Mission over the Taiwan Strait. Source: Naval History and Heritage Command Archives

Lockheed EP-3E Airborne Reconnaissance Integrated Electronic System (ARIES). These aircraft could do an even better job conducting electronic intelligence even while flying farther out to sea. Before these new airframes were fully developed, however, signal-intelligence missions were also conducted by specially outfitted USN ships. Once the PRC acquired submarines from the USSR, locating these assets soon became a focus of concern.

INITIATING ANTISUBMARINE-WARFARE EXERCISES

The potential submarine threat from the PRC greatly concerned the U.S. Navy. When the PRC was founded in 1949, it did not have a well-trained surface-ship navy, much less a submarine force. The northern fleet of the PLAN, called the North Sea Fleet, created China's first submarine corps on June 19, 1954.[37] Between 1953 and 1955, the USSR transferred to the PLAN a total of thirteen submarines, twelve large submarine chasers, and over fifty motor torpedo boats. By 1956, the U.S. Navy's Office of Naval Intelligence warned that China's growing submarine fleet "undoubtedly constitutes its greatest offensive potential as a Far Eastern naval force."[38] This made it more difficult for U.S. submarines to operate with the former impunity that they had enjoyed.

Throughout the mid-1950s, Moscow provided crucial assistance to Beijing's submarine program.[39] By early 1958, the Royal Navy estimated that the USSR had 112 submarines in the Pacific, with twenty more in the PLAN.[40] In 1960, the PRC's active submarine fleet had grown to twenty-five. China's submarines were mainly based at Qingdao and Shanghai, with the exception of a few training vessels based far to the north at Lüshun. But Chinese submarines were also observed operating as far south as Yulin, near Hainan Island, and so were most likely transiting the Taiwan Strait, as well as operating in waters near Taiwan.[41]

From the early 1950s onward, the conduct of U.S. naval exercises either in or near the Taiwan Strait was intended to send a clear signal to the PRC that USN vessels were ready to repel any submarine-led or -supported invasion of Taiwan. According to USN battle-plan assumptions, any PRC invasion would be preceded by air and submarine attacks against surface ships.[42] Submarine attacks were particularly deadly, so it was determined that "Unidentified submarines may be attacked and driven off by all means available in self-defense or when offensive action against our force is indicated. Continued submergence of any unidentified submarine in position to attack our force is considered to indicate offensive action."[43]

Since the rules of engagement (ROE) allowed for attacking unidentified submarines, combined antisubmarine exercises were particularly important. In the event of a real invasion there could be chaos and confusion due to the fact that U.S. and Nationalist crewmembers, particularly aircraft pilots and communication personnel, had not been provided with an opportunity to familiarize themselves with local conditions.[44] Later, "Shark Hunt" or hunter-killer (HUK) exercises were adopted to practice antisubmarine operations.

By the mid-1960s, combined exercises were regularly held between U.S. and Nationalist ships. Even after regular patrols were discontinued in 1969, USS *Caliente* (AO 53) conducted a training exercise on June 22, 1972, called SHARK HUNT II, with ships from Taiwan. From July 22 to 28 of that year, *Wiltsie* followed suit. During the early summer of 1973, the destroyers *Wiltsie, Southerland* (DD 743), and *McKean* (DD 784), sailed to Taiwan and participated in SHARK HUNT III with Nationalist destroyers. The U.S.–Taiwan combined training exercises continued all the way up until the late 1970s. In May of 1977, for example, USS *Buchanan* (DDG 14) was reportedly ordered to proceed to Kaohsiung to participate in exercise SHARK HUNT XXII.[45] The final exercise of this series, SHARK HUNT XXVIII, took place on November 6, 1978.[46]

This 1978 event proved to be one of the final combined U.S.–Taiwan surface and antisubmarine-warfare exercises. With the U.S. decision to recognize the PRC in 1979, these combined exercises had to be called to a halt. But other important strategic concerns, such as the possible use of atomic weapons, continued to have an enormous influence on relations between the United States and the Republic of China on Taiwan. From the early 1950s onward, there was almost constant debate in Washington over whether nuclear weapons could be used in response to a PRC invasion of Taiwan. In addition, the U.S. Navy had to conduct war games on the possible use of atomic weapons against an approaching surface- and subsurface-invasion force.

THE NUCLEAR OPTION

During the early 1950s, atomic bombs were often thought of much like regular bombs. The use of the A-bomb was considered in Korea, and later in Vietnam during the Dien Bien Phu crisis. With regard to Taiwan, in July of 1950 President Truman authorized the movement of B-29 bombers to Guam. They were capable of carrying atomic bombs, and the air unit in Guam was given control of nonradioactive atomic bomb components, with the nuclear core to be provided only during an emergency. This information was leaked to the *New York Times* so as to give the PRC pause before they decided to attack Taiwan.[47]

It is still unclear whether the U.S. government would have actually used A-bombs to halt a PRC invasion of Taiwan. In 1950, MacArthur told Averell Harriman during their talks on August 6 through 8 that if there were an attack, then Seventh Fleet ships, fighter jets from the Philippines and Okinawa, B-29s, and other aircraft could destroy any invasion attempt that might be made. He further stated that it would be a one-sided battle: "Should the Communists be so foolhardy as to make such an attempt, it would be the bloodiest victory in Far East history."[48] Although use of the A-bomb may not have been specifically discussed during these meetings, the fact that the A-bomb-equipped B-29s were mentioned by MacArthur suggests that he had their use in mind.

Even if MacArthur had not been referring to use of the A-bomb in 1950, the use of atomic weapons was certainly considered later during the 1950s. On September 12, 1954, during the first Taiwan Strait crisis, the U.S. Joint Chiefs of Staff (JCS) recommended considering using nuclear weapons against China. On March 10, 1955, Dulles stated at a National Security Council (NSC) meeting that the U.S. might use nuclear weapons against China, and on March 16 Eisenhower publicly confirmed that "A-bombs can be used . . . as you would use a bullet." About ten days later, on March 25, the CNO, Admiral Robert B. Carney, stated that the president was planning to destroy Red China's military potential, which certainly implied use of the atomic bomb.[49]

If these statements were intended to reach the ears of China's leaders, they succeeded. In February 1955, Mao Zedong warned the Finnish ambassador to China that "if the Americans atomic bombed Shanghai or Peking, 'they' [meaning the Soviets] would retaliate by wiping out American cities, which would cause the replacement of the present leaders of the United States." When the Finnish Ambassador double-checked with the Soviet Ambassador to China, he was assured that "if the Americans bombed the Chinese mainland, the Soviet Government would give the Chinese all possible support under the Sino–Soviet Agreement."[50] Certainly, the use of the phrase *all possible support* implied that the USSR might resort to nuclear weapons.

Because of its close proximity, Japan was particularly concerned that the United States's first use of atomic weapons might result in Soviet retaliation. A 1955 USN memorandum, summarizing a longer report by the U.S. ambassador to Japan, even warned that while the Japanese would support U.S. efforts to defend Taiwan and the Penghu Islands, they would expect that hostilities could be localized and that nuclear weapons would not be used. If fighting broke out over the smaller offshore islands, including over Jinmen and Mazu, the Japanese public would be far less supportive. USN involvement in these offshore-island disputes could jeopardize its entire position in Japan, especially if "we were to employ nuclear weapons."[51]

As commander in chief of the Pacific Command (CinCPac), Admiral Harry Felt, later recounted, by the end of the 1950s "at that time we had plans for use of tactical nuclear weapons."[52] Many military officers did not believe that tactical nuclear weapons would lead to a larger war. On September 2, 1958, General Twining, chairman of the JCS, explained to

Dulles that a seven- to ten-kiloton airburst bomb would have a lethal range of three to four miles, but there would be "virtually no fallout." If tensions over the Taiwan Strait got out of hand, it might be necessary to use tactical weapons against the PRC: "The initial attack would be only on five coast airfields (with one bomb being used per airfield)."[53] In January of 1958, Vice Admiral Austin K. Doyle, commander of the United States Taiwan Defense Command (USTDC), also reported that Matador missiles had been stationed in Taiwan and were ready for action. Although Doyle refused to say whether atomic weapons had been stockpiled in Taiwan, it was public knowledge that the Matador missiles were capable of delivering nuclear payloads in the forty- to fifty-kiloton range.[54]

Many civilian leaders in Washington were not as optimistic as their military counterparts about using atomic bombs as if they were conventional weapons. But, as Dulles told Prime Minister Macmillan in September of 1958, "It seems that the Sino–Soviet strategy is designed to put strains upon us at many separate places, and our various commitments to NATO, in Korea, to individual allies, are spreading our forces too thin for comfort—certainly unless atomic weapons are to be used."[55] Due to fears that first use of atomic weapons could lead to reprisals, Admiral Felt was eventually directed to draw up a plan for use of only conventional weapons.[56]

The United States' nuclear policy directly impacted Taiwan. During the mid-1960s, the Nationalists began their own nuclear-weapons program. According to declassified reports, the U.S. military stored atomic bombs in Taiwan, and these weapons were not removed until the early 1970s.[57] In 1976, under pressure from the U.S. government, Taiwan agreed to dismantle its nuclear program. Following the 1995 and 1996 Taiwan Strait crisis, President Lee Teng-hui proposed reactivating Taiwan's nuclear program, but he later backed down.

Although the nuclear aspect of U.S. policy toward the Taiwan Strait was always kept highly secret, it was clear from 1950 onward that atomic weapons were kept available in the region should they be needed to prevent a PRC invasion of Taiwan. Over time, however, more precise conventional weapons began to replace atomic bombs. To what degree Taiwan was able to make use of American help to build its own nuclear weapons is still unclear. Certainly this lack of clarity contributes to the importance of keeping tensions in the Taiwan Strait under tight control.

CONCLUSIONS

Spurred on by war on the Korean peninsula, the USN's patrols of the Taiwan Strait were intended to prevent the Chinese Communists from invading Taiwan. Moreover, as part of their neutralization function, they also discouraged the Nationalists from mounting a major attack of the Chinese mainland. A typical patrol in the Taiwan Strait might begin in waters just south of Japan, pass the Penghu Islands, and then cruise by southern Taiwan. Meanwhile, other ships were usually patrolling in the opposite direction heading north. By the mid-1950s, rising tensions between the PRC and Taiwan meant that the Taiwan Patrol Force operated substantially farther to the north. In 1955, for example, during the first Taiwan Strait crisis, USS *Wiltsie* (DD 716) even found herself within twelve nautical miles of Shanghai, right off the mouth of the Yangzi River.[58]

The Taiwan Patrol Force was conducted in a highly sensitive part of Asia. Since the primary goal was to dissuade an invasion from either side, the patrols often had the appearance of steaming up and down aimlessly.[59] The ultimate goal was to limit the possible spread of the Korean conflict farther to the south, which might then escalate into a world war between the United States and the USSR. Success was measured by what did not happen, so no news was good news. To ensure that a cross-strait conflict did not occur, the Taiwan Patrol Force had to take into account a number of special strategic concerns, including possible PRC attacks on the surface, in the air, and underwater and use of nuclear weapons by China's ally, the USSR, and—after Beijing exploded its own atomic bomb in 1964—by the PRC. USN vessels conducting patrols had to always be aware of the PRC's hostile intentions. As the early warning picket, these USN ships had to remain in continuous radio contact. If contact was broken, this could indicate an attack was in progress.

The USN crews had to be on constant watch for signs of an impending PRC cross-strait attack aimed at Taiwan. They were the first barrier in the defense of Taiwan.[60] James Barber probably put it best when he said that "The patrol's primary purpose was symbolic, to indicate an intention to come to Taiwan's aid if it were threatened by mainland China. Two DERs with two three-inch guns apiece did not constitute much of a military presence, but as a symbol of commitment the Patrol undoubtedly had value."[61] Or, as Doug Hatfield ironically recalled, "The Chinese Communists would have to go through us (Lots of Luck!) to invade Taiwan."[62] It was fairly certain, therefore, that the first USN ship to be attacked would be severely damaged if not destroyed. As later recounted by Paul Romanski, who served as Combat Information Center (CIC) officer in *Hissem* during late 1968 and early 1969, the USN ROE clearly stated that they could only use their weapons to defend themselves. This meant that the first USN ship to be attacked by Communist forces would necessarily become the proverbial "sacrificial anode."[63] Once the first USN ship was attacked, then others could be called in to respond in force. U.S.–PRC tensions remained high for more than two decades, and every sailor on a U.S. ship knew very well that World War III might erupt out of an incident that occurred in the Taiwan Strait. This situation was made even more tense by significant policy differences between the United States and United Kingdom regarding trade with the PRC.

NOTES

1. U.S. Office of Naval Intelligence, "The Southeast China Coast Today," *ONI Review* (February 1953): 51–60.
2. Charles H. Bogart, "Christmas in the Formosa Straits," *Dennis J. Buckley* and Other Navy Links (accessed December 13, 2010), http://djbuckley.com/bogy1.htm.
3. "Statement by the President," January 5, 1950, TNA/UK, PREM 8/1408.
4. James F. Schnabel, "The Relief of MacArthur," chap. 20 in *Policy and Direction: The First Year* (Washington, DC: U.S. Army Center of Military History, 1992) (accessed March 14, 2011), http://www.history.army.mil/books/pd-c-20.htm.
5. During the 1930s, a somewhat similar U.S. diplomatic policy directed against Japan's invasion of Manchuria was called the "nonrecognition" policy. The United States did not denounce Japan's aggression but did not recognize its gains either. The Taiwan neutralization order was designed to give U.S. policy makers maximum flexibility.
6. U.S. Navy Operation Order, ComCruDivONE No. 7-50, October 7, 1950, NHHC Archives, Post-1946 Operation Plans, Task Force 72.
7. Schnabel, "The Relief of MacArthur."
8. "Cabinet: Formosa, Memorandum by the Secretary of State for Foreign Affairs (Secret)," August 31, 1950, TNA/UK, PREM 8/1408.
9. Schnabel, "The Relief of MacArthur."
10. Jay Pryor interview with author, April 28, 2009.
11. Ibid. USS *Denny J* is short for USS *Dennis J. Buckley* (DDR 808).
12. James Barber interview with author, May 2, 2009.
13. "Operation Order 201 (Confidential)," Commander Task Force Seventy-Two, November 1, 1974, NHHC Archives, Post-1946 Operation Plans, Task Force 72, July 1968–1972, Box 290, B-II-10.
14. Bogart, "Christmas in the Formosa Straits."
15. Michael Westmoreland interview with author, April 29, 2009.
16. Doug Hatfield interview with author, April 29, 2009.
17. Paul Romanski interview with author, April 1 2009.
18. James Barber interview.
19. Commander Task Force Seventy-Two "Operation Order 201 (Confidential)," November 1, 1974, NHHC Archives, Post-1946 Operation Plans, Task Force 72, July 1968-1972, Box 290, B-II-10.
20. Paul Romanski interview.
21. Commander Task Force Seventy-Two, "Operation Order 201 (Confidential)," November 1, 1974, NHHC Archives, Post-1946 Operation Plans, Task Force 72, July 1968-1972, Box 290, B-II-10.
22. U.S. Navy Operation Order, ComCruDivONE No. 7-50, October 7, 1950, NHHC Archives, Post-1946 Operation Plans, Task Force 72.
23. Edward J. Marolda, "Invasion Patrol: The Seventh Fleet in Chinese Waters." Naval History and Heritage Command. Accessed December 13, 2010. http://www.history.navy.mil/colloquia/cch3c.htm.
24. "Annex A: Battle Plan (Confidential)," U.S. Navy Operation Order, ComCruDivONE No. 7-50, October 7, 1950, NHHC Archives, Post-1946 Operation Plans, Task Force 72.
25. Edward J. Marolda, "The U.S. Navy and the Chinese Civil War, 1945–1952," PhD diss. (The George Washington University, 1990), 193.
26. Marolda, "Invasion Patrol."
27. Ibid.

28. U.S. Navy Patrol Squadrons, "VP-28 History" (accessed December 13, 2010), http://www.vpnavy.com/vp28_1950.html.
29. Marolda, "Invasion Patrol."
30. "VP-46: History of VP-46," *History of the Grey Knights* (accessed October 16, 2014),http://www.vp46.navy.mil/history.html.
31. Marolda, "The U.S. Navy and the Chinese Civil War," 176.
32. VP-1 later replaced seaplanes with other airframes and after 1985 was known as the "Screaming Eagles."
33. Naval Historical Center, "Patrol Squadron (VP) Histories; VP-1 to VP-153," chap. 3 in *Dictionary of American Naval Aviation Squadrons*, vol. 2 (Washington, DC: Naval Historical Center, Department of the Navy, 2000) (accessed December 13, 2010), http://www.history.navy.mil/avh-vol2/chap3-1.pdf.
34. Edward J. Marolda, *The Approaching Storm: Conflict in Asia, 1945–1965* (Washington, DC: Government Printing Office, 2009), 14.
35. George W. Anderson Jr., *Reminiscences of Admiral George W. Anderson, Jr., U.S. Navy (Retired)*, Oral History 42 (Annapolis, MD: U.S. Naval Institute, 1983), 314. In fact, seaplanes continued to be used in Vietnam during the mid-1960s but never regained their former prominence.
36. Arleigh A. Burke, *Recollections of Admiral Arleigh A. Burke, U.S. Navy (Retired)*, Oral History 64 (Annapolis, MD: U.S. Naval Institute, 1973), 42.
37. Srikanth Kondapalli, *China's Naval Power* (New Delhi: Knowledge World, 2001), 36.
38. U.S. Office of Naval Intelligence, "The Red Chinese Navy," *ONI Review*, secret supplement (Summer 1956): 5–8.
39. James Bussert and Bruce A. Elleman, *People's Liberation Army Navy (PLAN): Combat Systems Technology, 1949–2010* (Annapolis, MD: Naval Institute Press, 2011), 63–65.
40. UK Consulate, Tamsui, to Foreign Office, January 27, 1958, TNA/UK, FO 371/33522.
41. U.S. Office of Naval Intelligence, "Current Trends in the Chinese Communist Navy," *ONI Review* (November 1960): 476–81.
42. "Annex A: Battle Plan (Confidential)," U.S. Navy Operation Order, ComCruDiv-ONE No. 7-50, October 7, 1950, NHHC Archives, Post-1946 Operation Plans, Task Force 72.
43. U.S. Navy Operation Order, ComDesDiv 112 No. 2-50, December 1, 1950, NHHC Archives, Post-1946 Operation Plans, Task Force 72.
44. Enclosure (1), "Comment on Modified Operational Instructions to CINCPAC," memorandum from Chief of Naval Operations, Admiral Robert B. Carney, to Joint Chiefs of Staff (top secret), Undated on March 19, 1953, Strategic Plans Division, NHHC Archives, Box 289.
45. "Commanding Officers Annual History Reports" (accessed October 16, 2014), http://www.uss-buchanan-ddg14.org/Annual%20History/History77.htm.
46. *U.S. Taiwan Defense Command Terminal History, Jan 1, 1978–30 April 1979*, 68.
47. Marolda, "The U.S. Navy and the Chinese Civil War," 180.
48. Ibid., 189–90.
49. GlobalSecurity.org, "First Taiwan Strait Crisis: Quemoy and Matsu Islands" (accessed December 14, 2010), http://www.globalsecurity.org/military/ops/quemoy_matsu.htm.
50. From UK Embassy in Peking to Foreign Office (secret), February 5, 1955, TNA/UK, PREM 11/867.
51. "Probable Japanese Reactions if U.S. Becomes Involved in Defense of Formosa and the Pescadores or the Offshore Islands," (top secret memorandum), W. K. Smedberg III, Director, Politico-Military Policy, Strategic Plans Division, NHHC Archives, Box 326. The Hoover Institution Archives announced on November 19, 2014, the existence of formerly secret documents proving that as many as 83 retired Japanese officers were covertly hired by Chiang Kai-shek during the 1950s to train Nationalist

officers. See http://www.hoover.org/news/new-japanese-materials-reveal-complicated-history-east-asia. My thanks to Stephen Kotkin for pointing this out.

52. Harry Donald Felt, *Reminiscences of Admiral Harry Donald Felt, U.S. Navy (Retired)*, Oral History 138 (Annapolis, MD: U.S. Naval Institute, 1974), 396.

53. Harriet Dashiell Schwar, ed., and Glen W. LaFantasie, gen. ed., "Memorandum of Conversation," September 2, 1958, in *Foreign Relations of the United States 1958–1960*, vol. 19, *China* (Washington, DC: United States Government Printing Office, 1996), 120.

54. UK Consulate, Tamsui, to Foreign Office, January 27, 1958, TNA/UK, FO 371/33522.

55. Letter from John Foster Dulles to Harold Macmillan (top secret), September 5, 1958, TNA/UK, CAB 21/3272.

56. Felt, *Reminiscences of Admiral Harry Donald Felt*, 396.

57. In 1974, all nuclear weapons were moved from Taiwan to Clark Air Base in the Philippines. Commander-in-Chief, U.S. Pacific Command, "CINCPAC Command History, 1974," vol. 1, accessed October 16, 2014, http://oldsite.nautilus.org/archives/library/security/foia/Japan/CINCPAC74Ip263.PDF; and find links for further documentation at Nautilus Institute, "Nuclear Strategy Project: Japan FOIA Documents," athttp://oldsite.nautilus.org/archives/library/security/foia/japanindex.html.

58. "USS *Wiltsie* DD-716." http://www.destroyersonline.com/usndd/dd716/ (accessed October 23, 2014).

59. Joe Claytor, "USS *Keppler* (DD-765)," Korean War Project (accessed December 13, 2010),http://www.koreanwar.org/html/units1/navy/uss_keppler.htm.

60. Several authors have argued that the PRC's invasion of Taiwan was "frustrated" by the presence of the U.S. Navy. John Gittings, *The Role of the Chinese Army* (New York: Oxford University Press, 1967), 40–44; Allen Whiting, *China Crosses the Yalu: The Decision to Enter the Korean War* (New York: Macmillan, 1960), 63–64.

61. James A. Barber interview.

62. Doug Hatfield interview.

63. Paul Romanski interview. A more corrosive metal placed near a less-active metal can protect it from corroding.

FOUR

Debates on the U.S.–China Policy

During the early 1950s, the United States and the United Kingdom carried out near-continuous discussions on their respective China policies. While the U.S. government supported a policy of refusing to recognize or trade with the PRC at all, the British had to be especially concerned about the fate of their colony of Hong Kong. At any point, the PRC could send in troops and take Hong Kong by force. Hong Kong's vulnerability led to the British decision to recognize the PRC on January 6, 1950, and to adopt a more liberal trade policy with China.

As argued persuasively by A. E. Franklin in January of 1951, "Hong Kong and its population of over two million Chinese are largely dependent on trade with China," and a complete embargo "would inevitably lead to serious discontentment and possibly even to loss of the Colony to China, which clearly would be harmful all round."[1] Furthermore, Hong Kong's strategic location could provide the West with crucial leverage over the PRC. It was of great value that Hong Kong should continue without undue economic dislocation as part of the free world, and they "must therefore insist on the importance of preventing economic distress which would foster popular unrest that might easily precipitate a dangerous state of affairs."[2]

The U.S. government was not immediately convinced by this reasoning, however, and ordered the U.S. Navy to conduct a number of studies on how effective a complete U.S. naval blockade of the PRC might be. During 1951, these studies tended to confirm Hong Kong's crucial strategic role and warned that any blockade of the PRC that did not include Hong Kong was bound to fail. So as to avoid undermining Anglo–American relations, it was eventually decided to rely more on the U.S. embargo of strategic goods, with help from the Nationalist Navy to enforce the embargo, to put economic pressure on China.

THE BRITISH DECISION TO RECOGNIZE THE PRC

In sharp contrast to the United States' support for the Nationalist blockade, the British government saw the continuation of trade between Hong Kong and the PRC as leaving the door open for China to move closer to the West. Unlike the United States, which did not have an empire to protect, the British had to be concerned with the safety of its colonies in India (which gained independence in 1947), Singapore, and Malaysia. Hong Kong's geographic position, just a stone's throw from the PRC, made conducting diplomatic talks between the UK and China particularly important. As a result, British recognition of the PRC broke with the United States.

Hong Kong was vulnerable to any fluctuations in trade. Its population thrived on international commerce with the PRC. A complete embargo would devastate these commercial enterprises, since approximately 45 percent of all of Hong Kong's exports went to China. During the first eleven months of 1950, for example, Hong Kong exports to China equaled 460 million Hong Kong dollars, with another 235 million Hong Kong dollars to Macao, much of which was re-exported to China. According to Hong Kong's governor, without this trade the "thriving, trading, financial, and insurance entrepôt of the Colony" would become "an economic desert."[3]

Another factor to keep in mind was Hong Kong's strategic maritime location. Assuming it ever fell to the Communists, Hong Kong would provide the PRC with a first-class naval base with valuable repair facilities for the PLAN, as well as one of the best airports in South China. If Russian forces were stationed there it could quickly become a threat to the U.S. bases in the Philippines. Finally, Hong Kong's fall would have huge Communist propaganda value and would assist the spread of Communism into Southeast Asia.[4] One British memo even warned that if Hong Kong fell into China's hands it "would be a useful base for operations against Formosa."[5]

There was always a chance that China would eventually reject monolithic Communism. As long as the PRC could expect to obtain certain supplies from the West, Beijing would not be completely dependent on the USSR and the East European satellites.[6] Britain's long-range goal vis-à-vis Hong Kong was to maintain a commercial and cultural foothold and to keep Western influence alive in the PRC.[7] While the U.S. policy might possibly result in throwing China into Russia's arms, Britain's recognition of the PRC sought to strengthen Mao's leverage in his negotiations with Stalin.[8] The British warned that the Western policy should not solidify against it the 700 million Russians and Chinese.[9] At some point, it was hoped that Britain's more friendly policy toward China might even pay dividends by "driving a wedge" between the PRC and the USSR.[10]

The U.S. government was forced to turn a blind eye to Hong Kong's commercial relations with China, since the danger of losing Hong Kong was greater than any possible trade benefits to the PRC. Meanwhile, the U.S. government's policy toward the PRC began to move closer and closer to the Nationalists. Beginning in summer 1949 and intensifying through early 1950, the U.S. adopted a policy of sealing the Communists into their continental territory by supporting a trade embargo.[11] During 1950, John Foster Dulles, the future secretary of state, began to argue that the best defense against Sino–Soviet military cooperation "lies in exploiting potential jealousies, rivalries, and disaffection within the present area of the Soviet Communist control so as to divert them from external adventures." Eisenhower later acknowledged that "trade might be a very useful tool" to "weaken the Sino–Soviet alliance."[12]

In sharp contrast to British recognition of the PRC, therefore, the U.S. government continued to recognize the exiled Nationalist officials on Taiwan. This political difference threatened to undermine Anglo–American cooperation. For example, during one October 1953 incident, the captain of a Nationalist warship even signaled to a British captain: "You should leave here at once. You were the enemy against the Communists in Korea, here you are their friends. Don't you feel ashamed of your honourable dead in Korea."[13] Beginning in January 1950, the U.S. imposed a strategic embargo against shipping certain goods to the PRC. But Washington did not want to become involved in a cross-strait war. Following the beginning of the Korean War, and in particular after the PRC's military intervention during the fall of 1950, however, the U.S. government for a short time even considered instituting a full naval blockade of its own against the PRC.

DEBATES OVER ESTABLISHING A U.S. NAVY BLOCKADE OF THE PRC

As the Korean War heated up during the fall of 1950, and following the intervention of Chinese forces during November of that year, the JCS ordered the U.S. Navy to study the prospects for adopting a full naval blockade of China.[14] As part of this order, the CNO was asked to estimate both the effects of a naval blockade on China and the USN force requirements to conduct such a blockade. After examining this question, it soon became apparent that adopting a full naval blockade of China might easily result in increased tensions not only with the USSR, which continued to occupy the ports of Lüshun and Dalian in Manchuria, but also with America's staunchest European ally, the United Kingdom, since such a blockade could only be truly effective if it cut off trade between Hong Kong and the PRC.

On January 6, 1951, the CNO, Admiral Forest Sherman, submitted a study, *Estimate of the Effects of a Naval Blockade of China*, to the JCS. This study concluded that for a naval blockade of China to be effective, it had to be applied equally to Hong Kong, the Portuguese island of Macao, and to the Soviet-controlled ports of Lüshun and Dalian. Blockading Manchuria would undoubtedly cause serious repercussions in the USSR, but if the blockade did not include Manchuria then it absolutely had to include Hong Kong and Macao, which would negatively impact U.S. relations with the UK and Portugal. For a U.S. blockade of the PRC to be truly effective, therefore, it would need to cut off all petroleum supplies, machinery and machine tools, railway equipment, rubber, and chemicals. Of course, many of these items could still be imported by land, and it was assumed that China would continue to receive economic and military assistance from the USSR. Given the available land routes, "Prevention of such imports by sea would leave China dependent upon the Soviet Bloc for these materials which are likewise in short supply in those countries."[15]

To conduct a full naval blockade of China, the U.S. Navy would need to close the ports of Hong Kong and Qingdao, plus close off the Korean Bay, the Bo Hai Gulf, and the mouth of the Yangzi River completely. For such a massive operation, a minimum of thirty-six destroyers, or other patrol vessels, would need to be allocated full time to be supported by five VP (U.S. Navy patrol) squadrons and anywhere from four to six submarines for occasional patrols as "opportunity, reconnaissance needs, and other circumstances dictate." An operation of this magnitude would also require huge logistical support, including at least four AV/AVP aircraft and seaplane tenders on station at all times.[16]

In his conclusions, the CNO reiterated that if ports in Manchuria were not included in the naval blockade, then Hong Kong and Macao would have to be blockaded. He listed nine possible positive outcomes of such a blockade operation:

1. Aid in the restoration of the prestige of the United States in the Far East and throughout the world.
2. Reduce the threat of amphibious invasion of Formosa, Japan, and other Far Eastern areas.
3. Keep Chinese Communist forces under surveillance and provide early warning of any movement by sea.
4. Permit the strengthening of Japan and Formosa without undue fear of Chinese Communist attack.
5. Impose an economic strain on the war-making potentialities of the Chinese Communists.
6. Overload and reduce the efficiency of the Chinese transportation system and place an additional strain on Russian transportation.

7. Encourage the Nationalist guerrilla forces now operating in south China and probably cause them to intensify their efforts while reducing Chinese Communist' ability to resist them.
8. Force the USSR to supply the major part of the equipment required by the Chinese Communists, thus interfering with the Russian armament program for her satellites in Europe.
9. Force certain United Nation members to recognize the fact that the United States refuses to continue the present conflict on a "business-as-usual" basis.[17]

Even though the CNO's nine concluding points were highly positive in nature, the political reality was that a U.S. blockade would either have to be focused on the Soviet Union or on the United Kingdom. Any U.S. naval blockade of Hong Kong would immediately undermine the long-standing Anglo–American alliance that was so important for propping up the NATO security system in Europe and for backing the UN military effort in Korea. For this reason, USN vessels patrolling the Taiwan Strait were warned beginning in December of 1950 to interrogate passing vessels discretely, since too thorough an interrogation might appear to be part of a blockade operation.[18] One USN study even cautioned that because the PRC was almost sure to retaliate with force if a full blockade were adopted, it was essential that "before establishing it [naval blockade] [e]nsure that Hong Kong is adequately defended."[19]

Given the assumption that a full U.S. blockade might lead to a break in diplomatic relations with Britain, on the one hand, or a PRC invasion of Hong Kong, on the other, it was not a coincidence that the CNO submitted his report to the JCS on January 6, 1951, the first anniversary of the British recognition of the PRC. Thus, even though the CNO began his letter by stating that he would not deal with political issues, the glaringly obvious political importance of retaining friendly U.S.–British relations virtually guaranteed that the U.S. Navy would never be ordered to institute a naval blockade of China that would include Hong Kong. Additionally, a strict naval blockade of the USSR's military bases in Manchuria might result in Soviet efforts to expand "Chinese Communist capabilities in submarine, air, and mine warfare."[20]

U.S.–LED STRATEGIC EMBARGO OF THE PRC

While the U.S. and Britain fought side by side with each other in Korea, the British traded freely with the PRC, while the U.S. did not. During early 1951, largely in response to China's armed intervention in the Korean War, but with due consideration for the Nationalist blockade, the British government considered halting trade with the PRC but rejected the idea. Because a full U.S. naval blockade of the PRC was politically infeasible due to the possible retaliation of the USSR, on the one hand,

and to Hong Kong's sensitive strategic position, on the other hand, beginning in December of 1950, the U.S. government instead began to impose a complete embargo on strategic goods to the PRC. This policy fell under the COCOM (Coordinating Committee for Multilateral Export Controls) trade control regime, which had previously been adopted in January of 1950. Although less effective than a full naval blockade, the U.S. government worked closely with the Nationalists to help enforce the strategic embargo.

The fifteen-country COCOM group was composed of the United States, all of the NATO countries, minus Iceland, and then also Japan. To convince other countries to conform to these proscriptions against China, Congress adopted the Mutual Defense Assistance Control Act of 1951. Commonly called the Battle Act, after its sponsor Congressman Laurie C. Battle, this legislation would terminate economic and military aid to countries that refused to cooperate with the control program.[21] During the fall of 1952, China Committee (CHINCOM) controls were instituted that were even tighter, embargoing industrial machinery, steel mill products, and metal of all types. Meanwhile, the U.S. embargo was also broadened to include more countries in COCOM and CHINCOM, such as Greece and Turkey in 1953, and bolstered by pledges of cooperation from Sweden and Switzerland, both important neutral countries.[22]

The Nationalist Navy fully cooperated in enforcing the U.S. sanctions program. For example, in early 1951 a Norwegian-owned ship, *Hoi Houw*, was reported to be carrying U.S.–made medicines and other manufactured goods to China.[23] These goods were originally shipped on American-flagged vessels from the United States to Bombay before a total embargo was instituted. Following the embargo's adoption, the goods were reloaded at Bombay onto the Norwegian ship for transport to the PRC. Upon hearing this news, the United States asked the United Kingdom to intercept the cargo when the ship docked in Hong Kong and halt its delivery to the PRC. But instead, the governor of Hong Kong arranged with the Norwegian consul in the Colony so that *Hoi Houw* would not call at Hong Kong.[24]

When *Hoi Houw* failed to stop in Hong Kong, this ignited a widespread search for the ship. Four USN destroyers and planes operated in the Taiwan Strait, and another three Nationalist destroyer escorts and planes patrolled east of Taiwan. When *Hoi Houw* passed sixty miles to the east of Taiwan, it was intercepted by the Nationalist Navy on February 11, 1951. Its cargo was impounded at Keelung, while the ship and crew were released on February 20, 1951.[25] As reported by Royal Navy Commander M. E. Lashmore, the interception and detention of *Hoi Houw* showed the close cooperation between the Americans and the Nationalists: "There can be little doubt that the Americans were behind the seizure and, whatever the cargo was, were determined to stop it reaching China. They were in the happy position of being able to get the Chinese

Nationalists to do their work for them and thus in theory being in no way connected with the incident." Later, U.S. government officials took their "ingenuous bluff" even further by asking authorities in Hong Kong for information on what was happening to *Hoi Houw* on Taiwan, "on the grounds that the U.S. authorities there did not know anything about her!"[26]

Officially, the U.S. government opposed the Nationalist blockade and so opposed the interception of neutral ships. According to a report from the British Consul in Taiwan, when U.S. government officials were asked about the matter, they said they could not "officially . . . approve the interception which contravened both International Law and the agreement between Nationalist China and America over the protection of Formosa, [but] they consider it most unlikely that they will be instructed to make any protest, as American public opinion obviously approves of the Nationalist action."[27]

Although a confidential 1955 USN report admitted that the strategic embargo was incomplete and that China obtained many goods through triangular deals and transshipments, the overall success of the embargo was shown by the fact that China's procurement was seriously hampered and higher costs had reduced the total amount of goods purchased.[28] A British report from February 1951 had likewise concluded that the U.S. sanctions program was quite effective and had produced a great shock to the mainland Chinese economy.[29] The Swedish ambassador confirmed that the strategic embargo was having the desired effect, since international "shipping was the Achilles heel of China and that if the amount of shipping engaged in trade with China would be drastically reduced it would have a serious effect on the Chinese economy."[30] The embargo's effectiveness had a negative impact on British trade with China, however, which led to a sharp increase in cross-strait tensions.

THE USE OF GUERRILLA BASES IN THE TAIWAN STRAIT

During the early 1950s, U.S. support for the Nationalist blockade shifted from opposing it at the beginning to lukewarm support to more active support for an air-based blockade in 1953. In order to avoid increasing diplomatic tension with the British and other neutral powers, the Nationalists largely depended on guerrillas in the Dachen Islands to enforce the blockade in the north. These blockade efforts were actively assisted by the United States. On the Lower Dachen Island, for example, the Central Intelligence Agency (CIA) Western Enterprises Incorporated (WEI) sent U.S. advisors to train the guerrillas. Lon Redman, a WEI advisor, even attempted to bulldoze an airstrip so that C-46 cargo planes could land. But this plan had to be abandoned once it became clear that they could not build a strip long enough to permit a C-46 unless they bulldozed almost down to sea level.[31]

The Nationalists portrayed these guerrilla bands as anti-Communist fighters. But to many foreign shippers, the pro-Nationalist guerrillas appeared little better than modern-day pirates. As reported by one British official in 1952, "Indications are that most of the piracies are done by Nationalist guerrillas not under the effective control of Taipei. The border line is obscure. In 1948 it was respectable for bandits to masquerade as Communist Liberation forces; in 1952 it is respectable for pirates to masquerade as the Nationalist Navy."[32]

The U.S. Navy's Office of Naval Intelligence (ONI) provided a good example of how the Nationalist-guerrilla blockade functioned. The British merchant ship *Admiral Hardy* was intercepted by guerrillas on September 8, 1952, trying to enter Fuzhou. Taken to White Dog Island, the guerrillas claimed that the ship was carrying strategic goods and so impounded its entire cargo. A $2,300 bribe was necessary to win the release of the ship and its crew. Before allowing the ship to leave, the head of the guerrilla group indicated that there would be no interference during any future trip if $15,000 were paid in advance to his agent in Hong Kong. This arrangement was to be secret, since the guerrillas were apparently "apprehensive lest the Nationalist Navy learn of this transaction."[33]

Sometimes these guerrilla units attacked the wrong ship, as occurred on February 11, 1951, when the British-registered *Wing Sang* sailing from Hong Kong to Taiwan was boarded and looted by Nationalist guerrillas. The Nationalist government immediately denied any connection with the guerrillas. After British protests via the U.S. embassy in Taipei, however, the Nationalists announced that the guerrilla leader responsible for the attack had been captured and executed. As one source noted, "In this case the [pro-Nationalist guerrilla] attackers made the mistake of attacking a ship engaged in trade with Formosa."[34]

The British government repeatedly protested against the Nationalist blockade policies and in particular against the illegal activities of Taiwanese warships and guerrillas interfering with British merchant shipping.[35] During the three years from 1951 to 1953, there were 141 reported incidents, including attacks from the sea (sixty-one), land batteries (fourteen), and air assaults (three) that resulted in four injuries and one death.[36] Over time, the Nationalist air blockade actually became tighter as U.S.–built, Nationalist-piloted planes were able to harass and even damage British-owned ships. As one British captain complained, "I can handle any two Nationalist warships. I don't mind their guns or their old planes. But I hate these jets! They come screaming out of nowhere, blast you, and then they're gone. You don't have a chance."[37]

With Chinese coastal shipping blocked by the Nationalists, much of the PRC's domestic north–south trade was diverted inland by train. Meanwhile, China's international maritime trade was largely conducted by either foreign-registered or Hong Kong ships, which—in theory at least—were neutral vessels. In response to these U.S.–imposed trade restrictions, the bulk of China's foreign trade now had to be conducted overland either with the Soviet Union directly or via the USSR with a number of friendly Eastern European countries. This put enormous strain on China's own railway system, not to mention the Trans-Siberian Railroad. As a result, by the late 1950s over half of China's foreign trade was with the USSR.[38]

CONCLUSIONS

In 1951, a full U.S. blockade of the PRC was discussed by U.S Navy planners, but fear of undermining the Anglo–American alliance both in Europe and in Korea overshadowed any possible benefits. During late 1953 and early 1954, therefore, the U.S. government provided the Nationalists with better equipment to enforce the blockade from the air. While about half of China's trade was at that point being conducted overland, mainly with the USSR, an estimated 1,000 foreign ship arrivals per year accounted for the rest of her foreign trade. With American training, equipment, and financial backing, it was hoped that the naval blockade would grow even more effective as the U.S. government helped build up the Nationalist naval and air forces.[39]

During 1953 and 1954, the Nationalist blockade gradually shifted away from patrol vessels to using more air power, mainly provided by the United States. In April 1953, Taipei also adopted more-stringent shipping regulations, largely in line with those already promulgated by the U.S. Maritime Shipping Association, which would prohibit any government-chartered foreign vessel from proceeding to any Communist country within a "sixty-day period after it had discharged its cargo at ports in Free China."[40] Incidents involving Nationalist ships steadily decreased even while airplane patrols became more common. During 1954, for example, there were a total of thirty-two incidents in which the Nationalist Air Force attacked British shipping.[41]

The British were upset by U.S. support for the Nationalist blockade of China, fearful that too strict an embargo might spark a war with the PRC.[42] But an even greater concern to London was that increasing Anglo–American friction might prejudice their world-wide cooperation, with possibly serious consequences to the security of Western Europe.[43] Given British reluctance to break openly with the U.S. government, it would be up to the PRC to stop the Nationalist air attacks. In 1954 and 1955, during the so-called first Taiwan Strait crisis, one of the PRC's most important objectives was to force the Nationalists to end their blockade of the Chinese coastline. USN ships assigned to the Taiwan Patrol Force were destined to play a crucial role during this crisis.

NOTES

1. Control of Exports from Hong Kong to China, A. E. Franklin, January 15, 1951, TNA/UK, FO 371/92274.
2. Memorandum from Washington to Foreign Office, January 9, 1951, TNA/UK, FO 371/92272.
3. "Sanctions against China. Probable economic political and strategic consequences in Hong Kong, Malaya and South East Asia generally," draft memorandum (top secret), undated (but most likely written in December 1950), TNA/UK, FO 371/92276.
4. Telegram 821 to Washington, discussing Hong Kong, March 1, 1951, TNA/UK, FO 371/92276.
5. "Secret" telegram from the Foreign Office to Washington, March 1, 1951, TNA/UK, FO 371/92276. This line was marked out of the telegram, perhaps because it made it sound like the British government was using Hong Kong's possible occupation by the PRC as a threat against U.S. support for Taiwan.
6. "Control of Experts from Hong Kong to China," A. A. E. Franklin, January 15, 1951, TNA/UK, FO 371/92274.
7. "Effects on Hong Kong of American Economic Action against China," N. C. C. Trench, January 13, 1951, TNA/UK, FO 371/92275.
8. "Conversation between the Foreign Secretary and Mr. Spender at the Foreign Office on 1st September, 1950," TNA/UK, PREM 8/1121.
9. "War with China," memorandum by UK Chiefs of Staff, undated (probably written during 1950), TNA/UK, PREM 8/1408.
10. Memo on China sanctions to R. A. Butler, October 21, 1952, TNA/UK, T 237/205.
11. Letter from H. A. Graves, British Embassy in Washington, to P. W. S. Y. Scarlett, Far Eastern Department (secret), February 4, 1950, TNA/UK, FO 371/83425.
12. Shu Guang Zhang, *Economic Cold War: America's Embargo against China and the Sino-Soviet Alliance, 1949–1963* (Stanford, CA: Stanford University Press, 2001), 115, 124.
13. "Formosa Strait Patrol—2nd to 6th October," R. D. Ritchie, Commander-in-Command, to the commodore in charge, Hong Kong, October 7, 1953, TNA/UK, ADM 1/24801.
14. JCS 92847 directed "CinCPac to develop a plan for a blockade of the China coast by naval forces." Cited in top-secret memorandum from the director of Strategic Plans to DCNO (Operations), June 14, 1951, Strategic Plans Division, NHHC Archives, Box 266.
15. "Estimate of the Effects of a Naval Blockade of China," top-secret study submitted by the chief of naval operations to the Joint Chiefs of Staff, January 6, 1951, Strategic Plans Division, NHHC Archives, Box 266.
16. Ibid.
17. Ibid.
18. U.S. Navy Operation Order, ComDesDiv 112 No. 2-50, December 1, 1950, NHHC Archives, Post-1946 Operation Plans, Task Force 72.
19. "Blockade of Communist China," memorandum for record, R. E. Stanley (top secret), February 12, 1953, Strategic Plans Division, NHHC Archives, Box 289.
20. "Estimate of the Effects of a Naval Blockade of China."
21. U.S. Office of Naval Intelligence, "The Southeast China Coast Today," *ONI Review* (February 1953): 51–60.
22. Sherman R. Abrahamson, "Intelligence for Economic Defense," Central Intelligence Agency, September 18, 1995, last updated August 3, 2011, https://www.cia.gov/library/center-for-the-study-of-intelligence/kent-csi/vol8no2/html/v08i2a03p_0001.htm.
23. The U.S. strategic embargo's effectiveness was shown by descriptions of how rare American medicines became in the PRC during the early 1950s, to the point where

only the Communist elite could obtain access to them. Jung Chang, *Wild Swans* (New York: Simon and Schuster, 1991), 175–76.

24. "*Hoi Houw*" minutes from N. C. C. Trench to Fitzmaurice, March 15, 1951, TNA/UK, FO 371/92277.

25. "Interception and Detention of MV *Hoi Houw*, 11th to 20th February, 1951 (Secret)," Commander M. E. Lashmore, Royal Navy, March 9, 1951, TNA/UK, FO 371/92278.

26. Ibid. Exclamation point in original.

27. Report from Consul E. T. Biggs, Tamsui, Formosa, to G. W. Aldington, Political Advisor, Hong Kong, February 24, 1951, TNA/UK, FO 371/92276.

28. "Memorandum of Information for the Secretary of the Navy," W. K. Smedberg, director, Politico-Military Policy (confidential), October 13, 1955, Strategic Plans Division, NHHC Archives, Box 326.

29. Letter from the China Association, London, to J. S. H. Shattock, Foreign Office, London, February 26, 1951, TNA/UK, FO 371/92276.

30. Telegram from the UK Delegation, New York, to Foreign Office, June 8, 1951, TNA/UK, FO 371/92280.

31. Frank Holober, *Raiders of the China Coast: CIA Covert Operations during the Korean War* (Annapolis, MD: Naval Institute Press, 1999), 113–14.

32. "Report on Visit to Hong Kong, 15–21 February, 1952," (secret), by D. F. Allen, TNA/UK, ADM 1/23217.

33. U.S. Office of Naval Intelligence, "The Southeast China Coast Today."

34. Ibid.

35. Memo on China sanctions to R. A. Butler, October 21, 1952, TNA/UK, T 237/205.

36. "Incidents involving British Merchant Ships Off the China Coast," July 18, 1955, TNA/UK, ADM 116/6245.

37. *U.S. News and World Report*, "A New Type of Formosa Warfare: Reds Spot British Cargo Ships for Chiang's Bombers," November 18, 1955.

38. Bruce A. Elleman and Stephen Kotkin, eds. *Manchurian Railways and the Opening of China: An International History* (Armonk, NY: M. E. Sharpe, 2010), 199.

39. *U.S. News and World Report*, "China Blockade: How It Works; Ships by the U.S.—Sailors by Chiang Kai-shek," February 20, 1953.

40. John Foster Dulles Papers, Princeton University, Reel 204/205, April 23, 1953, 88971.

41. "China: Interference with British Merchant Shipping (Secret)," 1955, TNA/UK, ADM 116/6245.

42. Edward J. Marolda, "The U.S. Navy and the Chinese Civil War, 1945–1952," PhD diss. (The George Washington University, 1990), 372.

43. "Strategic Implications of the Application of Economic Sanctions against China," annex (top secret), undated (but most likely written in February 1951), TNA/UK, FO 371/92276.

FIVE

The First Taiwan Strait Crisis, 1954 to 1955

By the summer of 1953, the Korean conflict had ended in an apparent stalemate. There were numerous reasons for signing the armistice, but Stalin's death on March 5, 1953, helped break the negotiating deadlock over the status of North Korean defectors. The Korean armistice was finally signed on July 27, 1953. Soon afterward, the PRC began to redeploy troops from north to south. Tensions gradually grew throughout the south, particularly in the Taiwan Strait region, with Secretary of State John Foster Dulles describing it as equivalent to "living over a volcano."[1]

On August 11, 1954, Zhou Enlai, the head of the PRC's foreign ministry, stated that the PRC must liberate Taiwan. Three weeks later, on September 3, 1954, PLA forces began to bombard Jinmen Island, killing two U.S. military advisors, Lt. Col. Alfred Mendendorp and Lt. Col. Frank W. Lynn. This renewed focus on the Taiwan Strait was intended to show Mao Zedong's independence from Moscow. But another important PRC goal was to interrupt the Nationalist blockade. During November of that year, Indian prime minister Jawaharlal Nehru explained that Chinese leaders had told him during his recent trip to Beijing that the Nationalist blockade was a major problem and that they were "faced with continuous pin-pricks and irritations of cumulative effect and he had the definite impression that they were determined not to tolerate this situation longer."[2]

The shelling of the offshore islands was also used as a cover to attack other Nationalist-controlled islands, in particular the most northerly of the Nationalist-held offshore island groups, the Dachens. In this overcharged political climate, the rapid response of the U.S. Navy helped to resolve this crisis. After Chiang Kai-shek agreed to evacuate the Dachens, the U.S. Navy provided the ships, training, and protection during the evacuation operations. The Taiwan Patrol Force also remained the first line of defense against any possible PRC cross-strait invasion.

THE CHANGING GOALS OF THE TAIWAN PATROL FORCE

Soon after the Communist victory in China and with the beginning of the Korean War, the U.S. government had instituted the Taiwan Patrol Force to neutralize the Taiwan Strait region. But, as the ongoing conflict in Korea had already shown, what the Communist forces lacked in technology and ordnance, they could more than make up for in sheer numbers. During the early 1950s, it was generally conceded that the Chinese Communists could take the disputed offshore islands along China's southeastern coastline whenever they wanted, so long as they were willing to devote the necessary manpower. The relatively small size of the Taiwan Patrol Force would, at the most, represent a temporary obstacle to any such invasion.

From 1950 through early 1953, the Taiwan Patrol Force was ordered to stop attacks from both sides of the strait. In this operation, USN ships were intended to play a neutral role by acting as a buffer between the PRC and ROC. While the PRC clearly resented the presence of USN ships in their offshore waters, at some point Beijing leaders must have appreciated the fact that the Nationalist forces were being actively dissuaded from attacking the mainland. The neutralization order, however, specifically did not include the many offshore islands controlled by the Nationalists: on October 7, 1950, it was clarified in Operation Order 7-50 that none of the Seventh Fleet vessels could participate in the "defense of any coastal islands held by the Nationalist Chinese, nor will they interfere with Nationalist Chinese operations from the coastal islands."[3]

Shortly after Dwight D. Eisenhower won the 1952 presidential election in the United States, the focus of the Taiwan Patrol Force began to change. At least at the beginning of his administration, Eisenhower heeded hard-liners' calls to "unleash" Chiang Kai-shek.[4] A Gallup poll from early in 1953 showed widespread public support for Eisenhower, with 61 percent of Americans in a nationwide survey supporting a policy of supplying more warships to Taiwan for use in blockading the Chinese coastline and more airplanes to bomb the mainland.[5]

Tensions were already high in the Taiwan Strait. From April 11 to 15, 1952, for example, the Nationalists and Communists fought over Nanri Island off of Fujian Province, about seventy miles south of Fuzhou. The Nationalists were eventually forced to abandon the island. But later that year approximately 4,000 regular Nationalist Fifth Army troops and about 1,000 guerrillas from Jinmen attacked again during the early morning of October 11, 1952. The raid failed, largely because the civilian junk crews used by the guerrilla army as amphibious lift ended up dropping the troops too far at sea and then left them stranded there.[6] The Nationalists were forced to withdraw on October 14, and in retaliation Communist forces attacked and took Nanpeng Island, part of the Lamock group of islands off the port of Shantou, in fighting that lasted from October 18 to 20. This Nationalist loss proved to be permanent, thus breaking the Nationalist blockade over Shantou and leaving Jinmen as the southernmost Nationalist island base.[7]

Carrying out his campaign promises, on February 2, 1953, Eisenhower lifted the U.S. Navy's previous orders to restrict the Nationalist forces. According to a U.S. government statement, the U.S. Seventh Fleet would "no longer be employed as a shield for the mainland of China."[8] One immediate result of this policy change was that the commander of the Seventh Fleet was ordered to remove the requirement that the Taiwan Patrol Force prevent the use of Taiwan and the Penghu Islands as a Nationalist base for operations against the Chinese mainland.[9] Interestingly, this change immediately led to the revision of previous orders. In particular, on paper copies of Operation Order 20-52, *Special Patrol Instructions*, the line "Large forces moving from Formosa toward the mainland will be reported to CTG 72.0" was scratched out.[10]

In April of 1953, talks were held in Taipei between Adlai Stevenson, a recent presidential candidate who had lost to Eisenhower, and Chiang Kai-shek. During this meeting, Chiang promised Stevenson that with continued U.S. military support his forces would be ready to return to the mainland within three years at the latest and that once they returned to China they would gain a significant domestic following within "three to six months."[11] The U.S. government agreed to support this plan. One reason later given by Dulles to the British ambassador was to "free the United States Navy from the obligation to protect the mainland against attack from Formosa."[12]

But another major reason for this U.S. policy change was to open a new peripheral theater in the south so as to put pressure on Beijing to sign a peace treaty ending the Korean War.[13] Washington's goal was to "make a diversionary threat at a time when fighting was going on in Korea so as to cause the Chinese Communists to transfer forces away from Korea towards Formosa."[14] Dulles even told a New Zealand delegation that "unleashing Chiang" would "encourage the Chinese [Communists] to retain substantial forces opposite Formosa."[15] Washington's strategic objective was to put additional military pressure on China's southern flank so that it would feel compelled to reduce the number of PLA troops in Korea.

The Nationalists seemed eager to carry out this new policy. The first raid mounted directly from Taiwan following Eisenhower's February 1953 deneutralization order was against Dongshan Island, which had been taken from the Nationalists on May 11, 1950, after PLA forces assaulted the island with more than 10,000 troops. In mid-July 1953, the

Nationalists tried to retake the island with approximately 6,500 guerrillas, marines, and paratroopers. Airplanes from the Chinese Nationalist Air Force (CNAF) dropped Nationalist paratroopers on the northwest coast. Meanwhile, the Jinmen-based amphibious force—called *Sea Guerrilla Task Force*—landed on the northeast coast and occupied Dongshan city.[16] This attack ultimately failed, however, and the Nationalist forces were forced to retreat, but the threat to the PRC was real.

Eisenhower's decision to open a peripheral campaign in the Taiwan Strait put pressure on Beijing. This in turn played a crucial role in the PRC's decision to come to terms in Korea. After the armistice was signed on July 27, 1953, the PRC immediately began to move troops to the south, stationing them across from Taiwan. This led to escalation on both sides of the Taiwan Strait, and during August 1954 Chiang Kai-shek ordered additional deployments of fifty-eight thousand troops to Jinmen and fifteen thousand more troops to Mazu. These troop movements had all of the outward appearances of supporting a Nationalist invasion of mainland China. The PRC was sufficiently concerned about this possibility to authorize PLA attacks against the Nationalist-held offshore islands, and in particular the northernmost islands of Yijiangshan and the Dachens.

THE BEGINNING OF THE 1954–1955 TAIWAN STRAIT CRISIS

After China intervened in the Korean War during the fall of 1950, the U.S. actively helped the Nationalists tighten their naval blockade of the PRC. With American military equipment, training, and financial backing, it was hoped that the blockade of strategic goods would become even tighter. The blockade was highly effective, and during November 1954 PRC leaders explained to visiting Indian prime minister Jawaharlal Nehru that the Nationalists from their offshore bases were conducting nuisance raids and were interfering with shipping. Upon his return, Nehru immediately warned the British high commissioner in India that China was determined to remedy this situation.[17]

During the early 1950s, the U.S. Navy and other military representatives helped equip Taiwan's navy and air force to conduct a more effective blockade.[18] But by late 1953, immediately before tensions erupted over control of Jinmen and Mazu islands, the Nationalist held only twenty-five offshore islands, down from thirty-two the year before.[19] The U.S. Navy supported Taiwan by sending aircraft carriers to patrol the region. For example, USS *Taussig* (DD 746), one of the first USN destroyers to carry out a patrol during early July 1950, departed on her first peacetime deployment to the Western Pacific on March 3, 1954, to escort the aircraft carrier USS *Boxer* (CV 21). The destroyer remained in the region for the next three months, screening *Boxer*, conducting various HUK antisubmarine warfare (ASW) exercises, and patrolling the Taiwan Strait.

After the PRC relocated troops from north to south following the reduction of tensions in Korea, the PRC began to shell Jinmen Island on September 3, 1954. PLA attacks also began against the Dachen Islands, which was an important guerrilla base for the Nationalist blockade. These attacks were aimed mainly at halting guerrilla activity. Taking the northernmost of the offshore islands in order to stage an invasion of Taiwan made little sense, since they were too far from Taiwan. According to Rear Admiral Samuel Frankel, "from the viewpoint of protecting Taiwan, I think that these islands have no significance at all."[20]

As early as July 15, 1953, Admiral Arthur W. Radford, dual-hatted as the commander in chief of the U.S. Pacific Command and commander in chief of the U.S. Pacific Fleet, had warned Chiang Kai-shek to bolster the sagging defense of the northern islands, but he reported back to Washington that Chiang was reluctant to deploy adequate forces. Radford was concerned that retaining the islands was psychologically important to Taiwan's defense and that they were strategically important for gathering intelligence on the PRC. For a time, Radford even considered proposing that these islands be put within the "U.S. defense perimeter."[21]

On July 21, 1953, the Eisenhower administration concluded that, "although the importance of these islands to Taiwan's defense is generally recognized here, the prevailing view is that the responsibility for their defense must remain with the Government of China."[22] On September 25, 1953, Admiral Joseph J. "Jocko" Clark, commander of the Seventh Fleet, stated that his instructions to protect Taiwan and the Penghus from aggression did not include the Nationalist-held islands close to China's coast.[23] Beginning in December of 1953, the ONI also began to warn that "the Nationalists now hold these coastal islands by default" and that the "Communists have not yet thought them of great enough value to tie down the necessary forces to take the area." This ONI report even suggested that "there has been some indication that the Nationalists are trying very hard to get the U.S. to make a statement obligating the Seventh Fleet to the protection of the offshore islands as well as Formosa."[24]

On June 1, 1954, the U.S. Seventh Fleet made a show of force in the Dachens, and later during the summer other Seventh Fleet ships paid a visit on August 18, 1954.[25] This was based on the calculated bluff that "the operation will create the impression that the U.S. is prepared to use force."[26] In this particular case, the PRC decided to call the U.S. bluff. As the U.S. military advisors had warned from July 1953 onward, PRC planes began to bomb and strafe the Dachen Islands on November 1, 1954. In early 1955, the PLA focused its attack to the northernmost of these islands, called Yijiangshan, only eight miles from the Dachens. Chinese Communist Air Force tactics reflected Soviet training, and on January 18, 1955, more than fifty PLA Air Force (PLAAF) planes attacked Yijiangshan. High winds disrupted the first air operation, but the second attack was evaluated as a "well-planned, well-organized, and well-executed operation." Yijiangshan fell on January 18. The PRC's victory convinced it to continue south to the next group of islands. On January 19, 1955, the PLAAF began to attack the Dachen Islands. Their raids included seventy attacking aircraft.[27]

This new attack spurred a U.S. decision to convince the Nationalists to abandon the Dachens. Chiang Kai-shek was initially reluctant, but by early 1955 increased PLA attacks had forced the Nationalists to evacuate the Dachen Islands.

THE DECISION TO EVACUATE THE DACHEN ISLANDS

In mid-January 1955, the Nationalists requested that the Seventh Fleet be moved closer to the Dachens to expedite the delivery of crucial logistics.[28] Later that month, they also asked for USN air support, which the U.S. ambassador to Taiwan backed in order to avoid undermining confidence in U.S. determination.[29] But defending the Dachen Islands permanently would be difficult, requiring two full-time USN aircraft carriers plus supporting ships. According to Dulles, the Dachens "were too far from Formosa, too vulnerable, and insufficiently important from the strategic point of view to justify an American commitment to defend them."[30]

On January 23, 1955, the U.S. recommended that the Dachen Islands be evacuated. Chiang only reluctantly agreed to withdraw, in particular because giving up a strong position like the Dachen Islands without a fight would "gravely affect troop and civilian morale." To avoid the impression that he was backing down, Chiang refused to agree to a ceasefire of any kind.[31] Facing overwhelming odds, the Nationalists finally agreed to evacuate. During this operation, the PRC was warned not to interfere, since USN forces were ordered "not to accept any tactical disadvantages." Or, put another way, U.S. pilots were not to get "altruistically shot down."[32]

The evacuation, called Operation KING KONG, proved to be a massive undertaking. The 209-man shore party included only eleven USN personnel, who were part of a reconnaissance team, while the majority was composed of U.S. Marines, including the 3d Shore Party Battalion and 3d Marine Division, supported by eighteen Chinese Nationalist interpreters. An on-island command group (twelve), supported by a radio-relay group (four) on the USS *Henrico* (APA 45), commanded two shore parties, with the majority (110) on the North Island and the rest (eighty-three) on the South Island. There were two evacuation beaches on each island. Tank-landing ships (LST) were beached during high tide and loaded and then embarked twelve hours later during the next high tide. From February 8 to 12, 1955, the marine teams evacuated "over 15,000 civilians, 11,000 military, 125 vehicles, 5,300 tons of material, 7,600 tons of ammunition, and 165 artillery pieces," while sustaining zero casualties to either U.S. or Nationalist personnel.[33]

To protect this massive evacuation, the Seventh Fleet assembled seventy vessels, including a "backbone" of six attack aircraft carriers (CVA) and one antisubmarine aircraft carrier (CVS). Many USN vessels assigned to the Taiwan Patrol, like the USS *Boyd* (DD 544), were involved in this operation.[34] During the early days of the crisis, *Carpenter* also patrolled the Taiwan Strait and helped convoy Nationalist forces as they evacuated the Dachen Islands. A total of twenty-two vessels, including seven aircraft carriers—*Bennington* (CVA 20), *Hancock* (CVA 19), *Midway* (CVA 41), *Princeton* (CVS 37), *Shangri-la* (CVA 38), *Lexington* (CVA 16), and *Ticonderoga* (CVA 14)—became eligible to receive the Armed Forces Expeditionary Medal–Taiwan Straits.[35]

Although the evacuation was a success, control over the operation was overly centralized, with local commanders "given grave responsibilities without the authority to exercise initiative and freedom of action in the execution of same." Poor vehicle maintenance and the lack of adequate traffic control were major problems, with the commander of the Tachen Defense Command Advisory Team (TDCAT), General John C. Macdonald, spending "better than an hour in the vicinity of Ta-Ao-Li personally unsnarling a traffic jam and acting as an MP." These shortfalls led to unexpected delays that could have jeopardized the entire operation: "Had the evacuation been opposed by the Communists, failure might well have been the result."[36]

After the evacuation, the flag of the Republic of China in the Dachen Islands was lowered by Chiang Ching-kuo, Chiang Kai-shek's son. The Zhejiang provincial government was also abolished in the Republic of China. This meant that Nationalist forces now held disputed mainland territory only in Fujian Province. Rather than pushing the United States and Taiwan further apart, however, as Beijing had undoubtedly hoped would happen, the evacuation of Dachen unexpectedly led to closer relations between Washington and Taipei.

NEW U.S.–ROC SECURITY ARRANGEMENTS

The political impact of the PRC attack on the Dachens was to spur discussions of a new U.S.–Taiwan security treaty; earlier in 1954, all U.S.–ROC talks on signing such a pact had ended in failure. While reaffirming the pledges made earlier by Truman and Eisenhower to defend Taiwan and the Penghu Islands against Communist attack, the new agreement was deliberately vague about the security status of the other offshore islands. Previous USN operation orders had even clarified that while the term *enemy forces* included all forces attacking Taiwan or the Penghus, it did not include forces attacking other offshore islands held by the Nationalists.[37]

The international reaction to the Dachen evacuation was mixed. To the Australians, the loss of the Dachens was compared to the 1938 fall of Czechoslovakia, while the PRC threat to invade Taiwan was compared to the 1939 invasion of Poland. In a February 1955 Gallup poll, 66 percent of Australians favored joining the United States in a war to prevent Chinese Communists from invading Taiwan. In a letter dated April 1955, Australian prime minister Menzies advocated the "desirability of giving Formosa military and political strength to ensure the future will be decided peacefully and not as a result of Communist policies of force."[38]

But public opinion in the United Kingdom opposed a war with China. Churchill, in a private letter to Eisenhower, warned that "a war to keep the coastal islands for China would not be defensible here."[39] The British ambassador to Washington further emphasized that, since the United Kingdom had recognized the PRC, it legally "recognized that these islands were part of China." This made it highly unlikely that Britain could support the United States in any fight over the offshore islands. This greatly concerned the British government, since, if war broke out, "The Western alliance might be split." The British Ambassador asked, "Were these islands really worth it?"[40]

Taking into consideration the differing views of its allies, the U.S. government adopted an intentionally ambiguous policy of keeping the Communists guessing about the true defense status of the offshore islands.[41] According to one press report, "The pact will be deliberately vague about how the U.S. might react if the Reds were to invade any of the other Nationalist-held islands off the China coast. The U.S. doesn't want the Reds to know which it will defend and which it will simply write off. It prefers to keep them guessing."[42] After lengthy negotiations, the two sides agreed to very specific wording. The treaty stated that the U.S. security guarantee was also "applicable to such other territories as may be determined by mutual agreement."[43] This deferred any decision on whether the offshore islands would be included in the treaty. The resulting U.S.–ROC mutual-defense treaty, which was signed on December 2, 1954, contained this ambiguous wording.

PRC attacks on the Dachen Islands the following January led to Eisenhower's request that Congress give him special powers to defend Taiwan. On January 29, 1955, the *Formosa Resolution* was passed by the Congress.[44] This resolution gave the president enormous latitude, since it stated that only the president could judge whether or not a PRC attack on the offshore islands was part of a more general assault on Taiwan.[45] The specific wording was left vague, and Congress agreed that the president could authorize "securing and protection of such related positions and territories of that area now in friendly hands."[46] Soon afterward, on February 9, 1955, the Senate accepted the defense pact and final ratifications were exchanged on March 3, 1955.

By leaving the status of the offshore islands vague, the president was left with the widest possible latitude to respond to future Communist attacks. In a top-secret letter to Churchill, Eisenhower explained that, for his part, Chiang Kai-shek had agreed that "he would not conduct any offensive operations against the mainland either from Formosa *or from his coastal positions*, except in agreement with us." This would allow Washington to stop Chiang from using his offshore bases to continue the "sporadic war against the mainland" or to support an "invasion of the mainland of China." According to Eisenhower, these agreements showed that the U.S. government has "done much more than seems generally realized."[47]

The true challenge for U.S. military and political leaders in the midst of the first Taiwan Strait crisis was to convince Chiang Kai-shek to settle the dispute over the offshore islands peacefully, preferably by abandoning them completely, without undermining the international community's faith in U.S. support for Taiwan. If the PRC took them by force, then Chiang Kai-shek would lose "prestige."[48] In the Asian context, this meant losing face. Eisenhower even reminded Churchill on January 25, 1955, that the United States had to be concerned with the "solidarity of the Island Barrier in the Western Pacific" and that if the United States were to desert Taiwan "a collapse of Asiatic resistance to the Communists" was risked.[49] This, in turn, would undermine the U.S. containment policy. However, if Chiang withdrew from the offshore islands on his own volition, then he would not lose face. In early 1955, various U.S. government and military officials attempted—without success—to convince Chiang to withdraw from the offshore islands.

FAILED U.S. ATTEMPTS TO FORCE CHIANG TO ABANDON THE OFFSHORE ISLANDS

With his last foothold in his home province of Zhejiang gone, Chiang Kai-shek was determined to retain the remaining offshore islands of Jinmen and Mazu at any cost. Giving up the last pieces of Nationalist-controlled mainland China might be interpreted by overseas Chinese as a sign that his resistance to Communism was collapsing. These concerns undermined a quick and easy settlement. One little-known aspect of the first Taiwan Strait crisis was that the United States repeatedly attempted to convince the Nationalists to abandon all of the offshore islands, including the most important Nationalist island bases on Jinmen and Mazu. One such attempt took place early in 1955, when Admiral Radford met with Chiang Kai-shek. This attempt failed. Later that year, Eisenhower authorized Dulles to repeat the offer, with equally poor results.

To many in Washington, the forced evacuation of the Dachens boded ill for the other Nationalist-occupied offshore islands. In early 1955, the newly appointed chairman of the JCS, Admiral Radford, along with Walter Robertson, assistant secretary of state for Far Eastern Affairs, met with Chiang Kai-shek. The two promised that the United States would supply better naval equipment to patrol the Nationalist blockade. In return for the equipment, Chiang would need to agree to give up the other disputed offshore islands. After leaving the room, supposedly to pray in the garden, Chiang returned and said, "I just want to tell you that I have prayerfully concluded that I cannot accept such a proposal because I do not have the faith in your government to sustain it."[50]

Chiang's refusal to retreat from these offshore islands left the United States with few options: they had either to support Chiang on his terms or else risk losing Taiwan as a dependable ally propping up the Cold War containment policy. In the spring of 1955, Washington once again asked Chiang to consider giving up Jinmen and Mazu islands, but he refused to agree.[51] In return for his acquiescence, Eisenhower even promised to create a joint U.S.–Taiwan defense zone from Shantou to Wenzhou in which the movement of all maritime traffic of a contraband or military character would be interdicted. In particular, the U.S. Navy would be responsible for setting mine fields that "would force coastwise junk traffic to come out where it also could be intercepted and controlled." [52]

But Chiang also vetoed this new U.S. proposal, since relinquishing control over additional offshore islands would make his government look weak. Furthermore, Chiang argued that once he gave up Jinmen and Mazu the U.S. might soon halt any "effective shipping-interdiction scheme in the face of strong and inevitable opposition by the British and others."[53] Certain USN leaders, including CNO Admiral Arleigh Burke (seen in figure 5.1), agreed with Chiang that defending the islands was necessary. Burke even told Eisenhower, "They don't mean anything; it's a purely symbolic thing; they don't mean anything except, Who's daddy? Who runs that part of the world—the Red Chinese or the Nationalist Chinese? But physically it doesn't make any difference. . . . These are Nationalist Chinese islands, and they have to be held, or they have to be abandoned voluntarily before they're threatened, before they're made to abandon them."[54] The big problem was that once the United States committed itself to defending the offshore islands, then it had to be "prepared to follow through in [the] event the Communists should decide to test U.S. willingness actually to participate in the defense of the islands."[55]

Even though the Dachens had been evacuated, the Nationalists retained control over Jinmen and Mazu islands, which were the two most important blockade bases. Rather than resort to force, the United States hoped to defuse military tensions and to focus instead on longer-term goals. During a February 10, 1955, talk with Taiwan foreign minister George K. C. Yeh, Dulles explained that the solution to the two-Chinas

Figure 5.1. Chief of Naval Operations Admiral Arleigh A. Burke Is Greeted by Generalissimo Chiang Kai-shek in a 1955 Visit to Taiwan. Source: Naval History and Heritage Command Archives

problem would take time. Instead of trying to force Chinese unification, the United States and Taiwan should instead focus on "the vulnerability of Communist regimes to economic and other pressures."[56] Ultimately, China's coercive tactics against Taiwan did not succeed, in large part because the USSR "failed to come to the PRC's rescue when it was intimidated by the United States."[57]

CONCLUSIONS

In a show of force, the PRC initiated the first Taiwan Strait crisis in early September of 1954. While merely shelling Jinmen Island, Communist forces overran Yijiangshan and attacked the Dachen Islands, which were evacuated by the Nationalists. During this period Washington repeatedly urged Taipei to abandon all the offshore islands, but Chiang Kai-shek refused. Not only would complete abandonment have forced Chiang to lose face, but so long as the Nationalists held these islands right off China's coast the Communists could not proclaim total victory over the mainland. In addition, Chinese history had shown that the Nationalists could always stage a future mainland invasion from their offshore bases, thereby using the disputed islands as stepping stones to retake control of China.

Scholars have argued that the PRC's primary motivation behind initiating this crisis was to test American resolve to defend Taiwan.[58] While the PRC could claim a limited victory because Nationalist troops had evacuated the Dachens and several other smaller offshore islands, from purely a strategic viewpoint the PRC's attacks backfired. In December of 1954, Taiwan and the United States signed a mutual security pact reaffirming that the United States would defend Taiwan and the Penghu Islands. As part of this agreement, Chiang Kai-shek promised that no offensive operations were to take place against the mainland without America's prior agreement. Recounting this discussion four years later in October 1958, Dulles said that Chiang "had maintained that limitation, and honourably maintained it."[59]

The 1954–1955 Taiwan Strait crisis also had important domestic consequences in the PRC. In December of 1953, the ONI had warned that Beijing's threats to attack the offshore islands, and especially to invade Taiwan, provided the Chinese leaders with an important propaganda "gimmick."[60] But, with the exception of regaining Yijiangshan and the Dachens—which were not considered strategically important in any future invasion of Taiwan—the PRC attacks had failed. Furthermore, the Soviet government showed that it would not give its full support to Beijing's military actions. Finally, rather than pushing the United States and Taiwan apart, the January 1955 Formosa Resolution provided even greater U.S. security guarantees to Taiwan and the offshore islands. Reflecting the new climate of improved U.S.–ROC military relations, the U.S. Navy also began to take on new responsibilities, including more robust naval funding and a more intensive training regime for the Nationalist Navy.

NOTES

1. Breakfast discussion with Secretary of State John Foster Dulles (top secret), July 22, 1955, TNA/UK, PREM 11/879.
2. Telegram from the UK Higher Commissioner in India to Commonwealth Relations Office (secret), November 10, 1954, TNA/UK, FO 371/ 110238.
3. U.S. Navy Operation Order, ComCruDivONE No. 7-50, October 7, 1950, NHHC Archives, Post-1946 Operation Plans, Task Force 72.
4. GlobalSecurity.org, "First Taiwan Strait Crisis: Quemoy and Matsu Islands" (accessed December 14, 2010), http://www.globalsecurity.org/military/ops/quemoy_matsu.htm.
5. Free China Information service, "U.S. to Send 100 Thunderjets, Warships to Free China," February 4, 1953, TNA/UK, FO 371/105272.
6. U.S. Office of Naval Intelligence, "The Struggle for the Coastal Islands of China," *ONI Review Supplement* (December 1953): i–ix.
7. U.S. Office of Naval Intelligence, "The Southeast China Coast Today," *ONI Review* (February 1953): 51–60.
8. UK Embassy, Washington, to Foreign Office (secret), January 30, 1953, TNA/UK, PREM 11/867.
9. U.S. Navy Operation Order, CTF 72 No. 2-A-53, May 1, 1954, NHHC Archives, Post-1946 Operation Plans, Task Force 72.
10. U.S. Navy Operation Order, CTG. 72.0 No. 20-52, December 3, 1952, NHHC Archives, Post-1946 Operation Plans, Task Force 72. There is no way to know when

this line was marked out, but most likely it was some time between January and March 1953.

11. John Foster Dulles Papers, Princeton University, Reel 204/205, April 8, 1953, 88851.

12. Telegram from UK Embassy, Washington, to Foreign Office (secret), October 18, 1954, TNA/UK, CAB 21/3272.

13. For more on opening new peripheral theaters, see Bruce A. Elleman and S. C. M. Paine, eds., *Naval Power and Expeditionary Warfare: Peripheral Campaigns and New Theatres of Naval Warfare* (London: Routledge Press, 2011), 197–212.

14. Telegram from UK Embassy, Washington, to Foreign Office (secret), October 18, 1954, TNA/UK, CAB 21/3272.

15. "Extract of New Zealand Delegation's Record of Discussions of Anzus Council Meeting in Washington, September 1953 (Secret)," TNA/UK, FO 371/105272.

16. U.S. Office of Naval Intelligence, "The Struggle for the Coastal Islands of China."

17. UK High Commissioner in India Report of Meeting with Prime Minister Nehru (secret), November 10, 1954, TNA/UK, FO 371/110238.

18. *U.S. News and World Report*, "China Blockade: How It Works; Ships by the U.S.— Sailors by Chiang Kai-shek," February 20, 1953.

19. U.S. Office of Naval Intelligence, "The Struggle for the Coastal Islands of China."

20. Samuel B. Frankel, *The Reminiscences of Rear Admiral Samuel B. Frankel, U.S. Navy (Retired)*, Oral History 325 (Annapolis, MD: U.S. Naval Institute, 1972), 359–60.

21. John Foster Dulles Papers, Princeton University, Reel 204/205, July 15, 1953, 89555.

22. Ibid.

23. Excerpt from a *South China Morning Post* article, dated September 25, 1953, TNA/UK, ADM 1/24789.

24. U.S. Office of Naval Intelligence, "The Struggle for the Coastal Islands of China."

25. Top-secret memorandum, "Information on the Offshore Islands Held by CHINATS," Robert L. Dennison, September 3, 1954, Strategic Plans Division, NHHC Archives, Box 306.

26. "Comments on Tachen Operation (Top Secret)," August 18, 1954, Strategic Plans Division, NHHC Archives, Box 289, 3.

27. U.S. Office of Naval Intelligence, "Aerial Tactics of the Chinese Communists in Naval Operations," *ONI Review* (February 1955): 85–87.

28. John Foster Dulles Papers, Princeton University, Reel 210/211, January 14, 1955, 92562.

29. John Foster Dulles Papers, Princeton University, Reel 210/211, January 20, 1955, 92599.

30. UK Ambassador, Washington, to Foreign Office (Secret), January 19, 1955, TNA/UK, PREM 11/867.

31. John Foster Dulles Papers, Princeton University, Reel 210/211, January 24, 1955, 92618.

32. UK Embassy, Washington, DC, to Foreign Office, February 6, 1955, TNA/UK, PREM 11/867.

33. Marine Corps History Division, "Report of Participation in Evacuation of China Civilians, Guerrillas, Military Personnel, Equipment and Supplies from the Tachen Islands," March 22, 1955, Taiwan Geographic File, Historical Reference Branch, Marine Corps History Division, Quantico, VA.

34. The National Association of Destroyer Veterans, "USS *Boyd* DD-544" (accessed October 16, 2014),http://www.destroyers.org/uss-boyd/history/start/43_58_boyd_history.htm.

35. Marine Corps History Division, "List of Units eligible for Armed Forces Exped Medal furnished CNO & Published in Ch-1/to SecNav P1650.1C of 16 Aug. 63," Tai-

wan Geographic File, Historical Reference Branch, Marine Corps History Division, Quantico, VA.

36. "Operation KING KONG: Evacuation of the Tachen Islands," ch. 3 in *History of the Army Section, MAAG, Taiwan* (1955), Army Center of Military History, Ft. McNair, Washington, DC.

37. U.S. Navy Operation Order, CTF 72 No. 2-A-53, 1 May 1954, NHHC Archives, Post-1946 Operation Plans, Task Force 72.

38. Telegram from UK High Commissioner in Australia to Commonwealth Relations Office (top secret), April 16, 1955, TNA/UK, DEFE 13/288.

39. Cited years later in a letter from Harold Macmillan to John Foster Dulles (top secret), September 5, 1958, TNA/UK, CAB 21/3272

40. UK Ambassador, Washington, to Foreign Office (secret), January 29, 1955, TNA/UK, PREM 11/867.

41. George W. Anderson Jr., *Reminiscences of Admiral George W. Anderson, Jr., U.S. Navy (Retired.)*, Oral History 42 (Annapolis, MD: U.S. Naval Institute, 1983), 272.

42. *Newsweek*, "Pressure and a Pact," December 13, 1954.

43. Hungdah Chiu, *China and the Taiwan Issue* (New York: Praeger Publishers, 1979), 160.

44. Ibid., 230. The full name of the Formosa Resolution is U.S. Congressional Authorization for the President to Employ the Armed Forces of the United States to Protect Formosa, the Pescadores, and Related Positions and Territories of That Area.

45. Harold C. Hinton, *China's Turbulent Quest* (New York: The Macmillan Company, 1972), 68.

46. Chiu, *China and the Taiwan Issue*, 231.

47. Letter from President Eisenhower to Prime Minister Churchill (top secret), February 19, 1955, TNA/UK, PREM 11/879, emphasis original. This provision was stipulated in a pair of notes exchanged at the same time as the treaty was signed. Foster Rhea Dulles, *American Policy toward Communist China, 1949–1969* (New York: Thomas Y. Crowell Company, 1972), 152.

48. Breakfast Discussion with Secretary of State John Foster Dulles (top secret), July 22, 1955, TNA/UK, PREM 11/879.

49. Letter from President Eisenhower to Prime Minister Churchill (top secret), January 25, 1955, TNA/UK, PREM 11/867.

50. Anderson, *Reminiscences of Admiral George W. Anderson, Jr.*, 280.

51. Warren I. Cohen, ed. *New Frontiers in American–East Asian Relations* (New York: Columbia University Press, 1983), 150–52.

52. Harriet D. Schwar and Louis J. Smith, eds., and John P. Glennon, gen. ed., "Memorandum for the Record, by the Ambassador in the Republic of China (Rankin)," April 29, 1955, 529–31, in *Foreign Relations of the United States, 1955–1957*, vol. 3, *China* (Washington, DC: U.S. Government Printing Office, 1986).

53. Ibid.

54. Arleigh A. Burke, *Recollections of Admiral Arleigh A. Burke, U.S. Navy (Retired)*, Oral History 64 (Annapolis, MD: U.S. Naval Institute, 1973), 44.

55. Appendix to "Security of the Offshore Islands Presently Held by the Nationalist Government of the Republic of China," memorandum from Chief of Naval Operations, Admiral Robert B. Carney, to Joint Chiefs of Staff (top secret), July 30, 1953, Strategic Plans Division, NHHC Archives, Box 289.

56. John Foster Dulles Papers, Princeton University, Reel 210/211, February 21, 1955, 92802.

57. John F. Copper, "The Origins of Conflict across the Taiwan Strait: The Problem of Differences in Perceptions," in *Across the Taiwan Strait: Mainland China, Taiwan, and the 1995–1996 Crisis*, ed. Suisheng Zhao, 49 (New York: Routledge Press, 1999); citing Weiqun Gu, *Conflicts of Divided Nations: The Case of China and Korea* (Westport, CT: Praeger, 1995), 26–28.

58. Thomas J. Christensen, *Useful Adversaries: Grand Strategy, Domestic Mobilization, and Sino–American Conflict, 1947–1958* (Princeton: Princeton University Press, 1996), 195.

59. Telegram from Foreign Office to UK Embassy, Washington, October 22, 1958, TNA/UK, PREM 11/3738.

60. U.S. Office of Naval Intelligence, "The Struggle for the Coastal Islands of China."

SIX
American Military and Financial Support for the Nationalists

While the Nationalist and Communist navies looked similar on paper during the early 1950s, in any actual encounter it would have been the officers' and crews' handling of the ships that would have made all the difference. Following the first Taiwan Strait crisis during 1954 and 1955 and in line with the new U.S.–ROC mutual-security pact, the U.S. Navy increased its funding and training efforts, particularly in the use of high-tech equipment. Over time, the Nationalist Navy's capabilities increased, to the point where many American officers considered them to be nearly on par with the U.S. Navy.[1] These improvements positively impacted the conduct of the Nationalist blockade, as well as kept the Nationalist Navy prepared to fight off a PRC invasion.

There were valid U.S. concerns that the Nationalists could not permanently retain their offshore island bases along the PRC coastline, much less use them to stage an invasion of the mainland. According to one ONI assessment from December 1953, the PLAN was more than a match for the Nationalists in the coastal waters of the Chinese mainland, since the Communist forces now had sufficient land-based air power to control the sky over the area. Since the two navies were now evenly matched, it was unclear why the Nationalists had been allowed to keep these coastal islands. The problem, from a military and strategic viewpoint, was that the coastal areas in Fujian Province were almost entirely cut off from the interior. Troops stationed there would be in a "deep freeze" and would be "immobile as far as the overall disposition of military forces in China are concerned." Therefore, any Communist invasion would require extremely large forces in order to occupy each and every offshore island.[2]

Any PRC decision to attack the offshore islands also depended on the international climate. A truce ending the Korean conflict could free up many PLA soldiers. According to one ONI assessment, "It is unlikely that the Chinese Communists will undertake to drive the Nationalists completely from the coastal islands of China as long as there is a possibility that the People's Liberation Army may again become actively engaged in the war in Korea. If a peace is concluded in Korea, or if the PLA is withdrawn from Korea, a campaign to 'liberate' the coastal islands would have great value to the Chinese Communists who have the capability to undertake and carry to a successful conclusion such a venture against the Nationalists."[3] Although the PRC had previously used mass forces to retake several crucial offshore islands, including Hainan, it needed to create a real navy if it hoped to take other islands so as to attack Taiwan itself. Early PLAN goals included (1) destroying the sea blockade of liberated China, (2) supporting the PLA in defense of Chinese soil, and (3) wiping out all "remnants of the reactionary forces" on Taiwan.[4]

THE U.S. NAVY TRAINING MISSION

During this PLAN buildup, the Nationalist Navy continued to carry out its blockade of the mainland. Through until 1954, the Communists had little choice but to bear up as best they could, since they did not have the naval assets necessary to stop them:

> The Chinese Communists have undoubtedly been inconvenienced by this activity, but their military activity in the coastal areas has been almost solely defensive in nature. They have from time to time taken retaliatory action in reprisal for Nationalist activity, but with the exception of the disastrous attempt by elements of the Third Field Army to recapture Quemoy [Jinmen] in October 1949, they have made no concerted effort to retake these islands. Rumors that the Communists are very apprehensive of Nationalist landings on the mainland have persisted, and reports indicate that they have made defensive preparations even including the razing of villages adjacent to the sea. Strategically, the area is of secondary importance to the Communists. The important ports of Shanghai and Canton are unaffected by Nationalist activity, and although shipping into Wenchow, Foochow, Amoy, and Swatow is interfered with, these ports have no accessibility to railroads and no significant industrial development. It is probable that the Communists are content to endure the Nationalist nuisance activity until they are ready to assert naval and air superiority in the area in preparation for an attack on Formosa.[5]

In the meantime, the PRC continued to obtain military hardware from the USSR.

To help solve the Nationalist Navy's operational problems, the U.S. Navy rapidly expanded its training mission in Taiwan. In May of 1951, the U.S. government created the Military Assistance Advisory Group (MAAG) for Taiwan and began to allocate funds for it to conduct operations. One estimate of U.S. military aid to Taiwan between 1950 and 1969 was $3.19 billion.[6] By 1951, the number of American advisors on Formosa totaled about 650, with about half of these associated with the MAAG and the other half with a variety of smaller organizations, including the aforementioned CIA–run Western Enterprises Incorporated, which was engaged in "guerrilla training and psychological warfare."[7] At any one time, about half of the U.S. advisors—anywhere from 250 to 300—were concentrating on assisting the Nationalist Navy.

Almost from the beginnings of the Taiwan Patrol Force, some basic training was provided for the Nationalist Navy. Civilian specialists, many of them retired USN officers, were hired by the Nationalists to help them operate the U.S. ships. According to Rear Admiral Walter Ansel, USN (ret.), when he arrived in Taiwan during the spring of 1950 as a civilian advisor to the Nationalist military, the State Department was not very enthusiastic about his mission, but this soon changed after the beginning of the Korean War. Ansel recounted how as an operational liaison he often went to sea with the Nationalist ships. While the Nationalists thought highly of the destroyers, going to sea and actually shooting and "really getting down to slugging" was not very popular. Among other innovations, Ansel helped set up round-the-clock watches, and he developed an English–Chinese signal book to be used in communications between U.S. and Nationalist ships. With the help of foreign advisors, the number of Nationalist destroyers available for operations rose from two of the eight to four, and finally to "six out of eight that you could call on and send over to the mainland, for instance, and the islands between Formosa and the mainland."[8]

While training for training purposes was important, it became even more crucial in battle. Perhaps the most intensive training mission occurred during the various Taiwan Strait crises, when the Nationalist Navy had to resupply the embattled islands. While USN ships could escort the supply ships most of the way, they stopped before reaching the three-mile territorial limit, as recognized by the U.S. government, to make sure that the isolated conflict did not turn into a larger war. When CNO Admiral Burke asked Eisenhower if the U.S. Navy could resupply the embattled islands, Eisenhower emphatically said no. However, the U.S. Navy was allowed to train the Nationalists to conduct these operations (see figure 6.1). According to Burke: "So we gave them lots of training and we gave them lots of [Dock Landing Ship] LSDs and ships, boats, to supply the thing." Although USN ships were only permitted to escort the Nationalist ships part of the way, with U.S. training and equipment the Nationalists "reinforced their garrisons and put their supplies in caves."[9]

Without this additional training by the U.S. Navy, it would have been difficult if not impossible for the Nationalists to fight off the PRC attacks against the offshore islands. As CinCPac Admiral Felt stated in a 1974

Figure 6.1.   USN Equipment and Training Helped the Nationalists Resupply Jinmen Island. Source: Naval History and Heritage Command Archives

interview, the American and Nationalist navies "devised ways and means and tactics and successfully did the job over a period of time. But it was touch and go there for a long, long time."[10] During these years, however, the USSR was busy transferring modern naval equipment to the PRC, and the PLAN's capabilities were rapidly improving. Therefore, the U.S. government also agreed to provide a wide range of new naval equipment to build up and sustain Taiwan's future military capabilities.

TRANSFERRING AMERICAN MILITARY EQUIPMENT

After initiating a comprehensive training program, the next step was to provide the Nationalists with better equipment, including more modern ships. The Nationalist Navy depended on the U.S. Navy for equipment and for training in how to use that equipment. As part of Public Law 188, signed on August 5, 1953, the United States was authorized to lend or give naval ships to friendly nations in the Far East. In order to assist the Nationalists in defending the offshore islands, the Joint Chiefs of Staff allocated (1) ten patrol-type craft, (2) two landing-craft repair ships (ARL), (3) about one hundred small landing craft—including both landing craft mechanized and landing craft vehicle personnel (LCM, LCVP)—and (4) approximately ten additional patrol-type craft.[11] The Nationalist need for more destroyers was questioned. One footnote in CNO Carney's memorandum to the JCS clarified that "Delivery of any additional destroyers . . . beyond the two now planned for FY 1954 will be affected only upon the clearly demonstrated capability of the NGRC [Nationalist Government of the Republic of China] to man and operate them."[12]

In addition to receiving a number of U.S. destroyers, by the mid-1950s the U.S. Navy had given Taiwan two old diesel submarines. According to Vice Admiral Philip Beshany, commander of U.S. Taiwan Defense Command from 1972 to 1974, the handpicked Nationalist crews were trained in New London, Connecticut. They were top caliber and absolutely excelled as students. The instructors later claimed that the Nationalist officers took to submarine operations "like ducks to water." While the U.S. government did not provide Taiwan with torpedoes, since their goal was for the two submarines to help train the Nationalist Navy in antisubmarine warfare, Beshany thoughtfully wondered "if they didn't somehow get some torpedoes from some other country."[13]

New airplanes were also crucial to Taiwan's defense. Of the $132 million in equipment deliveries between 1951 and 1954, fully two-thirds of this was comprised of aircraft and aircraft spares, while another 18 percent was for bombs, rockets, and ammunition. In 1954 alone, the United States shipped $48.3 million in equipment to Taiwan. By December 1954, 456 of the 657 aircraft promised to Taiwan had been delivered, 131 of them during that year alone. These included seventy-two F-84Gs, twenty-five F-86Fs, sixteen T-33s, and five RT-33s.[14]

Another example of providing Taiwan with high-tech equipment was the U.S. decision to deliver F-104s to Taiwan by means of cargo planes. According to Admiral Felt, it was the "first time it had ever been done, I guess. They took the little old stub wings off of them and flew them out to Taiwan, unloaded them, stuck the wings on, and there we had an F-104 squadron!"[15] The first F-104s arrived in early 1960, and eventually Taiwan acquired 247 of them, mainly from the United States but also purchasing them second-hand from Belgium, Canada, Denmark, Germany, and Japan. One of their primary missions was to patrol the Taiwan Strait. On January 13, 1967, ROC Air Force Major Shih-Lin Hu and Captain Bei-Puo Shih each shot down a PLAAF MiG-19, which was the first ever F-104 combat victory.[16]

The delivery of high-tech equipment, as well as U.S. military training on how to use it, proved indispensible. As later recounted by Admiral George Anderson, who in 1955 was head of the Taiwan Patrol Force, "it was a fascinating job because, in addition to everything else, you really had the Chinese Navy even if not under direct command you had the primary influence on the Chinese Navy, and the great respect of the Chinese military, including their navy, including Chiang Kai-shek."[17] When not actually engaged in patrol or training duties, USN ships scheduled combined naval exercises with Nationalist vessels just to make sure the two navies could cooperate with each other in a crisis.

COMBINED U.S.–ROC NAVAL EXERCISES

While training Nationalist naval officers was a top priority of the U.S. Navy, combined naval exercises were equally important to cover all phases of operations necessary to ensuring that U.S. and Nationalist naval forces were ready to defend Taiwan and the Penghu islands.[18] Combined exercises were held between the USN destroyers on the Taiwan Patrol Force and several of the Nationalist destroyers. During one night exercise, five U.S. ships tried to penetrate the Taiwan Strait and were quickly intercepted by the Nationalist vessels. In another exercise, the destroyers grouped together and tried to protect the flagship against a submarine attack, but the submarine managed to slip by twice and torpedo the flagship. According to Admiral Stroop, "This was the first time I'd ever attempted to maneuver—work—combined operations with U.S. and Chinese forces, and I was pleased that they were fairly successful."[19]

Beginning in 1954, many training duties initially carried out by the CIA through such groups as the WEI were transferred by presidential directive to the Department of Defense (DOD). This required assigning about fifty new USN personnel, mostly to the MAAG in Taipei. For example, one top-secret memo noted that three officers and five enlisted personnel would be assigned to help train a 14,500–man Marine Corps division and a three thousand–man Guerrilla Parachute Command. It was expected that some of these U.S. naval advisors would even be stationed on various offshore islands.[20]

The U.S. Navy actively assisted the Nationalist amphibious operations by participating in combined training for landing exercises. According to Captain Phil Bucklew, these exercises took place along Taiwan's southeast coastline so as to keep the American officers away from the actual staging areas on the west coast of the island. Still, he was very impressed with the Nationalist training, calling it thorough and strenuous. Bucklew even stated that "in many ways, their operation was even more demanding than ours in training and qualifications." As a result, he concluded, "Their general capabilities, I thought, were among the best in the Far East. The amphibious exercise in which we participated jointly with them was a very good show."[21]

While the U.S. Navy conducted shipboard training, the U.S. Air Force was assigned to train Nationalist pilots. According to Admiral Felt,

> We had an air force section of the MAAG down there, the Military Assistance Group, which trained our Chinese friends, and they were well trained, every bit as good tactically as the U.S. Air Force or naval air fighters. They'd go out on these patrols, out over the straits, and just loiter at their best fighting altitude, more or less presenting themselves as bait. The Chinese would come out at higher altitudes and finally couldn't resist the temptation to come down, and when they came down they got took. Also, it was the first combat introduction of the

Sidewinder, which had been given to the Chinese. I can't remember the numbers, but I think it was something like twenty of the Communist planes shot down and success for the Sidewinders—not 100 percent, but a very fine performance.

As a result of superior U.S. equipment and training, the Nationalist pilots could exert air control and the "Red Chinese weren't much interested in challenging in the air."[22]

Finally, although the U.S. government gave Taiwan U.S.-made destroyers, submarines, and airplanes, it was a generally acknowledged fact the Nationalist Navy still did not have very much equipment. In the event of war the Nationalist Navy would be "dependent, really, on the Seventh Fleet." The decision to train better pilots and provide Taiwan with Sidewinder missiles was probably the single most important factor adding to the Nationalist military's capabilities. In addition to giving Taiwan new offensive weapons, U.S. advisors in Taiwan helped build airfields and provided better radar equipment. All of these U.S. efforts would allow the Nationalists to provide a measure of air control should the PRC decide to attack the offshore islands again.[23]

Throughout the Taiwan Patrol Force's existence, morale building—for the Nationalists—and frequent R & R (rest and recreation) visits—for visiting USN crews—were an important function of the patrols. As Eisenhower put it to Churchill in a March 1955 eyes-only, top-secret letter, the only way to avoid losing Taiwan, which would "doom the Philippines and eventually the remainder of the region" to Communism, was to "sustain a high morale among Chiang's forces."[24]

During the early 1950s, morale was particularly low within the Nationalist Navy. According to one ONI report, officers' attitudes toward shipboard life left something to be desired, as did their "lack of interest in the training and advancement of their juniors." Moreover, there was still a sense of "aimlessness and idleness" among the Nationalist crews while under way.[25] Morale building included showing the U.S. flag, so as to prove that the U.S. Navy was backing Taiwan. Morale building could also include USN personnel participating in sporting events, such as softball or baseball, with local teams.

Taiwan's morale was also closely linked to its economic wellbeing. U.S. government financial aid and preferential trade rights were crucial for building up the ROC economy during the early to mid-1950s. Since Taiwan was virtually cut off from mainland China, traditionally one of its greatest trade partners, Taiwan businessmen had to conduct correspondingly greater trade with Hong Kong, Japan, and the United States. Military-to-military relations directly added to Taiwan's security, which indirectly helped sponsor greater trade and commercial links between Taiwan and the United States. In this effort, visiting USN vessels in Taiwan contributed to the island's economic growth.

Chapter 6

POLITICAL AND ECONOMIC IMPACT OF U.S. AID

Following their defeat, the Nationalists were well aware of the precariousness of their existence on Taiwan. Japan had renounced its sovereignty over Taiwan at the end of World War II, while the United States had facilitated the evacuation of Nationalists troops to the island. Unlike mainland China, Taiwan's economy had not been shattered. The Japanese had maintained stability during their rule, and the U.S. bombing campaign to defeat Japan had largely bypassed the island. When the first Nationalist troops arrived in October of 1945, they encountered immediate problems with the local population, many of whom did not feel a common identity with the Nationalist refugees from the Asian mainland. Most educated Taiwanese used Japanese. Although they also spoke a Chinese dialect, it was the South China language of Fujian Province, largely unintelligible to speakers of the North China language of Mandarin or to Chiang's allies from Shanghai or Guangzhou.

A major anti-Nationalist uprising broke out on February 28, 1947 — the so-called February 28 Incident — during a police crackdown on cigarette smuggling. Investigators tried to confiscate one woman's cigarettes, and when she resisted one of the policemen hit her. Locals rioted, and sympathetic rioting spread across Taipei, its port city of Keelung, and then quickly on to other cities throughout Taiwan. These demonstrations resulted in the deaths or injury of approximately one thousand recent pro-Nationalist immigrants from the mainland. In retaliation, government repression led to the death or injury of over eight thousand Taiwanese. Tensions remained high. The only bright side was that in sharp contrast to Nationalist practices on the mainland, which tended to ignore such incidents, this time the embattled leadership concluded that the army general in charge of suppressing the unrest had used excessive force and subsequently had him executed.

The Nationalist Party had learned certain lessons from its defeat on the mainland. It was well aware of the precariousness of its existence. While it monopolized politics on the national level until the 1980s, it held local elections starting in 1946 and elections for the provincial assembly starting in 1951. Thus, the Nationalist Party early on in Taiwan created a hybrid government that mixed elements of a democracy with its autocratic one-party rule. To avoid widespread corruption and hyperinflation that had alienated public support on the mainland, Taiwan supported economic growth through price stability and land reform. The Nationalist Party was urged by the U.S. government to create a hybrid government mixing elements of democracy with one-party rule, even while adopting a market-driven economy. To support this transition, between 1952 and 1960 approximately $100 million in economic aid was given to Taiwan each year.[26] One estimate of total U.S. economic aid between 1950 and 1969 was $2.2 billion.[27]

Learning from their many mistakes fighting the Chinese Communists, the Nationalist government on Taiwan successfully merged basic democratic principles and low government corruption with economic growth and price stability. For example, the Nationalists embarked on land reform in Taiwan in 1948, with the sale of public land that had formerly belonged to Japanese landlords. During the early 1950s, the percentage of farmers on Taiwan owning land rose from 25 to 35 percent.[28] This Nationalist redistribution policy paralleled the highly successful Communist land practices on the mainland, but without fomenting class hatred.

The U.S. government played a major role in spurring Taiwan's economic growth. In 1951 alone, U.S. economic aid to Taiwan amounted to 10 percent of the island's entire gross national product (GNP).[29] Between 1951 and 1954, U.S. grants totaled $375 million.[30] However, it was assumed that this U.S. support could not last forever. During 1953, the U.S. embassy in Taipei reported that the Nationalists had just adopted a four-year plan that sought to make the ROC economically independent of the United States by 1957.[31]

The Taiwanese economic plan was ambitious. To promote rapid industrial development, the Nationalists focused on import substitution. By erecting a tariff wall to protect infant industries, they could substitute locally made consumer goods for imported ones. In addition, they sought to develop export industries to profit from value-added processing of raw materials. Taiwan also focused on the development of light industry and the production of consumer goods that would improve the local standard of living. It would not focus on heavy industry until the 1960s. These economic policies stood in stark contrast to the Soviet model for industrial development followed by mainland China, which emphasized developing heavy industry first.

U.S. economic support had a dramatic impact on Taiwan. On May 3, 1951, E. H. Jacobs-Larkcom, the British consul in Taiwan, reported on the positive benefits of this American aid, saying that, "it was not until the accelerated American aid programme of 1949–'50 that the Formosans found an administration to their taste. The Americans have insisted on political and social reform—e.g., a measure of democratic self-government has been granted, and land rentals have been reduced to fair levels. In addition, American material aid really reaches the common people, and at fair prices. I think it may be stated, therefore, that what the bulk of the native population desire is a continuation of the present American colonial regime."[32] In March 1955, British observers remained impressed, positively commenting that the Nationalists were gradually bringing about a more democratic climate, although the government "is still a dictatorship, albeit a benevolent and—insofar as the president was elected and his emergency powers were approved by the National Assembly—a constitutional one."[33]

Considering that these years of extremely high economic growth on Taiwan corresponded with the presence of the Taiwan Patrol Force, it is undeniable that the U.S. Navy provided the necessary security that helped promote the origins of the so-called Taiwan miracle. Because the Seventh Fleet had such a wide range of duties to perform, and could not focus all of its efforts on Taiwan, it was important that Nationalist morale be kept as high as possible. The U.S. embassy kept close track of how these U.S. Navy missions impacted local morale.

USN MORALE-BUILDING ACTIVITIES

It was feared that the 1955 decision to evacuate the Dachens had a serious psychological impact on the Nationalists, gravely undermining their morale. The U.S. government had to be concerned about these trends, and the U.S. embassy in Taipei played an important role in coordinating the ongoing morale-building effort. Throughout the 1950s, there were grave concerns that the morale of Taiwanese citizens was waning; after all, they were a small island nation facing an enormous continental power. As U.S. Ambassador Karl L. Rankin explained to a British visitor in 1953, "the Chinese Nationalists on Formosa represented the only case where a sizeable element of a Communist-dominated country had escaped from behind the Iron Curtain and was conducting his affairs as an independent government." Taiwan's success or failure could have a dramatic effect on "the whole anti-Communist problem . . . in the ultimate showdown." Because of Taiwan's "unique position," it required "great vision and foresight in framing our future policy toward Communism as a whole and, in particular, towards the situation in the Far East."[34]

One important USN goals was sustaining high morale on Taiwan. It was a delicate balancing act keeping the Nationalists happy while not giving them too much leeway. In a February 10, 1955, top-secret, eyes-only letter, Eisenhower described this problem to Churchill:

> To defend Formosa, the United States has been engaged in a long and costly program of arming and sustaining the Nationalist troops on the island. Those troops, however, and Chiang himself, are not content, *now*, to accept irrevocably and permanently the status of "prisoners" on the island. They are held together by a conviction that some day they will go back to the mainland.
>
> As a consequence, their attitude toward Quemoy [Jinmen] and the Matsus [Mazus], which they deem the stepping stones between the two hostile regions, is that the surrender of those islands would destroy the reason for the existence of the Nationalist forces on Formosa. This, then, would mean the almost-immediate conversion of that asset into a deadly danger, because the Communists would immediately take it over.

The Formosa Resolution, as passed by the Congress, is our publicly stated position; the problem now is how to make it work. The morale of the Chinese Nationalists is important to us, so for the moment, and under existing conditions, we feel they must have certain assurances with respect to the offshore islands. But these must be less binding on us than the terms of the Chino-American Treaty, which was overwhelmingly passed yesterday by the Senate. We must remain ready, until some better solution can be found, to move promptly against any Communist force that is manifestly preparing to attack Formosa. And we must make a distinction—(this is a difficult one)—between an attack that has *only* as its objective the capture of an offshore island and one that is primarily a preliminary movement to an all-out attack on Formosa.

Whatever now is to happen, I know that nothing could be worse than global war.... I devoutly hope that history's inflexible yardstick will show that we have done everything in our power, and everything that is right, to prevent the awful catastrophe of another major war.[35]

As Eisenhower emphasized in a later letter to Churchill, in some ways the U.S. government had actually gained much less than it wanted in negotiations with Taipei, since it had to be careful not to coerce Chiang Kai-shek, lest they undermine the "morale and the loyalty of the non-Communist forces on Formosa."[36]

The U.S. embassy on Taiwan was primarily responsible for tracking morale. In a March 31, 1955, memo it reported that to an average native on Taiwan the recent U.S.–Taiwan mutual-security treaty had increased the security of their island. But mainland Chinese living in exile on Taiwan were upset over U.S. attempts to sign a cease-fire that would permanently pacify the Taiwan Strait area, as well as over the U.S. failure to commit itself fully to the defense of Jinmen and Mazu islands.[37] An April 1955 assessment was more optimistic, concluding that "The Embassy believes we can count on the determination and fighting spirit of the Nationalists until they are convinced the U.S. has abandoned their cause."[38] In June of that year, however, Chiang Kai-shek informed Dulles that he wanted to reinforce the offshore islands by sending an additional division. But before taking action, he wanted to learn Washington's view, since should the public and military learn that Washington opposed reinforcing the island garrisons, they might "deduce that we are thinking of urging another Dachen-like withdrawal."[39]

Concerns about low morale among the Nationalists also affected the overseas Chinese. According to Eisenhower, there were millions of ethnic Chinese living in the Philippines, Indonesia, Malaya, and Hong Kong who were looking to Chiang Kai-shek. "If the Chinese National Government should disappear," said Eisenhower, "these émigré Chinese will certainly deem themselves subjects of the Chinese Communist Government and they will quickly add to the difficulties of their adopted countries."[40] A British report confirmed that overseas Chinese support would disappear if Taiwan were completely neutralized with "no stake at all in mainland China."[41] Frequent U.S. Navy port calls were another highly visible method of boosting morale on Taiwan. Fortunately, the U.S. Navy retained a generally good record with the locals. Nationalist newspapers wrote flattering articles concerning the fine conduct of USN crew members on liberty.[42] In July 1955, therefore, a British observer was able to report that "morale is high and Nationalist naval and air strength growing."[43] These elements would prove to be highly important during the next few years, when a second crisis with the PRC rocked the Taiwan Strait.

CONCLUSIONS

With equipment and training from the U.S. Navy, the Nationalist Navy gradually improved. From the early 1950s onward, USN ships often came to Taiwan to conduct combined training exercises, both to pass on their expertise and to ensure that the two navies could cooperate together if a war ever broke out over the Taiwan Strait. The U.S. government also authorized the transfer of high-tech naval equipment to Taiwan. After the first Taiwan Strait crisis during 1954 and 1955, the U.S. Navy's training mission became more intense. The Nationalist Navy was able to receive more advanced equipment, including additional destroyers and diesel submarines. More importantly, the U.S. military transferred high-tech aircraft and Sidewinder missiles to Taiwan. These technological developments allowed the Nationalist to adopt a more offensive policy, including on occasion using marine forces trained by U.S. Navy advisors to mount attacks against the mainland and Communist-held islands.

It was no longer clear that the PLAN could defeat the Nationalist Navy in a fleet-on-fleet battle at sea. The USN efforts largely matched the Soviet Union's ongoing attempts to build up the Chinese Communist fleet, which effectively denied Beijing leaders the expected military benefits of their alliance with Moscow. To further bolster Taiwan's security, USN ships also carried out naval demonstrations and morale-building exercises and scheduled frequent R & R visits to Taiwan to help build up Taiwan's economy. With American political and financial support, Taiwan experienced rapid economic growth from the early 1950s through the 1970s. By the mid-1980s, Taiwan's GNP was approximately half the PRC's, even though it had less than one-fiftieth of China's population. Taiwan was also well on its way to adopting a truly democratic government.

The U.S. Navy played an especially important role during these years by helping to maintain Nationalist morale. This was all part and parcel of a larger U.S. economic program intended to put Taiwan on its feet. Considering Taiwan's geographic isolation, high morale in Taiwan could, in turn, have a significant impact on the overseas Chinese communities throughout East Asia and Southeast Asia, who were looking to Taiwan for moral and political leadership. The people on Taiwan clearly appreciated U.S. Navy efforts to protect them from invasion across the Taiwan Strait. In fact, during its decades-long existence, the USN patrol ships on the Taiwan Patrol Force were the most obvious and visible sign of U.S. government support for Taiwan. All of these political, economic, and psychological factors were to play an especially important role during the second Taiwan Strait crisis in 1958.

NOTES

1. Jay Pryor interview with author, April 28, 2009.
2. U.S. Office of Naval Intelligence, "The Struggle for the Coastal Islands of China," *ONI Review Supplement* (December 1953): i–ix.
3. Ibid.
4. David Muller, *China as a Maritime Power* (Boulder, CO: Westview Press, 1983), 14.
5. U.S. Office of Naval Intelligence, "The Southeast China Coast Today," *ONI Review* (February 1953): 51–60.
6. Gabe T. Wang, *China and the Taiwan Issue: Impending War at Taiwan Strait* (Lanham, MD: University Press of America, 2006), 160.
7. "American Military Activity in Taiwan (Secret Guard)," Naval Liaison Office, British Consulate, Tamsui, October 5, 1951, TNA/UK, FO 371/92300.
8. Walter Ansel, *The Reminiscences of Rear Admiral Walter C. W. Ansel, U.S. Navy (Retired)*, Oral History 74 (Annapolis, MD: U.S. Naval Institute, 1972), 230–41.
9. Arleigh A. Burke, *Recollections of Admiral Arleigh A. Burke, U.S. Navy (Retired)*, Oral History 64 (Annapolis, MD: U.S. Naval Institute, 1973), 43–44.
10. Harry Donald Felt, *Reminiscences of Admiral Harry Donald Felt, U.S. Navy (Retired)*, Oral History 138 (Annapolis, MD: U.S. Naval Institute, 1974), 392.
11. "Security of the Offshore Islands Presently Held by the Nationalist Government of the Republic of China," memorandum from Chief of Naval Operations, Admiral Robert B. Carney, to Joint Chiefs of Staff (top secret), August 20, 1953, Strategic Plans Division, NHHC Archives, Box 289.
12. "Review of Chinese Nationalist Forces," memorandum from Chief of Naval Operations, Admiral Robert B. Carney, to Join Chiefs of Staff (top secret), December 16, 1953, Strategic Plans Division, NHHC Archives, Box 289.
13. Philip A. Beshany, *The Reminiscences of Vice Admiral Philip A. Beshany, U.S. Navy (Retired)*, Oral History 45 (Annapolis, MD: U.S. Naval Institute, 1983), 887–88.
14. "Summary of NDAP Support (Secret)," March 24, 1955, Strategic Plans Division, NHHC Archives, Box 326.
15. Beshany, *The Reminiscences of Vice Admiral Philip A. Beshany*, 395.
16. TaiwanAirPower.org, "ROCAF F-104 Retirement," last updated August 24, 2005 (accessed December 15, 2010), http://www.taiwanairpower.org/history/f104ret.html.
17. George W. Anderson Jr., *Reminiscences of Admiral George W. Anderson, Jr., U.S. Navy (Retired.)*, Oral History 42 (Annapolis, MD: U.S. Naval Institute, 1983), 307.
18. U.S. Navy Operation Order, CTF 72 No. 2-56, October 1, 1956, NHHC Archives, Post-1946 Operation Plans, Task Force 72.
19. Paul D. Stroop, *The Reminiscences of Vice Admrial Paul D. Stroop, U.S. Navy (Retired)*, Oral History 139 (Annapolis, MD: U.S. Naval Institute, 1970), 278–79.

20. "Transfer of Responsibility for Support of and Training for Coastal Raiding and Maritime Interdiction Operations (China)," top-secret memorandum, Robert L. Dennison, July 21, 1954, Strategic Plans Division, NHHC Archives, Box 306.

21. Phil H. Bucklew, *Reminiscences of Captain Phil H. Bucklew, U.S. Navy (Retired)*, Oral History 34 (Annapolis, MD: U.S. Naval Institute, 1982), 300–4.

22. Felt, *Reminiscences of Admiral Harry Donald Felt*, 391.

23. Anderson Jr., *Reminiscences of Admiral George W. Anderson, Jr.*, 310–11.

24. Personal letter from President Eisenhower to Prime Minister Churchill (eyes only, top secret), March 29, 1955, TNA/UK, PREM 11/879.

25. U.S. Office of Naval Intelligence, "Intelligence Briefs: China," *ONI Review* (August 1952): 336.

26. Dennis Van Vranken Hickey, *United States–Taiwan Security Ties: From Cold War to Beyond Containment* (Westport, CT: Praeger, 1994), 21.

27. Wang, *China and the Taiwan Issue*, 160.

28. Bruce A. Elleman and S. C. M. Paine, *Modern China: Continuity and Change, 1644 to the Present* (Upper Saddle River, NJ: Prentice-Hall, 2010), 363.

29. Ibid., 364.

30. Hickey, *United States–Taiwan Security Ties*, 21.

31. John Foster Dulles Papers, Princeton University, Reel 204/205, April 15, 1953, 88908; citing an April 8, 1953, memo of conversation, "Chinese Nationalist Program for Economic Self-Support in Four Years."

32. Secret and personal letter from E. H. Jacobs-Larkom, Consul, British Consulate, Tamsui, Formosa, to R. H. Scott, Foreign Office, London, May 3, 1951, TNA/UK, FO 371/92225.

33. Letter from A. H. B. Hermann, British Consulate, Tamsui, to Sir Anthony Eden, Foreign Office (Secret and Guard), March 1, 1955, TNA/UK, FO 371/115042.

34. Letter from M. Shoosmith to Headquarters, United Nations Command, Office of the Deputy Chief of Staff (secret), March 30, 1953, TNA/UK, FO 371/105323.

35. Letter from President Eisenhower to Prime Minister Churchill (top secret, eyes only), February 10, 1955, TNA/UK, PREM 11/879; emphasis original.

36. Letter from President Eisenhower to Prime Minister Churchill (top secret), February 19, 1955, TNA/UK, PREM 11/879.

37. John Foster Dulles Papers, Princeton University, Reel 210/211, March 31, 1955, 93065.

38. John Foster Dulles Papers, Princeton University, Reel 210/211, April 4, 1955, 93088.

39. John Foster Dulles Papers, Princeton University, Reel 210/211, June 29, 1955, 93578.

40. Personal letter from President Eisenhower to Prime Minister Churchill (eyes only, top secret), March 29, 1955, TNA/UK, PREM 11/879.

41. Report from John Ogle, Lieutenant Commander, Royal Navy, British Consulate, Tamsui, July 7, 1955, TNA/UK, FO 371/115077.

42. Jim Osenton, ed., "USS *Manatee* (AO-58)," Unofficial USS *Manatee* Homepage (accessed December 13, 2010), http://www.ussmanatee.org/mohhist.htm.

43. Report from John Ogle, Lieutenant Commander, Royal Navy, British Consulate, Tamsui, July 7, 1955, FO 371/115077.

SEVEN

The Second Taiwan Strait Crisis, 1958

Tensions between mainland China and Taiwan remained high after the first Taiwan Strait crisis in 1954 and 1955. The Nationalist blockade of the PRC continued, although it halted a lower percentage of international shipping with the PRC, since its range was limited to southeast China. However, the blockade plus the U.S.–sponsored strategic embargo that lasted through 1971 together had a significant impact on the PRC. One scholar has even concluded, "It is no exaggeration that the U.S. embargo in part prompted the Three-Anti's and Five-Anti's campaigns, the Socialist Transformation, the Anti-Rightist movements, and the Great Leap Forward, which precipitated both economic disaster and political disorder in China."[1]

To make up for the loss of international seaborne commerce, the PRC was forced to turn to the USSR, conducting an ever-larger share of trade via the Trans-Siberian Railroad. China's debts to the USSR had grown to well over a billion U.S. dollars, with one estimate of China's total debt equaling 1.5 billion rubles, or almost $2 billion in 1962 dollars.[2] During the late 1950s, the PRC sought to break away from its overreliance on the USSR. In 1957 the British tried to help China diversify its trade by shipping a wider range of goods. In response, the Nationalist blockade tightened. On June 7, 1957, the Nationalist minister for foreign affairs pledged that his government would stand firm on its mainland "port-closure order" whether or not the British used warships to escort merchant ships into the Communist ports.[3]

Occurring as it did in the midst of the Nationalist retightening the blockade, the second Taiwan Strait crisis during 1958 was precipitated by the PRC's attempt to halt the blockade once and for all, thereby diversifying its international trade away from the USSR. To try to catch up with the West, Mao Zedong even adopted unsound economic policies like the

Great Leap Forward, which eventually produced a nationwide famine that killed millions of Chinese. Beijing's renewed attacks during 1958 on Jinmen—the Nationalists' main blockade base—put extreme pressure on Taiwan to end the blockade. Similar to the first crisis during 1954 and 1955, the Taiwan Patrol Force was put right in the midst of this dispute.

THE GRADUAL DECLINE OF THE NATIONALIST BLOCKADE

During the early 1950s, the U.S. government actively supported the Nationalist blockade, in particular when its enforcement helped to strengthen the U.S.–led strategic embargo of the PRC. By contrast, the British government opposed the blockade with its own Formosa Patrol Force and in 1957 even announced that it was planning to increase trade with China. Meanwhile, in 1954, the Nationalist Navy unwittingly sparked a diplomatic furor when it detained *Tuapse*, a Soviet-flagged tanker. The bad publicity about the poor treatment of the Russian crew eventually led to a sharp reduction in U.S. congressional support for the Nationalist blockade.

By 1957, the Nationalist blockade was under attack by the British, who protested its interference with Hong Kong's trade with China. During the year and a half between 1954 and mid-1955, there were thirty-five reported incidents against British shipping; the number of serious attacks from the sea (nine), land (two), and air (three) dropped to a total of fourteen, however, with no reported injuries or deaths.[4] The British Formosa Strait Patrol, unlike its American counterpart, operated more sporadically during the mid-1950s. Usually one Royal Navy ship was engaged on a patrol, and each patrol only lasted two to three days. During a five-month period in late 1954, for example, only seven ships patrolled the Taiwan Strait, each for two to three days, which meant ships were only present during twenty-four out of about 150 days, or about 16 percent of the period.[5]

Unlike the complex duties carried out by USN vessels, which included patrolling, training, and morale building, the Royal Navy sought to protect British shipping from interference by the Nationalists and their guerrilla allies. During a chance encounter in a Taipei bar, the commanding officer of a British ship showed his orders signed by the First Lord of the Admiralty: "You will uphold the Queen's interests in the Formosa Straits." This differed from USN practices, which tended to outline every possible contingency, prompting the U.S. officer to say, "I presume he may also have been given verbal guidance, but it was *not* in writing, so he had complete latitude in deciding how to act. Now that's the way to run a Navy!"[6]

One sure sign of the British patrol's impact appeared on September 8, 1955, when the Nationalist government's Department of Defense ordered that attacks on shipping off the coast of China must be confined to Communist vessels and that no neutral ships should be molested unless it was necessary for self-defense. This sole exception would appear to be covering a hypothetical situation where a neutral vessel "happened to be in the way of a bona fide attack on a Communist vessel."[7] Although British-flagged vessels continued to be stopped and searched from time to time, during July 1956 it was reported that so far that year no British ship had sustained damage or casualties either as a result of Nationalist air and naval action or by shore batteries from coastal islands.[8] Almost a year after that, in May 1957, it was further reported that since December 1955 not a single British ship had been damaged and that there were no casualties.[9]

The loosening of the Nationalist blockade against British shipping also corresponded with a gradual decline in U.S. congressional support. This was largely due to the June 1954 seizure by the Nationalists of the Soviet oil tanker *Tuapse*. Moscow immediately protested that a U.S. destroyer had conducted the operation, but Washington denied this accusation. Rather, the ship's capture was described by one specialist as Chiang's "first act of revenge" against the Soviet Union for supporting the Chinese Communists.[10] After *Tuapse* was taken to Taiwan, its crew was released. While most of the Russian crew members were eventually returned to the Soviet Union, eleven elected to remain in Taiwan, and nine later asked for and were eventually granted political asylum in the United States. In 1956, the Soviet embassy requested that it be allowed to interview the nine defectors. Initially, the U.S. government refused, presenting "letters from all nine crew members stating they did not wish to talk with any Soviet official."[11]

When the nine crew members arrived in the United States, however, they were allowed to meet with Soviet diplomats. Five of the nine were convinced to return home, perhaps when family members back in the USSR were threatened with punishment. Upon their return to the USSR, the sailors then claimed in the Soviet press that they had been little better than hostages in Taiwan. When they asked to be returned home, for example, they were put in solitary confinement, where they were "cruelly beaten and abused almost every day for two months."[12]

The bad publicity surrounding this incident increased U.S.–Soviet diplomatic tensions, which undermined congressional support for the Nationalist blockade. The Senate Internal Subcommittee, in particular, blamed the U.S. government for letting Soviet officials put pressure on the sailors to redefect. The generally negative press reports of this incident created a bad impression in the United States and abroad, since it seemed to many that the Soviet crew members had been forced to defect first to Taiwan and then later to the United States. After the *Tuapse* incident, there were many fewer cases of search, seizure, and attack by Nationalist warships.

By 1957, the Nationalist blockade of the PRC had been underway for almost ten years. A combination of British protests, plus the presence of the Royal Navy, gradually limited the usefulness of the Nationalist blockade against British shipping. However, on May 31, 1957, the thirty-third anniversary of the 1924 Sino–Soviet Treaty opening diplomatic relations between the USSR and China, a Nationalist naval squadron sank a 1,500–ton Communist transport ship off the Xiamen coastline.[13] As late as June 1957, the Nationalist government was still publicly warning foreign ships entering Communist ports that they did so at their own risk.[14]

In June 1957, after years of internal debate and discussion, the British government finally decided to eliminate its support for the U.S.–led embargo. Beginning in early 1958, both the total size of the Sino–British trade, plus the total number of items traded, began to increase dramatically. This prompted the U.S. embassy in Taipei to warn in the summer of 1957 that "the Chinese Communists may wish to neutralize it [Jinmen] in order to facilitate a greater use of the harbor following the British action on trade controls."[15] PRC attempts to neutralize Jinmen Island resulted in the second Taiwan Strait crisis.

THE SECOND TAIWAN STRAIT CRISIS, 1958

As the U.S. Embassy had predicted, one of the PRC's top priorities in 1958 was to increase its trade with Britain. The key to making this new trade policy effective was to eliminate the threat from the Nationalist base on Jinmen. Since the mid-1950s, an estimated seven hundred fifty thousand PLA troops had been permanently stationed along the mainland coast opposite the offshore islands. This deployment was a constant drain on the PRC and definitely slowed down any PLA military probing elsewhere.[16] According to Joseph Bouchard, therefore, the PRC's "first objective" during the second Taiwan Strait crisis "was to deter the Nationalists from using the offshore islands for harassment of the mainland or as a base for a future invasion of the mainland."[17]

On August 23, 1958, Communist forces began shelling Jinmen Island, using an estimated forty thousand shells during the first attack. Scholars have argued that the timing of China's attack was linked to the ongoing crisis in the Middle East (where the United States ended up sending troops into Lebanon to protect President Chamoun's pro-Western regime against civil war).[18] Although it is true that Beijing hoped that U.S. military, overextended by the Middle East crisis, would be unable to respond to the offshore attack, the British decision to liberalize trade with China was also an important contributing factor. For example, in August 1958, Prince Norodom Sihanouk, the president of the Council of Ministers of Cambodia, visited China to mediate with Mao Zedong and Zhou Enlai, and in mid-September he explained to Walter S. Robertson, assistant secretary to the U.S. Mission to the UN, that the PRC leaders were "concerned by the fact that the offshore islands are being used to mount Commando attacks on the mainland and to impose a blockade."[19]

Immediately after the shelling began, the Nationalists requested full U.S. military support. Vice Admiral Roland N. Smoot, commander of the USTDC from 1958 to 1962, had no choice but to tell Chiang that according to the U.S.–ROC defense treaty the USN could not get directly involved. However, the U.S. military did assist in other ways: "We could and did take over military defense of Taiwan itself, thus releasing his military forces to defend and resupply the offshore islands."[20] In addition, a number of flyovers were conducted to show the PRC that the U.S. Navy was in the area. In demonstrations carried out in September 1958, the aircraft-carrier group commanders were too enthusiastic, and the "navy paid a price for the show of force put on by the combat air patrol over the Taiwan Strait, losing four planes and three pilots in accidents."[21]

The PRC attack on Jinmen immediately drew in the Seventh Fleet. A direct Sino–U.S. conflict was narrowly avoided when, on September 24, 1958, USS *Hopewell* (DD 681) went to the assistance of a Nationalist tank landing ship (LST) being attacked by Communist torpedo boats. Its orders were to remain clear of the fighting and to not fire unless fired upon. Although the Communist patrol boats circled *Hopewell*, the Chinese ships also elected to not fire. As one account of this standoff concluded, "Thus, caution on both sides averted the first potential clash between Communist and American forces in the Strait."[22]

By mid-September 1958, the U.S. Navy had positioned five carriers and their escort ships near Taiwan, and another two were on their way. A clear message was sent to the PRC when it was revealed on October 1 that a number of eight-inch howitzers, capable of firing nuclear shells, had been delivered to Jinmen Island.[23] In addition, the Nationalist Air Force was provided with advanced Sidewinder air-to-air missiles. In one air battle on September 24, 1958, the Nationalist F-86s shot down an impressive ten MiGs, with two other probable hits, without sustaining a single loss.[24] These were the first ever kills by these air-to-air missiles.[25]

Most importantly, the U.S. Navy helped protect the shipping lanes supplying Jinmen. In early September 1958, the Taiwan Patrol Force was ordered to assist the Nationalist effort to resupply Jinmen by providing landing ships plus escort and support forces to protect the Nationalist convoy vessels. On September 6, the first United States–escorted Nationalist convoy, code named *LIGHTNING*, reached Jinmen with crucial supplies. The Taiwan Patrol Force escort included four destroyers and two cruisers, including the USS *Helena* (CA 75). By September 19, a total of nine convoys had reached Jinmen; the final four were able to land an average of 151 tons of supplies.[26] With USN assistance, Nationalist supply ships began to reach Jinmen in sufficiently large numbers that by mid-September they successfully broke what was being called a PRC artillery blockade of the island.

Of particular importance was safeguarding the supply ships' arrival and withdrawal from the area. To assist this effort, aircraft were provided for ASW and surface reconnaissance within twenty-five miles of Jinmen Island. While U.S. aircraft were told to stay at least twenty miles off the Chinese coastline, USN vessels were ordered to remain at least three miles from shore. U.S. Navy ships were particularly warned not to shoot at the mainland.[27] However, a special ROE was issued, stating that "U.S. commanders are authorized to engage hostile surface vessels in territorial or international waters if they are attacking the RCN [Republic of China Navy] forces."[28] Meanwhile, intensive training was undertaken by USN personnel to ensure that the Nationalists could carry out a successful convoy operation. A September 15, 1958, map showed how USN ships—stationed in the dotted boxes—protected Nationalist ships resupplying Jinmen (see figure 7.1).

Washington's support for the Nationalists was not unconditional. For example, when Chiang told Admiral Smoot that he wanted to use Taiwanese planes to bomb the mainland, Washington was concerned this might escalate the conflict. According to Admiral Smoot, the U.S. Navy "developed a study [that] proved to them that for every one of those guns that they might silence by the type of bombing they had available, they'd probably lose almost a squadron of planes. This, of course was too big a price to pay, and they were convinced of the proposal's infeasibility."[29]

During late September of 1958, the PRC sent a message through Indian intermediaries that if the Nationalists withdrew from the islands they would not be attacked and that Beijing would not press immediately its claims to Taiwan.[30] The Chinese leaders were clearly concerned about further U.S. intervention: they warned the artillery units firing on Jinmen that "no strike should be aimed at American ships."[31] However, Mao refused to accept U.S. demands that a cease-fire precede Sino–U.S. talks to resolve the crisis.[32] For this reason, a negotiated settlement appeared unlikely.

GROWING SINO–SOVIET ECONOMIC TENSIONS

Behind the scenes, there were several important diplomatic factors that contributed to the second cross-strait crisis. The PRC was determined to break the Nationalist blockade. This decision was in turn linked to growing Sino–Soviet tensions over the PRC's recently adopted economic plan, called the Great Leap Forward. Mao's decision to shell Jinmen without first seeking Soviet approval has even been described as "a challenge not just to Taipei and Washington but to Moscow's domination of the international Communist movement as well."[33]

The Second Taiwan Strait Crisis, 1958   95

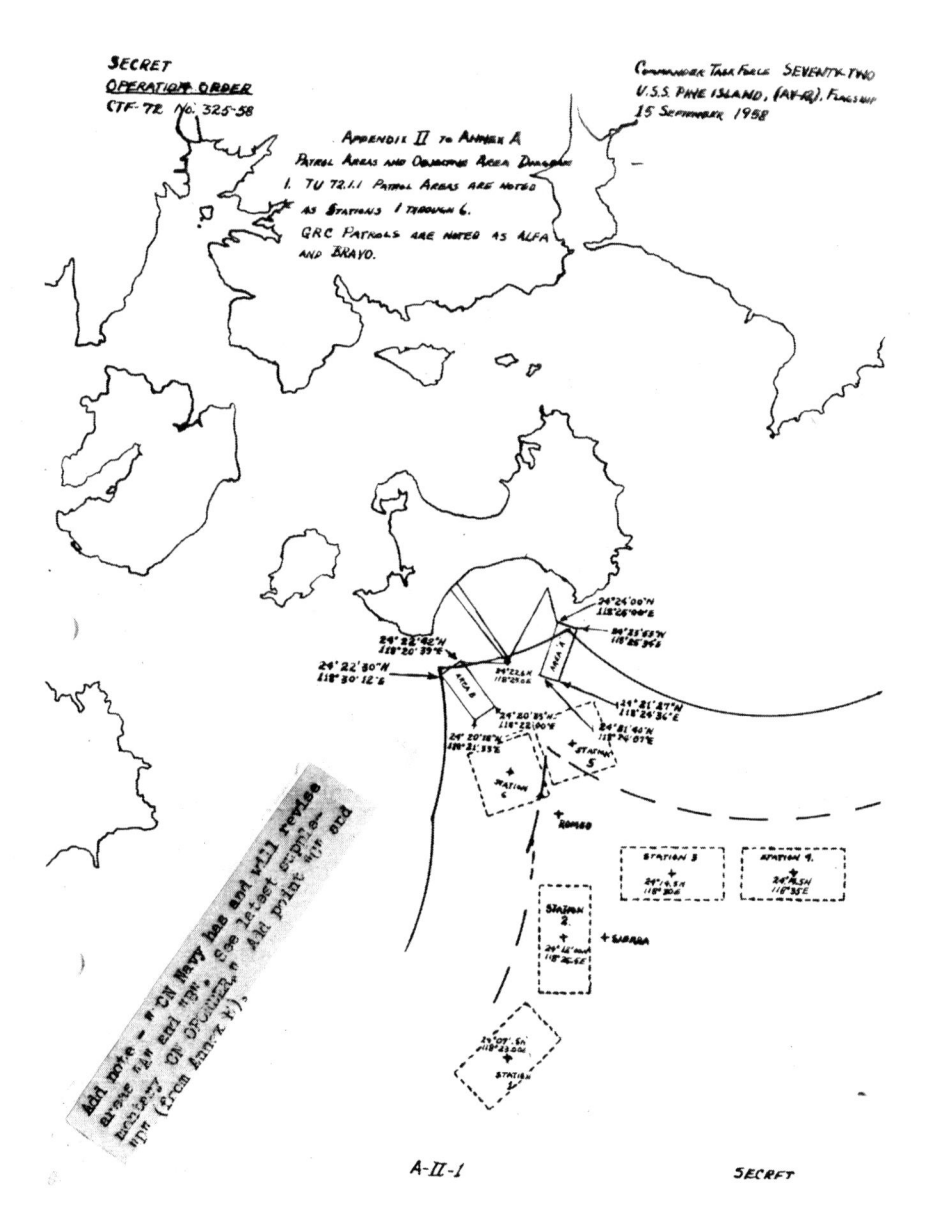

Figure 7.1. U.S. Navy's Jinmen Convoy Operations. Source: Naval History and Heritage Command Archives

Due in large measure to the U.S.–led economic embargo of China, the PRC's economic dependency on the USSR grew rapidly throughout the 1950s. Since 1950, when the PRC had borrowed three hundred million U.S. dollars from the USSR, a sum that was clearly insufficient to solve China's many economic problems, it had fallen further into debt to Moscow. The PRC's fall 1950 intervention in the Korean War not only led to huge military losses but to even greater debts to the USSR, since, to "add insult to injury," Stalin also demanded that China pay for all the Soviet military equipment sent to Korea.[34]

During August of 1958, Mao initiated a new phase of the Great Leap Forward. Due to the Nationalist blockade and the U.S. embargo, Mao was forced to rely mainly on Soviet imports, which rose by an "astounding 70 percent in 1958 and 1959," to support his industrialization plans.[35] But Beijing's constant demands on Moscow entailed political costs. During the summer of 1958, when Mao requested that Khrushchev provide nuclear submarines, Khrushchev in turn pressured Mao to agree to allow Soviet submarine bases in China. This proposal was a clear throwback to tsarist Russian imperialism undermining China's sovereignty. Friction over Soviet bases, plus over the artillery attack on Jinmen, were major factors in the resulting Sino–Soviet rift.[36] To pay back China's debt to the USSR, beginning in 1959 the PRC began to export millions of tons of grain, worth an estimated U.S. $935 million, largely to fund its purchases from the USSR.[37] About three-quarters of all famine-related deaths in China occurred during 1960, which corresponds with the periods seeing the highest grain exports.[38]

In order to increase grain sales to pay for the Great Leap Forward, Beijing desperately needed to increase its maritime trade. PRC officials attempted to exploit Anglo–American differences in trade policy to achieve this goal. Mao also put pressure on Taiwan to give up its last offshore island bases, which were the only part of the mainland the Nationalists still controlled.[39] Not only would this undermine Chiang's goal of returning to the mainland, but the PRC could also finally claim to have reunified all of mainland China. All of these foreign-policy, economic, and political factors contributed to Mao's decision in August of 1958 to attack Jinmen Island.

DULLES HALTS THE NATIONALIST BLOCKADE

Washington was concerned that fighting in the Taiwan Strait might escalate into all-out war. In October of 1958, Dulles tried to persuade Chiang to reduce the number of Nationalist forces on the islands so as to halt the Nationalist commando raids and naval blockade.[40] Although left unstated, any decision to cut forces from the offshore islands would also necessarily result in the termination of the Nationalists' decade-long naval blockade of China. Chiang was opposed to this proposal.

In October, Dulles flew to Taiwan to convince Chiang to withdraw from the offshore islands.[41] During private talks, Chiang refused to withdraw, rejecting any proposal that seemed to him to suggest "retreat from his position as head of the only legitimate Chinese government."[42] Dulles instead urged him to renounce the use of force to reunify China.[43] Included in this plan would be a substantial reduction of forces on Jinmen and Mazu.[44]

Decreasing forces on the offshore islands would be tantamount to stopping the Nationalist blockade. Dulles told the British Foreign Office this was one of his goals immediately before he left for Taiwan to meet with Chiang Kai-shek.[45] The blockade was no longer considered necessary, since the PRC was experiencing an economic implosion due to the Great Leap Forward. Meanwhile, it was well-known in Washington that Sino–Soviet diplomatic relations were already under increasing stress.[46] It was no coincidence that the Nationalist blockade ended in 1958, just as the first hint emerged of what would soon be called the Sino–Soviet split.[47]

After forty-four days, the PRC halted shelling on October 6, 1958. Civilian casualties on Jinmen were 138 dead and 324 injured, while the number of dead and wounded soldiers numbered close to three thousand. In addition, an estimated seven thousand buildings on Jinmen were either damaged or destroyed.[48] Artillery fire continued for the next twenty years, ending for good only in January 1979 after the United States and the PRC recognized each other. Firing took place on alternate days of the week, and the shells mainly contained propaganda leaflets. An estimated one million steel shell casings were fired at Jinmen, making it the longest sustained artillery barrage in world history.[49]

All U.S. attempts to resolve PRC–Taiwan differences peacefully failed. On October 27, 1958, British Foreign Secretary Selwyn Lloyd even wrote to Dulles that the Chinese seemed not to be in any hurry to make peace with Taiwan and would pursue their aims by whatever political means they could think of. "They do not want mediation," wrote Lloyd, "and their ultimate goal appears to be some direct arrangement with the Nationalists." He concluded by predicting, with great accuracy from the viewpoint of a half a century later, that "We are, therefore, likely to be in for a fairly long period of such tactics."[50]

THE ECONOMIC IMPACT OF THE SECOND TAIWAN STRAIT CRISIS

Following the end of the Nationalist blockade, China's international maritime trade gradually began to recover. For example, between 1957 and 1959 there was almost a doubling of imports from Britain and almost a tripling of imports from West Germany.[51] Much of China's foreign trade with Europe was still being funneled through the USSR by means of the Trans-Siberian Railroad, which gave a false appearance that Sino–Soviet trade was continuing. But once the Sino–Soviet split occurred, there was a complete shift away from the Soviet Union toward the West beginning in August 1960.[52]

By 1960, the PRC was facing a domestic financial disaster as a result of the Great Leap Forward. As soon as the Sino–Soviet split became public, however, Beijing insisted on repaying its estimated billion-plus-ruble debt to the USSR. Mao's actions were reportedly a desperate attempt to break away from the USSR-dominated economic system.[53] Enormous Chinese grain exports in 1959 and 1960 helped fund these repayments. The end result of Mao's ill-conceived economic policies was a nationwide famine in China. During 1961, the PRC finally began to import more grain than it exported.[54] But according to one study, almost half a billion rubles were repaid to the USSR during 1960 and 1962, right as tens of millions of Chinese died during the famine. By ignoring the dire plight of the Chinese people, Beijing managed to repay its entire debt to Moscow ahead of schedule, by 1965.[55]

In the aftermath of the 1958 Taiwan Strait crisis, Sino–Soviet trade began to decline, just as China's trade with the West began to grow. According to one view of the U.S. embargo, "China's dependence on Soviet assistance inevitably created heavy economic burdens on Moscow and could slow down Soviet development, thus making the Moscow–Beijing alliance quite costly. On the other hand, Sino–Soviet economic leverage placed the Kremlin in a politically favorable position from which to dictate relations within the alliance and influence the CCP's domestic and foreign policies. This paradoxical situation turned out to be a major contributor to the collapse of the Soviet economic cooperation and the eventual deterioration of the alliance between the two Communist powers." Thus, the indirect and long-term effects of the U.S. strategic embargo produced sufficiently high tensions in Beijing's economic relations with Moscow that by 1960 it helped lead to the disintegration of the Sino–Soviet alliance.[56]

The destruction of this so-called "monolith" was a major victory in the Cold War. This political outcome largely achieved one of Dulles's prime strategic goals of pushing the USSR and the PRC together so as to tear them apart. The Nationalist blockade of China, which was actively supported by the U.S. Navy with equipment and training, played a major role in bringing about this strategic victory.

CONCLUSIONS

The second Taiwan Strait crisis ended the Nationalist blockade of the PRC. The blockade had already lasted ten years and, in combination with the ongoing U.S. strategic embargo, had exerted extreme economic pressure on the PRC. Sino–Soviet economic tensions eventually forced a major realignment in the PRC's foreign trade. In the immediate aftermath of the Sino–Soviet split, Chinese trade with the USSR dropped sharply right as imports soared—especially much-needed grain from Canada and Australia to offset the effects of the Great Famine.

During the 1958 crisis, the Taiwan Patrol Force "accomplished one of the most important missions of her career by playing a major role in aiding the Chinese Nationalists."[57] But according to Dulles, the real dispute was not geography but human wills. If the United States "seems afraid, and loses 'face' in any way, the consequences will be far-reaching, extending from Viet Nam in the south to Japan and Korea in the north."[58] Periodic PLA attacks against Jinmen were intended to make it a whipping boy for Taiwan itself.[59] Since the PRC leaders were pursuing mainly a political, not a military, strategy, they intended to play a cat-and-mouse game with the offshore islands. To Dulles, therefore, the PRC announcement that shelling of Jinmen might switch from even-numbered days to odd-numbered days seemed to substantiate his previous assessment of the situation: "This rather fantastic statement seems to confirm our analysis of the Chinese Communist attitude as being essentially political and propaganda rather than military."[60]

Meanwhile, the U.S. government's announcements remained intentionally vague about Washington's decision not to use military force to support the Nationalist bases on Jinmen and Mazu. However, a secret December 26, 1959, Operation Order, while admitting that the offshore islands were not covered under this agreement, did acknowledge that the United States had committed itself to the defense of Taiwan, the Penghu Islands, and—most importantly—to the offshore islands of Mazu and Jinmen, insofar as a threat to these islands was considered to be a threat to Taiwan and the Penghus.[61] The U.S. government decision to defend any offshore island that posed a direct threat to Taiwan virtually guaranteed that the Nationalists would survive, even while ensuring that the Taiwan Patrol Force would continue for some time to come.

NOTES

1. Shu Guang Zhang, *Economic Cold War: America's Embargo against China and the Sino–Soviet Alliance, 1949–1963* (Stanford, CA: Stanford University Press, 2001), 268.

2. Frank Dikötter, *Mao's Great Famine: The History of China's Most Devastating Catastrophe, 1958–1962* (New York: Walker and Co., 2010), 105.

3. Telegram from Tamsui, Formosa, to Foreign Office, June 9, 1957, TNA/UK, ADM 116/6245.

4. "Incidents Involving British Merchant Ships Off the China Coast," July 18, 1955, TNA/UK, ADM 116/6245.

5. Letter from A. H. E. Allingham to P. Wilkinson, Far Eastern Department, Foreign Office, March 24, 1955, TNA/UK, ADM 1/26157.

6. Ben Simonton, "Leadership in Frustration, a Sea Story," *Gather*, June 3, 2006 (accessed December 13, 2010),http://webcache.googleusercontent.com/search?q=cache:VUwGylXk-J0J:www.gather.com/viewArticle.action%3FarticleId=281474976757231+&cd=2&hl=en&ct=clnk&gl=us&client=firefox-a. Emphasis original.

7. Telegram from the United States to the United Kingdom informing them of the Nationalist order to halt attacks on neutral shipping, September 8, 1955, TNA/UK, ADM 116/6245.

8. Telegram from Tamsui, Formosa, to Foreign Office, July 6, 1956, TNA/UK, ADM 116/6245.

9. Telegram from Tamsui, Formosa, to Foreign Office, May 31, 1957, TNA/UK, ADM 116/6245.

10. Shin Kawashima, "Soviet–Taiwanese Relations during the Early Cold War," Wilson Center, Cold War International History Project, September 23, 2009 (accessed December 14, 2010), http://www.wilsoncenter.org/event/soviet-taiwanese-relations-during-the-early-cold-war.

11. John Foster Dulles Papers, Princeton University, Reel 212/213, March 6, 1956, 949–55.

12. *Current Digest of the Russian Press*, "Report by Soviet Sailors of the Tanker *Tuapse*," 10, no. 25 (July 30, 1958), available online at http://dlib.eastview.com/browse/doc/13821870 (accessed December 14, 2010).

13. "Navy Commander Says Warships Continue to Seal Off Red Ports," *China News*, June 11, 1957, TNA/UK, FO 371/127500.

14. *New York Times*, June 6, 1957.

15. John Foster Dulles Papers, Princeton University, Reel 217/218, June 26, 1957, 97827.

16. UK Consulate, Tamsui, to Foreign Office, January 27, 1958, TNA/UK, FO 371/33522.

17. Joseph F. Bouchard, *Command in Crisis: Four Case Studies* (New York: Columbia University Press, 1991), 59.

18. Jian Chen, *Mao's China and the Cold War* (Chapel Hill: University of North Carolina Press, 2001), 175.

19. Harriet Dashiell Schwar, ed., and Glen W. LaFantasie, gen. ed, "Memorandum of Conversation," September 16, 1958, in *Foreign Relations of the United States, 1958–1960*, vol. 19, *China*, 201–3 (Washington, DC: United States Government Printing Office, 1996).

20. Vice Admiral Roland N. Smoot, "As I Recall . . . The U.S. Taiwan Defense Command." *Proceedings* 110/9/979 (September 1984): 56–59.

21. Bouchard, *Command in Crisis*, 76–77.

22. Ibid., 69.

23. Chang-Kwoun Park, "Consequences of U.S. Naval Shows of Force, 1946–1989," PhD diss., University of Missouri–Columbia, 1995, 257–60.

24. Robert Keng, "Republic of China F-86's in Battle," Aircraft Resource Center, 2003 (accessed March 22, 2011), http://www.aircraftresourcecenter.com/Stories1/001-100/021_TaiwanF-86_Keng/story021.htm.

25. Edward J., "Confrontation in the Taiwan Straits," in *U.S. Navy: A Complete History*, ed. M. Hill Goodspeed (Washington, DC: Naval Historical Foundation, 2003).

26. Bouchard, *Command in Crisis*, 74.

27. Smoot, "As I Recall," 56–59.

28. U.S. Navy Operation Order, CTF 72 No. 325–58, September 15, 1958, NHHC Archives, Post-1946 Operation Plans, Task Force 72.

29. Smoot, "As I Recall," 56–59.

30. "Secret" telegram from Peking to Foreign Office, September 25, 1958, TNA/UK, PREM 11/3738. This offer appears to have been mentioned by Zhou Enlai to Parthasarathi during a meeting held Sunday, September 21, 1958.

31. Chen, *Mao's China and the Cold War*, 190–91.

32. Ibid., 193–96.

33. Ibid., 179.

34. Dikötter, *Mao's Great Famine*, 5.

35. Ibid., 73–83.

36. John R. Thomas, "The Limits of Alliance: The Quemoy Crisis of 1958," in *Sino–Soviet Military Relations*, ed. Raymond L. Garthoff, 120–24, (New York: Frederick A Praeger, 1966).

37. Jung Chang and Jon Halliday, *Mao: The Unknown Story* (New York: Alfred A, Knopf, 2005), 428.

38. Lorenz M. Lüthi, *The Sino–Soviet Split: Cold War in the Communist World* (Princeton, NJ: Princeton University Press, 2008), 158.

39. Telegram from Washington to Foreign Office (top secret), September 5, 1958, TNA/UK, CAB 21/3272.

40. Foreign Office to Washington (secret), October 22, 1958, TNA/UK, PREM 11/3738.

41. Telegram from the UK Embassy, Washington, to Foreign Office (secret), October 17, 1958, TNA/UK, PREM 11/3738.

42. Letter from President Eisenhower to Prime Minister Macmillan (top secret), September 6, 1958, TNA/UK, CAB 21/3272.

43. Letter from John Foster Dulles to British Ambassador (secret), October 25, 1958, TNA/UK, FO 371/133543.

44. Letter from John Foster Dulles to Selwyn Lloyd (secret), October 25, 1958, TNA/UK, PREM 11/3738.

45. Telegram from Foreign Office to UK Embassy, Washington, October 22, 1958, TNA/UK, PREM 11/3738.

46. As Gordan Chang has pointed out, Eisenhower was careful not to comment on the Sino–Soviet relationship for fear of strengthening it. For example, *The White House Years: Mandate for Change, 1953–1956*, Eisenhower's 1963 memoir, barely mentioned Sino–Soviet tensions so as "to avoid saying anything that could hinder the emergence of the Sino–Soviet split." Gordan H. Chang, *Friends and Enemies: The United States, China, and the Soviet Union, 1948–1972* (Stanford: Stanford University Press, 1990), 331, note 24.

47. Bruce A. Elleman, "The Nationalists' Blockade of the PRC, 1949–58," in *Naval Blockades and Seapower: Strategies and Counter-Strategies, 1805–2005*, ed. Bruce A. Elleman and S. C. M. Paine, 142 (London: Routledge Press, 2006).

48. Michael Szonyi, *Cold War Island: Quemoy on the Front Line* (New York: Cambridge University Press, 2008), 76–77.

49. Xiaobing Li, "PLA Attacks and Amphibious Operations during the Taiwan Strait Crises of 1954–55 and 1958," in *Chinese Warfighting*, ed. Mark A. Ryan, David Finkelstein, and Michael Devitt, 167 (Armonk, NY: M. E. Sharpe, 2003).

50. "Secret" letter from Foreign Secretary Selwyn Lloyd to Secretary of State John Foster Dulles, October 27, 1958, PREM 11/3738.

51. Dikötter, *Mao's Great Famine*, 75.

52. Ibid., 116.

53. Zhang, *Economic Cold War*, 221–22.

54. Lüthi, *The Sino–Soviet Split*, 195.

55. Dikötter, *Mao's Great Famine*, 105.

56. Zhang, *Economic Cold War*, 268–69.

57. "Post-1946, Command File, Taiwan Patrol Force," NHHC Archives, Box 784, 7–8.

58. Telegram from John Foster Dulles to Harold Macmillan (top secret), September 13, 1958, TNA/UK, CAB 21/3272.

59. Telegram from the UK Embassy in Washington to the Foreign Office, October 25, 1958, TNA/UK, PREM 11/3738.

60. Letter from John Foster Dulles to Selwyn Lloyd (secret), October 25, 1958, TNA/UK, PREM 11/3738.

61. U.S. Navy Operation Order, CTF 72 No. 201-60 (secret), December 26, 1959, NHHC Archives, Post-1946 Operation Plans, Task Force 72.

EIGHT
The Third Taiwan Strait Crisis and Sino–American Rapprochement

Following the public acknowledgment of the Sino–Soviet split in 1960, the PRC's main source of modern military equipment disappeared. There was a belated Taiwan Strait crisis in 1962, which was settled diplomatically rather than by fighting. Over time, however, the military rift with the USSR negatively impacted the PLA Navy's technical capabilities, which undermined the PRC's ability to invade Taiwan. The chaos surrounding the 1966–1976 Cultural Revolution exacerbated this situation, since Beijing could not focus as many scarce resources on naval development.

This lower threat level resulted in significant changes to the Taiwan Patrol Force during the 1960s, including assigning fewer and smaller vessels. However, USN ships did remain on patrol duty in the Taiwan Strait. These duties continued throughout all of the 1960s and well into the 1970s. With the escalation of U.S. actions in Vietnam, the Taiwan Patrol Force and the U.S. interdiction program off North Vietnam became more and more closely linked. Sino–U.S tensions also remained high throughout most of the 1960s because of the Vietnam War.

The 1969 Sino–Soviet dispute provided a long-awaited opportunity to improve Sino–U.S. relations. Soon afterward, National Security Advisor Henry Kissinger ordered the U.S. ambassador in Taiwan to tell Vice Premier Chiang Ching-kuo that modifications to the Taiwan Strait Patrol would occur in November of 1969. When Taiwan protested, Kissinger replied that "the decision to change patrol from permanent to intermittent status is not subject to change."[1] This naval de-escalation sent a potent message to Beijing, as did Washington's simultaneous decision to modify the terms of the U.S. embargo on strategic goods. According to Kissinger's memoir, these were messages that "Peking had understood."[2]

Even after Nixon's historic 1972 visit to Beijing, however, the Taiwan Patrol Force continued for another seven years, through the opening of official Sino–U.S. diplomatic relations in 1979.

THE THIRD TAIWAN STRAIT CRISIS, 1962

Tensions in the Taiwan Strait remained high after 1958. During the 1960 U.S. presidential elections, the offshore islands became a hotly debated political issue. Richard Nixon even accused fellow candidate John F. Kennedy of lacking the resolve to protect the offshore islands with force. By the early 1960s there was a significant PLA buildup across from Jinmen Island, and during the spring of 1962 the PRC began to deploy additional troops to the Taiwan Strait region. This incident, often referred to as the third Taiwan Strait crisis, prompted a rapid U.S. diplomatic response.

The background to this third incident was the severe famine brought about by Mao's determination to pay back China's debts to the USSR. Estimates vary, but tens of millions of Chinese died in the Great Famine between 1958 and 1961. Food shortages continued well into 1962. Beginning in May 1962, more than 100,000 refugees flooded across the border into Hong Kong. Taking advantage of this crisis, the Nationalist government agreed to accept all refugees who wished to move to Taiwan. Two days later the U.S. government agreed to accept several thousand Chinese refugees.[3]

When the Kennedy administration came into office, it considered—and then rejected—any suggestion of relaxing trade controls with China due to the unfolding Sino–Soviet split or because of the humanitarian crisis caused by the famine.[4] In fact, Admiral Smoot admitted that the Nationalists were doing all they could to exacerbate the crisis. With U.S. approval, teams of ten to twenty men were transported to the PRC to conduct sabotage missions: "They'd take a midget submarine and twenty or thirty men ashore at night, then they'd go over where the Communists had a bunch of guns annoying the offshore islands. The men would go and cut the throats of all the gun crews and then disappear. The Communists would wonder why the guns weren't firing and in their investigations would find all the crews with their throats cut." But Smoot admitted that these sabotage missions were simply to harass the enemy and were not a Nationalist attempt "to return to the mainland in force."[5]

In reaction to the flood of refugees, and fearful that Taiwan might be contemplating offensive operations against the mainland to take advantage of the general collapse of the Great Leap Forward, the PLA moved additional divisions across from Jinmen and Mazu islands.[6] During the spring of 1962, Secretary of State Dean Rusk was able to confirm that U.S. intelligence services had determined that the PLA had moved six or eight divisions to the coastal areas opposite Taiwan. However, there was as yet no sign that junks were assembling, so he concluded that the Chinese moves were probably precautionary in nature.[7]

On June 23, 1962, the American ambassador to Poland met his Chinese counterpart in Warsaw to ask about this unexplained buildup. The Chinese claimed it was due to the threatening posture of the Taiwan authorities. Averell Harriman, the former U.S. ambassador to the USSR, immediately warned the Soviet ambassador to the U.S., Anatoly Dobrynin, of the extreme dangers in any attempt by the Chinese Communists to attack the offshore islands. Harriman also explained that Washington was giving Chiang Kai-shek no encouragement to pursue reckless policies against the PRC. When Dobrynin questioned whether America would support Taiwan in a conflict, especially considering what Kennedy had said during his presidential campaign, Harriman cautioned this would be a most unwise conclusion to draw and that any move against the islands by the Communists ran "terrible risks."[8]

On June 27, 1962, the twelfth anniversary of the founding of the Taiwan Patrol Force, Kennedy warned that if the PRC attacked the offshore islands, then his administration would stand by the 1955 Formosa Resolution to guarantee the defense of Taiwan. He reiterated that "Any threat to the offshore islands ... must be judged in relation to its wider meaning for the safety of Formosa and the peace of the area."[9] Meanwhile, Beijing was also reassured by U.S. officials that Washington would not support a Nationalist attack against the mainland. The U.S. ambassador to Taiwan even warned Chiang Kai-shek that the U.S.–ROC mutual-defense treaty did not say the United States would support a Taiwanese counterattack against China and that it would be "a mistake to create [an] impression in the minds of the people that [the] U.S. has any such obligations."[10]

Although tensions remained high, there was no military conflict. Arguably, the so-called third Taiwan Strait crisis was resolved by the Kennedy administration with diplomacy, although backed up by the USN forces in the region. By utilizing the ambiguity in the wording of the mutual-defense treaty, the U.S. government succeeded in de-escalating rising tensions in the Taiwan Strait. However, to help ensure that Taiwan could adequately defend itself, during the early 1960s the U.S. also began to provide the Nationalist military with more powerful missiles to defend the Taiwan Strait. Highly visible Nationalist missile tests were intended to send a warning to the PRC to not attempt a cross-strait invasion.

NATIONALIST MISSILE TESTS OVER THE TAIWAN STRAIT

In response to renewed Taiwan Strait tensions in 1962, the U.S. military transferred to Taiwan additional high-tech weaponry, including Nike and Hawk missiles. The Nike Hercules missile had a range of about 100 miles and was considered a highly effective air-defense weapon.[11] By contrast, the MIM-23 Hawk missile was a low- to medium-altitude air-defense missile with a range of only about fifteen miles.[12] Put together, however, these two missile systems gave Taiwan unchallenged air control over the Taiwan Strait.

To send a highly public warning to the PRC to not attempt an attack against Taiwan or the offshore islands, a series of missile tests was announced by the Taiwanese government during the spring of 1965. In April of that year, the Nationalist military carried out tests under the technical guidance of U.S. experts. Taiwan announced that for a fifteen-day period in mid-April ships should refrain from sailing in the "danger area."[13] During this period, Taiwan fired four missiles north of Taiwan (see figure 8.1).

Although most international-shipping companies ignored these missile tests, Alfred Holt and Co. of Liverpool complained to the British government that the tests violated freedom of the seas. On October 29, 1965, the UK's Ministry of Defence determined that while these tests were a hindrance to shipping, and therefore appeared to violate the principle of freedom of the seas, a formal protest did not seem necessary. Instead, it recommended that further questions be directed to either the Chinese Nationalists or to the Americans. It also asked the Board of Trade to inquire whether any other British shipping companies had been adversely affected.[14]

Working through the British Chamber of Shipping, which took a poll of those shipping companies impacted by the missile tests, the Board of Trade determined that, "although we cannot claim there has been actual inconvenience to our shipping, so far there is no doubt that if the range is used more extensively in the future it will cause inconvenience." Depending on when the tests were conducted, British ships could experience delays of up to ten hours or be forced to "proceed by way of the east coast of Taiwan, incurring extra distance and time." In addition to requesting that the direction of the tests be changed to fire over a comparatively little used section of the China Sea, it was also recommended that warnings of future missile tests be circulated by Nationalist authorities well in advance, both by issuing Notices to Mariners and by broadcasting radio warnings.[15]

In the end, nothing seems to have been done; there are no copies of official protests in the British archives. However, it is important to reiterate that the British Foreign Office considered these tests to be a violation of freedom of the seas. As such, it was determined that the Taiwan missile range as it was declared in 1965 appears "to violate a principle, and every reasonable endeavour should be made to prevent such violations. Even if their immediate practical effects are not great, they all add nails to the coffin of the freedom of the high seas."[16]

China's comparative naval weakness helped Taiwan during the 1960s, since the Nationalist government could allocate fewer maritime resources

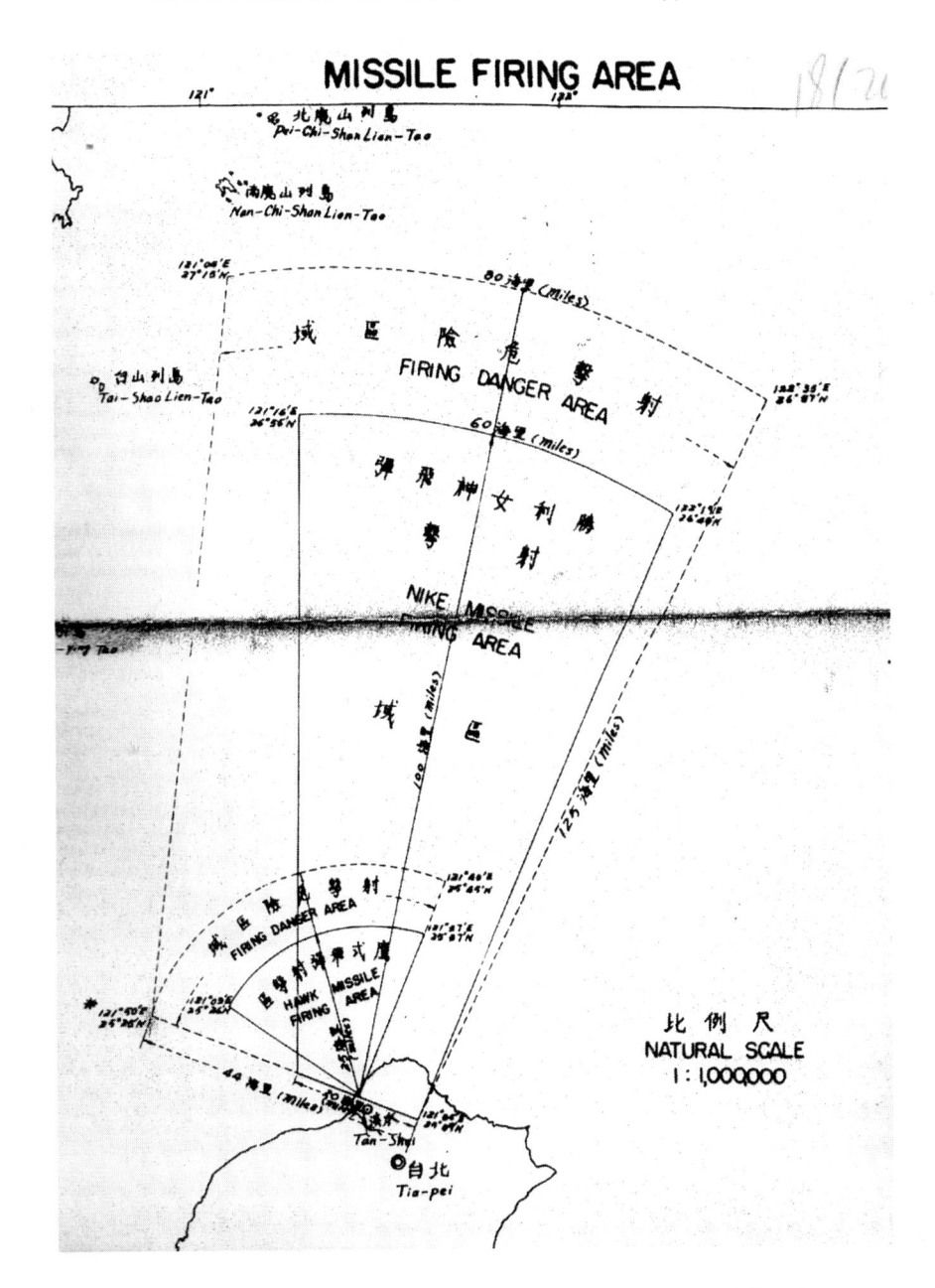

The Third Taiwan Strait Crisis and Sino–American Rapprochement 107

Figure 8.1. Missile Testing Zones North of Taiwan. Source: UK National Archives

to protecting Taiwan from a naval invasion. Meanwhile, public missile tests sent a potent warning to the PLA not to stage an attack. Still, the PRC had a large military force opposite Taiwan, and cross-strait relations remained tense. Faced with these fundamental differences on Taiwan's international status, the U.S. strategic embargo continued throughout the 1960s. Meanwhile, the Taiwan Patrol Force was called upon to broaden its patrol duties to include waters off Vietnam.

TAIWAN DURING THE VIETNAM WAR

By the mid-1960s, PRC intervention in Southeast Asia had a major impact on the Taiwan Patrol Force. Although the U.S. Navy began to assign significant naval assets to waters off Vietnam, the Taiwan Patrol Force continued to function throughout this period, even during the height of the Vietnam War. In November 1965, while patrolling the Taiwan Strait, the USS *O'Brien* arrived just after an attack on two Nationalist patrol boats near Wuchiu Island by PLAN torpedo and gun boats. One Nationalist vessel, PCE-61, was sunk. *O'Brien* rescued survivors and transported them back to land. The PRC's November 14, 1965, "serious warning" was No. 395.[17]

With the escalation of the Vietnam War, the Taiwan Patrol Force became more closely linked with other ongoing naval operations. 1965's Operation MARKET TIME was adopted to interdict the delivery of supplies and weapons to the Viet Cong by infiltration trawlers. This navy operation was destined to impact the Taiwan Patrol Force, since many USN vessels were assigned to carry out both duties. By the mid- to late 1960s, the destroyers would often split their time between Taiwan and Vietnam, breaking midway in Hong Kong for rest and recreation (R & R) between the Taiwan Patrol and the Vietnamese MARKET TIME interdiction program. During 1966 and 1967, U.S. and South Vietnamese patrol boats inspected or boarded more than 700,000 vessels.[18]

USN destroyers could be out patrolling for five days, a week, or as long as ten days at a time, at which point they would return to Keelung or Kaohsiung for supplies and then go out again for another patrol. During lax periods, rather than four destroyers, two smaller DERs would be assigned to the patrol at a time. The usual operating pattern was for one to be at sea for a week, while the other was on call in either Kaohsiung or Keelung, with turnovers normally conducted at sea. Readiness was paramount, since tensions in the Taiwan Strait could run high. The hours were long, and the crew had to work at peak efficiency. During actual patrols, the crew would take any chance opportunity for food and sleep. According to one account, "I remember going to the mess deck for supper and being served eggs and getting extremely mad at the cooks for serving such an evening meal. I was informed by them that it was 0700 and that as a result breakfast was being served and not supper. In Combat Information Center (CIC) we lived by Greenwich time and seldom went out on deck. Actual time would became meaningless for Operations Department during the patrol."[19]

According to James Barber, Captain of the USS *Hissem* (DE 400), during one patrol in late 1968 the weather was particularly memorable:

> During the winter the Taiwan Strait can be some very rough water. Several times the weather was severe enough that we were restricted to little more than survival, making minimum speed both upwind and downwind. The characteristics of the DER engineering plant dictated that our minimum speed was the idling speed of a diesel, which under normal circumstances gave us about seven knots through the water. During the rough weather we would actually make something like three knots going into the wind and eleven knots going down wind. Thus we were spending about a quarter of the time on the somewhat more comfortable downwind leg and the rest of the time slamming into head seas on the upwind leg. The steep seas made reversing course an adventure, since if we got caught in the trough of the waves we could be in serious trouble. I made it a practice to come to the bridge for every reversal. We would watch for a temporary slackening, then come about with full speed and full rudder. When the weather was like this about all we could do was hang on. I had broken a finger playing touch football during one of our in-port periods, and the doctor had fitted me with a large and clumsy cast that made it impossible to use that hand to hang on to railings while moving about the ship. After just a few hours at sea in heavy weather it became evident that my inability to hang on because of the cast risked life and limb, and I ordered our hospital corpsman to remove the cast. One mental picture I retain is of a super tanker plowing into the seas with spray coming over her bridge but with the ship looking like an island and hardly being moved by the waves, at the same time we were being beaten up in three dimensions by the same seas. That made the difference between two hundred thousand tons and 1,500 tons abundantly clear.[20]

Because the patrol ships were so small, it was common for sailors to fall overboard and never be seen again.[21] In 1968, *Hissem* assisted a damaged Chinese trawler (see figure 8.2).

Serving meals during bad weather could be especially problematic. As one former supply officer recalled, "The seas were so rough that on many occasions we used one bowl and a spoon with meals . . . hang on to the table and bowl with one hand, eat with the other."[22] Since the wardroom table could be especially hazardous in heavy weather, it was considered to be a severe breach of etiquette to allow your meal to end up in someone else's lap.[23] To make sure the bowls did not slide off the smooth table, stewards would place wet hand towels under the bowls.[24]

One of the USN's greatest concerns was to not antagonize the PRC. USN ships were ordered that "Operations could not be conducted within

Figure 8.2. Crew of *Hissem* **Assisting Damaged Chinese Fishing Boat. Source: Jay Prior, personal photo**

thirty nautical miles of the Chinese border for fear of provoking Chinese intervention in the war."[25] Strict orders were given to all USN vessels in these waters not to enter China's territorial waters:

> While *Hissem* was assigned to MARKET TIME, I would guess in February of 1968, U.S. Navy P3s had been tracking a trawler in the South China Sea headed for Vietnam. The trawler, aware that he was being tracked, reversed course to return home, and the U.S. commanders wanted to discover where his home was. *Hissem* was assigned to take an over-the-horizon radar turnover from a P3 and follow the trawler home without his knowing he was being tracked. We followed him around the southern side of Hainan Island, up the eastern side of the island, and into the channel between Hainan and the mainland. As we approached Chinese territorial waters, three high-speed gunboats came out to look us over. Since this was shortly after the *Pueblo* incident, things were a bit tense. We were at General Quarters but did not train our weapons to avoid looking threatening. Our orders were to not enter Chinese territorial waters but to track the trawler as long as we could. This we did until the trawler disappeared from radar.[26]

According to Captain Barber, as *Hissem* disengaged, Chinese gunboats followed the ship but then finally broke off. During this incident, the ship was bombarded by an enormous volume of communications from everyone in the chain of command, including the "national command authority." The operations officer, Meredith Musick, did a "superb job of managing this inundation and bringing to my attention only those things I really needed to see. Otherwise it would have made my primary job of being ready to fight much more difficult." The ship was especially vulnerable because there was no air cover.[27]

Since the PRC was the real focus of both operations, the United States and Taiwan worked closely during the Vietnam War. Because of the huge logistical needs of the U.S. Navy, Taiwan became a major support base. In October 1962, a memorandum of understanding was signed for the U.S. Air Force to build air bases on Taiwan. The largest was located outside of Taizhong, in central Taiwan, and was called Ching Chuan Kang (CCK). Beginning in 1966, three squadrons of C-130 transport planes were deployed to CCK on a permanent basis, and by 1972 this had grown to four. By the end of the 1960s, quite a few different air assets were operating out of Taiwan, including several squadrons of F-100 fighter aircraft, EC-121 electronic warfare aircraft, and KC-135 tankers intended for mid-air refueling.[28]

During the late 1960s and early 1970s, the Nationalists also acted as an unofficial military depot. In the final years of the Vietnam War, for example, about fifty F-5A aircraft donated by Taiwan were flown to South Vietnam to help prop up the failing government while Taiwan was later reimbursed with more modern F-5Es.[29] As Admiral Beshany later recalled, "I can tell you this that every plane was there exactly on schedule. They didn't miss one flight of some fifty-odd aircraft that they transferred, which was a big part of their Air Force. It was all the modern aircraft that they had. That was a personal sacrifice on their part, and it's one we can't kid ourselves about." Later, during November 1972, Kissinger even sent a letter of thanks to the Nationalists for their "help and assistance in getting those aircraft over to Vietnam."[30]

As part of the global Cold War to contain the spread of Communism, Taiwan reportedly became an important, albeit unofficial, U.S. nuclear base in the Western Pacific. Recent declassification efforts have confirmed that the U.S. military stored nuclear weapons at Tainan Air Base, Taiwan.[31] When called on to assist, the Nationalist government could also be counted on to support other Asian countries fighting their own Communist insurgencies. But beginning in 1969, this close U.S.–ROC defense relationship began to change as a result of border clashes between the PRC and USSR. These events soon led to a dramatic warming in Sino–U.S. diplomatic relations.

TAIWAN AND THE OPENING OF SINO–U.S. DIPLOMATIC RELATIONS

By the late 1960s, Sino–Soviet tensions had gone from bad to worse, including active fighting along their lengthy borders. Facing the threat of nuclear war with the USSR, in 1972 Mao Zedong invited Richard Nixon to Beijing to begin opening Sino–U.S. diplomatic relations. Seven years later, on January 1, 1979, President Jimmy Carter completed the gradual transition from Taiwan to the PRC by officially recognizing Beijing. Recognition also marked the official termination of the Taiwan Patrol Force.

Increased Sino–Soviet tensions during the late 1960s gave Washington a long-awaited opportunity to combine forces with China to exert greater military and economic pressure on the USSR. As early as 1956, the British embassy in China had speculated on the possible effect of rising Sino–Soviet tensions on improving Sino–U.S. relations. It concluded that any relaxation of PRC ties with the Soviets could lead to improved relations with the United States rather than with the UK. In support of this view, the paper cited the "traditional American friendship for China as opposed to the traditional British imperialist role in China."[32]

Even though the Sino–Soviet monolith publicly split in 1960, U.S. leaders patiently waited until Sino–Soviet relations reached a crisis. After all, Washington's policy was not simply to break China and the USSR apart but to force China to play by U.S. rules.[33] John W. Garver has confirmed that Washington's measured response to the Taiwan Strait crises played a role in this gradual PRC transition: "It is also likely that the restrained use of U.S. power during the various Taiwan Strait crises of 1955, 1958, and 1962 somewhat moderated Chinese fear of U.S. attack."[34] On August 4, 1969, during the height of the Sino–Soviet border conflict, the time finally seemed ripe. President Nixon made his intentions to Beijing clear when he called Moscow the main aggressor and suggested that the PRC's defeat would not be in the best interests of the United States. This statement indicated a dramatic shift from the former U.S. policy of isolating China.

Next, National Security Adviser Henry Kissinger sent the PRC a potent signal by ordering the suspension of the Seventh Fleet's regular patrols of the Taiwan Strait. The official USN explanation was that the U.S. government had ordered a 100-ship reduction in worldwide USN deployment due to a $3 billion reduction in defense expenditures.[35] On November 15, 1969, a U.S. Navy order changed the Taiwan Strait Patrol "from a continuous patrol composed of DD types permanently assigned to Task Group 72.1 to a random patrol composed of various combatant and auxiliary units."[36]

These highly public changes in U.S. policy greatly concerned Taiwan. In response to Nationalist protests, the CinCPac privately reassured Taiwan's Ministry of National Defense that an average of fifteen ships per month would still transit the Taiwan Strait.[37] On December 17, 1969, Ambassador Walter P. McConaughy reassured Chiang Kai-shek that most of the USN ships in the Far East would also be ordered to transit the Taiwan Strait rather than travel along the East Coast of Taiwan. This would mean a higher number of transits than before and therefore "a more thorough naval observation of the Strait under the new procedure than when the two DEs [destroyer escorts] were on regular patrol."[38] In addition, the primary duty of the patrol would remain the same—to "Detect and report Communist Chinese (CHINCOM) shipping preparing for, or actually attempting an invasion of, Taiwan and/or the Penghu Islands."[39]

The real reason for changing the Taiwan Patrol Force was to send a highly visible signal to Beijing that Washington was willing to open talks. In addition to making this message clear via unofficial discussions in Warsaw, the State Department wanted to make the same "pitch" to a Chinese official in Hong Kong, just to "make sure that Peking gets the message."[40] So as to ensure that the PRC did not misunderstand what the United States intended, "Kissinger told Beijing, via Pakistani President Yahya Khan, that the basic U.S. commitment to Taiwan's defense remained unchanged." The termination of the patrols was intended more as a "gesture intended to remove an irritant in relations."[41] In fact, Kissinger's offer to end the patrol was intended to give Beijing leaders "face" rather than reflect any substantive change in the operations of the Taiwan Patrol Force.[42]

This diplomatic ploy proved to be highly successful, and in 1971 Henry Kissinger made a secret trip to Beijing in order to prepare for Nixon's historic visit the next year to meet with Mao Zedong. As a second concession to Beijing, the U.S. embargo on strategic goods, which had been adopted on December 8, 1950, was finally terminated on June 10, 1971.[43] Earlier that year, in February 1971, Washington publicly reiterated that America's commitment to Taiwan's defense remained unchanged.[44] USN ships still visited Taiwanese ports, and combined exercises between the U.S. Navy and Nationalist ships continued to be conducted throughout the 1970s. Intermittent patrols were still being conducted by the Taiwan Patrol Force, but the new "Commander U.S. Taiwan Patrol Force is largely a planning function," whose job was to plan and provide "designated forces as the Naval Component Commander of the Taiwan Defense Command in the event that wide ranging hostilities break out between the Communist and Nationalist Chinese."[45]

In what must have seemed to many Chinese as an American tributary mission to China, President Nixon flew to Beijing in 1972 to meet with Mao. They signed the Shanghai Communiqué, the first of three communiqués issued in 1972, 1979, and 1982. The Shanghai Communiqué provided two interpretations of the status of Taiwan. While China again declared Taiwan to be its province, the United States agreed not to challenge the view shared by "all Chinese" on both sides of the Taiwan Strait that "there is but one China and that Taiwan is part of China." The Shanghai Communiqué also provided for exchanges between the United States and China (see appendix 5).

Nixon's visit to China resulted in a rapid change in U.S. foreign policy toward Taiwan. The U.S. government continued to have representatives in Taiwan, naval officers could attend the U.S. Naval War College, and American arms sales to Taiwan continued unchanged. Although the U.S. embassy in Taiwan closed, the two countries quickly established semi-official organizations that functioned as embassies. Previously, the Nationalist government had proclaimed there was only one China and that the ROC was the official government. Over the next decades, however, particularly after the Taiwanese government allowed its citizens to visit China in 1987, many Taiwanese changed their minds to conclude that the one China did not include Taiwan. This spurred the creation of an independence movement.

After visiting Beijing, President Nixon next visited Moscow, where he warned General Secretary Leonid Brezhnev that attacking China would adversely affect U.S. interests. Beginning in the mid-1970s, the U.S. and Chinese militaries began to work closely together against the Soviet Union. In particular, U.S. companies were allowed to sell naval equipment to improve the PLAN's ability to monitor Soviet ships. Increased military and naval cooperation enabled China and the U.S. to encircle the USSR on the East and the West, forcing higher rates of Soviet militarization than its woefully inefficient economy could support.

While formal Sino–American diplomatic relations would not be reestablished until 1979, the subject of the second communiqué, the long period of Sino–American estrangement had ended. On October 25, 1971, Taiwan lost its seat at the United Nations, and the PRC obtained it. Henceforth, the PRC sat on the Security Council as one of the five privileged nations to possess veto power, along with the Soviet Union, the United States, France, and Great Britain, the victorious powers at the end of World War II when the United Nations was established. A third communiqué would limit U.S. arms sales to Taiwan.

When Jimmy Carter and Deng Xiaoping recognized each other's governments on January 1, 1979, the U.S.'s 1954 mutual-defense treaty with Taiwan was unilaterally terminated. This elicited an angry Nationalist statement on January 2, 1979.[46] The USS *Midway* was the last U.S. Navy aircraft carrier to visit Taiwan as part of the BLUESKY combined exercise on November 18, 1978, less than six weeks before the U.S. officially recognized the PRC.[47] Meanwhile, combined Shark Hunt exercises between U.S. and Taiwanese naval vessels also continued through November 1978. However, all future combined exercises between the U.S. Navy and the Nationalist Navy were canceled, marking January 1, 1979, as the termination date of the Taiwan Patrol Force.[48]

CONCLUSIONS

Following U.S. recognition of the PRC, the American embassy in Taipei closed its doors on February 28, 1979.[49] Although it appeared that the U.S. had abandoned Taiwan, on April 10, 1979, Congress passed the Taiwan Relations Act. This codified Taiwan's unique position as part of "one China," even while existing outside of PRC sovereignty claims. A Sino–U.S. communiqué signed on August 17, 1982, appeared to promise that U.S. arms sales to Taiwan would gradually diminish, but there was no set date for ending the sales. Secretly, the Reagan administration reassured Taiwan that it would continue to monitor PRC military deployments and that if the PRC attacked Taiwan then "U.S. commitments would become invalidated."[50]

Meanwhile, U.S. recognition of the PRC in 1979 allowed for a two-front strategy, with NATO on the USSR's western flank and China on her eastern flank. During the late 1970s, China's new leader, Deng Xiaoping, announced his open-door policy, which sponsored greater economic interaction with the West. The PRC's economic development also began to adopt its own version of Taiwan's earlier, highly successful, trade policies.[51] China's gradual shift to a market economy validated the U.S. policy first proposed during the summer of 1949, and later supported by the 1950 creation of the Taiwan Patrol Force, to use the U.S. Navy to exert military, economic, and political pressure on the PRC.

The combination of this new East–West strategic threat, plus China's rapid economic growth based on free-market reforms, put enormous pressure on the USSR. During the mid- to late 1980s, Mikhail Gorbachev tried, but failed, to adopt similar Westernizing reforms in the USSR. Among other successes, Sino–American military cooperation has been cited as one of the major factors in forcing the Soviet withdrawal from Afghanistan during February 1989.[52] This military failure was correctly perceived by the USSR's client states in Eastern Europe as a sign of weakness. With the fall of the Berlin Wall in November 1989, and following the December 1991 collapse of the USSR, the Taiwan Patrol Force's original strategic purpose appeared to be over for good. However, during the mid-1990s, tensions over the Taiwan Strait once again mounted.

NOTES

1. "CINCPAC Command History 1969," vol. 1, NHHC Archives, 142.

2. Henry Kissinger, *White House Years* (Boston: Little, Brown, and Company, 1979), 178–80.

3. Ta Jen Liu, *U.S.–China Relations, 1784–1992* (Lanham, MD: University Press of America, 1997), 261, note 18.

4. Shu Guang Zhang, *Economic Cold War: America's Embargo against China and the Sino–Soviet Alliance, 1949–1963* (Stanford, CA: Stanford University Press, 2001), 267.

5. Vice Admiral Roland N. Smoot, "As I Recall . . . The U.S. Taiwan Defense Command," *Proceedings* 110/9/979 (September 1984): 59.

6. Stephen P. Gibert and William M. Carpenter, *America and Island China: A Documentary History* (Lanham, MD: University Press of America, 1989), 11.

7. "Record of a Conversation after Dinner at 1 Carlton Gardens on June 24, 1962," TNA/UK, PREM 11/3738. This troop buildup preceded by several months China's attack against India, far to the west, so in hindsight China's decision to beef up the PLA forces along the Taiwan Strait might have been intended to ensure Taiwan could not take military advantage of the Sino–Indian conflict.

8. Telegram from Sir D. Ormsby Gore, Washington, to Foreign Office, London, June 25, 1962, TNA/UK, PREM 11/3738.

9. Liu, *U.S.–China Relations*, 261.

10. Nancy Bernkopf Tucker, "Strategic Ambiguity or Strategic Clarity?" in *Dangerous Strait: The U.S.–Taiwan–China Crisis*, ed. Nancy Bernkopf Tucker, 192 (New York: Columbia University Press, 2005); citing 611.93/7-562 #22 Kirk, Taipei, *Foreign Relations of the United States, 1961–1963*, 22: 288.

11. Donald E. Bender, "The Nike Missile System: A Concise Historical Overview," last modified May 2, 2004 (accessed December 16, 2010), http://alpha.fdu.edu/~bender/N-view.html.

12. Federation of American Scientists, Space Policy Project: Special Weapons Monitor, "Hawk" (accessed December 20, 2010), http://www.fas.org/spp/starwars/program/hawk.htm.

13. Confidential letter from R. F. McKeever, H. M. Consul, British Consulate, Tamsui, to R. C. Samuel, Foreign Office, London, June 16, 1965, TNA/UK, FO 371/181207.

14. Restricted letter from Masters, Ministry of Defence to J. Flynn, Foreign Office, London, October 29, 1965, TNA/UK, FO 371/181207.

15. Letter from N. R. Swann, Board of Trade, to D. N. Wood, Foreign Office, London, December 10, 1965, TNA/UK, FO 371/181207.

16. Restricted letter from Masters, Ministry of Defence to J. Flynn, Foreign Office, London, October 29, 1965, TNA/UK, FO 371/181207.

17. Commander C.S. Christensen and Ensign J. B. Hattendorf, "O'Brien's Odyssey: One Destroyer's Duty in the Seventh Fleet," *Our Navy* Vol. 61, No. 9 (September 1966), 2–4, 60:60.

18. Edward J. Marolda, *By Sea, Air, and Land: An Illustrated History of the U.S. Navy and the War in Southeast Asia* (Washington, DC: Government Printing Office, 1994), 151.

19. Charles H. Bogart, "Christmas in the Formosa Straits," Dennis J. Buckley and Other Navy Links (accessed December 13, 2010), http://djbuckley.com/bogy1.htm.

20. James Barber interview with author, May 2, 2009.

21. Robert McCurley, "USS *Fletcher* DDE-445 Chronology 1952," USS *Fletcher* Home Page (accessed December 13, 2010), http://www.ussfletcher.org/history/1952.html.

22. Bob Chamberlin interview with author, May 4, 2009.

23. James Barber interview with author, May 5, 2009.

24. Jay Pryor interview with author, May 5, 2009.

25. R. L. Schreadley, *From the Rivers to the Sea: The United States Navy in Vietnam* (Annapolis, MD: Naval Institute Press, 1992), 120.

26. James Barber interview, May 2, 2009.

27. Ibid.

28. John W. Garver, *The Sino–American Alliance: Nationalist China and American Cold War Strategy in Asia* (Armonk, NY: M. E. Sharpe, 1997), 208.

29. Philip A. Beshany, *The Reminiscences of Vice Admiral Philip A. Beshany, U.S. Navy (Retired)*, Oral History 45 (Annapolis, MD: U.S. Naval Institute, 1983), 925–27.

30. Ibid., 927, 934.

31. Commander-in-Chief, U.S. Pacific Command, "CINCPAC Command History, 1974," vol. 1 (accessed on October 16, 2014), http://oldsite.nautilus.org/archives/library/security/foia/Japan/CINCPAC74Ip263.PDF.

32. John Foster Dulles Papers, Princeton University, Reel 212/213, March 14, 1956, 95016.

33. British Consulate-General, Canton, to Political Adviser, Hong Kong, July 25, 1949 (Confidential), TNA/UK, FO 371/75810-75815.

34. John W. Garver, *China's Decision for Rapprochement with the United States, 1968–1971* (Boulder, CO: Westview Press, 1982), 52.

35. "Telegram from the Department of State to the Embassy in the Republic of China and Commander, U.S. Taiwan Defense Command," September 23, 1969. Found in Steven E. Philips, ed., Edward C. Keefer, gen. ed., *Foreign Relations of the United States, 1969–1976*, vol. 17, *China 1969–1972*, 89 (Washington, DC: U.S. Government Printing Office, 2006).

36. "Operation Order 201 (Confidential)," Commander Task Force Seventy-Two, November 1, 1974, Post-1946 Operation Plans, Task Force 72, July 1968–1972, NHHC Archives, Box 290, B-II-1.

37. "CINCPAC Command History 1969 (Top Secret)," vol. 1, NHHC Archives, 143.

38. "Memorandum of Conversation," December 17, 1969. Found in Philips, ed., *Foreign Relations of the United States, 1969–1976*, 151.

39. "Operation Order 201 (Confidential)," Commander Task Force Seventy-Two, November 1, 1974, Post-1946 Operation Plans, Task Force 72, July 1968–1972, NHHC Archives, Box 290, B-II-1.

40. "Memorandum from John H. Holdridge of the National Security Council Staff to the President's Assistant for National Security Affairs (Kissinger)," November 21, 1969. Found in Philips, ed., *Foreign Relations of the United States, 1969–1976*, 138.

41. Garver, *The Sino–American Alliance*, 267.

42. For more on the practical uses of *giving face*, especially in a public setting, see Bruce A. Elleman and S. C. M. Paine, *Modern China: Continuity and Change, 1644 to the Present* (Upper Saddle River, NJ: Prentice-Hall, 2010), 11.

43. Robert B. Semple Jr., "President Ends 21-Year Embargo on Peking Trade," *New York Times*, June 11, 1971.

44. David Muller, *China as a Maritime Power* (Boulder, CO: Westview Press, 1983), 175.

45. "Taiwan Patrol-Command History," March 5, 1971.

46. "Document 33: ROC Statement on U.S. Termination of Mutual Defense Treaty, January 2, 1979," Chiu, 264–65.

47. GlobalSecurity.org, "Taiwan Strait: 21 July 1995 to 23 March 1996" (accessed October 16, 2014), http://www.globalsecurity.org/military/ops/taiwan_strait.htm. *Turner Joy* may have been one of the last USN ships to transit the Taiwan Strait. See Hullnumber.com, "USS *Turner Joy* (DD-951)" (accessed October 16, 2014), http://www.hullnumber.com/DD-951.

48. Although the U.S.–ROC treaty officially ended on January 1, 1980, all U.S.–ROC exercises ended on January 1, 1979. Edward Marolda has stated, "I completely agree with the 1979 date. . . . Even if patrols were infrequent during the 1970s, we still had a treaty obligation to defend the island." E-mail exchange with author, December 12, 2010.

49. This was the thirty-second anniversary of the February 28, 1947, massacre of Taiwanese by Nationalist troops, perhaps sending a signal to the Nationalist leadership concerning the need for greater democratic reforms on Taiwan.

50. Tucker, "Strategic Ambiguity or Strategic Clarity?" 194.

51. Sheppard Glass, "Some Aspects of Formosa's Economic Growth," in *Formosa Today*, ed. Mark Mancall, 70 (New York: Frederick A. Praeger, 1964).

52. John J. Tkacik Jr., "Strategy Deficit: U.S. Security in the Pacific and the Future of Taiwan," in *Reshaping the Taiwan Strait*, ed. John J. Tkacik Jr., 13 (Washington, DC: Heritage Foundation, 2007).

NINE

PRC Economic Development, Tiananmen, and the Fourth Taiwan Strait Crisis, 1995 to 1996

From 1979 through 1989, the United States and the People's Republic of China actively cooperated against the Soviet Union, including authorizing high-tech U.S. naval equipment sales to China. This focus on Russia helped to limit tensions in the Taiwan Strait. In fact, any need for a Taiwan Patrol Force seemed to be long past. However, even after the U.S. government recognized the PRC, it maintained a strong interest in Taiwan's defense, including the continued sale of weapons.[1] While the PRC's economic reforms were a success, the Communist government cracked down on student demonstrators seeking democracy. An unknown number of students—purportedly as many as 10,000—died in the Tiananmen massacre.

The delicate balance of power in the Taiwan Strait once again began to shift after the end of the Cold War in 1989, followed soon afterward by the 1991 collapse of the USSR. These events gave Beijing an unforeseen opportunity to expand its naval influence in Asia. Following the collapse of the Soviet Union, the PRC rapidly begin to build up its naval forces, in part to fill the military vacuum following the USSR's retreat. With the help of Russia, mainly through sales of advanced naval equipment, including Sovremenny destroyers and Kilo submarines, the PLAN began a long period of growth.[2] The PRC also developed a large conventional-missile force, deployed mainly against Taiwan. Arguably, it has been this rapid military growth that has upset the delicate PRC–Taiwan military balance.

The growth of the PLAN has, in turn, created a strategic shift that appears in some ways to be an unofficial reinstitution of the Taiwan

Patrol Force. Throughout 1995 and 1996, as a result of PRC missile testing off Taiwan, the U.S. Navy once again responded by sending USN aircraft carriers and destroyers into the region. This naval demonstration was similar to the USN's response to previous Taiwan Strait crises during the 1950s and early 1960s. These events have been discussed as the fourth Taiwan Strait crisis.[3]

CHINA'S NEW "OPEN DOOR" ECONOMIC POLICIES

Since 1949, Taiwan prospered with American financial aid and foreign investment. With a GNP half that of the entire PRC, Taiwan was an island with one-fiftieth of the mainland's population, less than 1/250th of its land mass, and no special resource endowment. The economic "miracle" in Taiwan put enormous pressure on the PRC to adopt economic reforms. To compete with Taiwan, Deng Xiaoping coupled Mao's foreign policy of rapprochement with the United States with a radical redirection of economic policy. These economic policies were known as the "Open Door" reforms.

In 1978, during the Third Plenum, Deng Xiaoping and his followers took power. They rode the wave of deep popular discontent beginning in late 1978 when Chinese citizens anonymously pasted big-character posters on city walls, called the Democracy Wall Movement, with messages critical of Mao's policies during the Cultural Revolution. In 1978, priority shifted from heavy to light industry. To create agricultural incentives, farm prices were increased while bonuses and piece rates were mandated. In 1979, enterprises were allowed to retain a portion of their profits to fund wage incentives.

Deng oversaw the dismantling over a five-year period of the commune system imposed during the Great Leap Forward. Individual families became responsible for agricultural production while the state set higher procurement prices. In 1985, the PRC government relaxed its procurement rules to introduce contract purchasing, creating a mix of state and market prices for agriculture. Households contracted with the state to rent land on a semi-permanent basis with the obligation to sell only a proportion of the crop output to the state. Decollectivizing agriculture from 1978 to 1984 created a one-time improvement in agricultural productivity that narrowed the gap in urban and rural standards of living. Whereas from 1957 to 1978 grain production had risen at a rate of 2.6 percent per annum, from 1979 to 1984 this rate doubled to 4.9 percent per annum, transforming China from a net importer into a net exporter of food. Cash incomes quadrupled, and standards of living rapidly improved. From 1978 to 1984 crop and livestock production increased by 49 percent. Rural poverty fell from 33 percent to 11 percent of the rural population during 1978 and 1984. This helped make possible the capital accumulation necessary for further economic growth.

In industry, Deng introduced the Industrial Responsibility System, allowing companies to retain a percentage of profits to reinvest at their own discretion. Plant managers could hire, fire, and set wages and prices within certain ranges. By 1984, only 30 to 40 percent of industrial production remained under central planning, while 20 percent was market driven. In 1980, China opened four Special Economic Zones to attract foreign investment. These zones were placed next to overseas Chinese communities: in Shenzhen on the border with Hong Kong; in Zhuhai outside of Macao; in Xiamen located in Fujian, the native province for many Taiwanese; and in Shantou, the native place of many other overseas Chinese. Tax exemptions, low wages, the freedom to hire and fire, and the prospect of joint Sino–foreign company ownership attracted Western and Japanese investment. Likewise, fourteen coastal cities were opened to foreign commerce. By the end of 1993, when the government prohibited the creation of additional Special Economic Zones, there were 9,000 of them. The Special Economic Zones provided a filter for the introduction of more market-oriented economic polices. Successful practices were then spread nationwide. This innovation proved breathtakingly successful.

China also attracted enormous foreign investments. In the late 1990s China absorbed 40 percent of the foreign investments made in all developing countries. Sino–foreign ventures accounted for half of China's imports and one-third of its exports. About two-thirds of this investment came from overseas Chinese and mainly from Hong Kong and Taiwan. On the eve of the reforms, foreign trade had accounted for 13 percent of the Chinese GDP, while, in terms of international trade, China ranked thirty-second in the world. Two decades later, in the late 1990s, trade had grown to 30 percent of the GDP, while China ranked tenth in international trade and possessed one of the world's largest merchant marines. Chinese trade had grown over ten times, and the PRC was no longer exporting primary products but manufactured goods.

To train professionals necessary to run a modern economy, for the first time since the 1930s China sent thousands of students to study abroad. These included the children of China's civil and military leadership. They would become China's Meiji generation of students, who would selectively apply what they had learned from their studies and seen in their travels. Increasing Western influence produced a short-lived campaign against Spiritual Pollution from the outside. However, the growing democracy movement in Taiwan was to put additional pressure on the PRC government to adopt political reforms.

GROWING DEMOCRACY IN TAIWAN

Chiang Kai-shek died in 1975, a year before Mao Zedong. Taiwan followed the imperial model for succession, with Chiang's son, Chiang Ching-kuo, assuming the presidency. This was potentially the end of the Chiang dynasty, however, since Chiang Ching-kuo had married a Russian woman while living in Moscow during the 1930s and his children looked Western. Perhaps as a result of this historical fluke, Taiwan intensified its transition to democracy during the late 1970s and 1980s.

Chiang Kai-shek's final years of rule had been marked by extensive economic reforms and a rapid rise in the general standard of living, but there had been little in the way of political reform, and Taiwan remained a police state under martial law. Taiwan had an active secret police, and only the Nationalist Party could legally compete in elections. The legislature, with representatives from all of the mainland provinces, was frozen in time, barring a highly unlikely conquest of the mainland. Thus its seats amounted to life terms.

Chiang Ching-kuo charted a new course for Taiwan. He had been born to Chiang Kai-shek's first wife of three, when his father was a relatively unknown twenty-three-year-old military student. In 1925, at only fifteen years of age, Chiang Ching-kuo had been sent to Moscow to be trained at the Sun Yat-sen University, where, after his father's purge of the Communists in 1927, he was denied the right to return home. As a student in Moscow, Chiang Ching-kuo became a devoted Trotskyite and denounced his own father. He also became a good friend of fellow student Deng Xiaoping. Stalin did not allow him to return home until 1937, after the formation of the Second United Front. After fleeing with his father to Taiwan in 1949, he held a variety of government positions, including minister of national defense, prime minister, and interim president following his father's death.

During these years living in Moscow, when he was little more than a hostage, Chiang had married a Russian woman, and they'd had several children. Because of their mixed marriage and the Russian and Chinese heritage of their children, the children appear to have been excluded from politics in virulently anti-Communist Taiwan. This chance circumstance may help explain Chiang Ching-kuo's willingness to promote democracy. In 1978, Chiang Ching-kuo became president for a six-year term, which was renewed in 1984, and his personal power ended only with his own death in 1988. In the mid-1970s, Chiang Ching-kuo embarked on anticorruption campaigns in the government and tried to bring more Taiwanese-born politicians into the Nationalist Party. A key beneficiary was his successor, Lee Teng-hui, a Cornell-educated PhD student, who became vice president in 1984.

During these years Taiwan was becoming increasingly prosperous. More Taiwanese began to demand political rights. Many suffered persecution in this period, including the first democratically elected president of Taiwan, Chen Shui-bian, and his running mate, Annette Lu. Chen Shui-bian's wife remains paralyzed from the waist down from an attempt, probably by Nationalist sympathizers, to run her over in a truck, while Chen served several months in prison for criticizing the regime. Annette Lu served a five-and-a-half-year prison term as a result of the political protests in 1979 that became violent and are known as the Kaohsiung Incident. Thus, a combination of pressure from below and leadership from above pushed Taiwan in the direction of democratization.

The end of the Vietnam War and the development of the Sino–Soviet split marginalized Taiwan. The U.S. recognition of the PRC and derecognition of Taiwan in 1979 created a radically different security environment, leaving Taiwan in international limbo. Although the Taiwan Relations Act passed by the U.S. Congress urged that the two-China problem be solved peacefully, in signing the act the United States promised to provide Taiwan military aid in the meantime, including potential U.S. protection in the event of a war, embargo, or boycott even though Taiwan lacks the status of a nation-state.

Taiwan had very few options given the enormous asymmetries of a small island defending its independence against the vast Chinese empire. Without the U.S. guarantees of security that Taiwan had enjoyed previously, Chiang Ching-kuo supported democratization. During 1979 and early 1980 there were public debates in Taiwan on promulgating new election rules. In November 1980, electoral campaigning was introduced. The election resulted in a landslide Nationalist Party victory, but in 1983 those opposing the Nationalist Party called themselves the *dangwai*— meaning "outside the party." In 1986, when Chiang allowed opposition parties to organize and compete in local elections, some *dangwai* members banded together to establish the Democratic Progressive Party (DPP) to create a two-party election. Chiang Ching-kuo also took steps toward implementing a truly parliamentary system of government. For the first time, the Nationalist Party faced genuine competition from other political parties.

In 1987, the government lifted martial law, which had given the government broad authority to arrest, imprison, and suppress dissent. For the first time, the government also allowed the general population to travel to China via the British colony of Hong Kong. Many Taiwanese were appalled when they saw the enormous disparity in living standards. Once they were able to visit the mainland, many Taiwanese began to question the wisdom of their government's one-China policy. Reunification under the best of circumstances would bring an implosion of Taiwanese living standards. Family members in the PRC who had survived Mao's many campaigns often believed that their far-richer Taiwanese relatives owed them recompense for their suffering.

PRC FAILURE TO ADOPT POLITICAL REFORMS

Deng Xiaoping accepted economic liberalization but rejected political liberalization. In March 1979, after a successful trip to the United States to normalize relations, Deng rapidly suppressed the Democracy Wall Movement, removing the posters and silencing their authors. In September 1980, he had the PRC constitution amended to revoke the right to display big-character posters. His concerns were validated only a decade later in the Soviet Union, when President Mikhail Gorbachev's call for *glasnost* (openness) ended in the collapse of the Communist government.

Deng sought to reduce tensions with the West to focus on domestic reforms. On January 11, 1982, he made clear that the One Country, Two Systems doctrine applied equally to Hong Kong and Taiwan, keeping tensions with Taiwan low during his tenure. His main legacies were an emphasis on technical expertise and the market-oriented economic reforms that lifted millions of Chinese from poverty. Deng's decade of economic reforms gave PRC citizens a wide variety of freedoms in economic life but no corresponding freedoms in political life.

The dramatic rise in the standard of living in the mainland was accompanied by greater corruption. Students, starting in Beijing, spearheaded demonstrations throughout China demanding reform. Soon the students were joined by workers hurt by inflation, by entrepreneurs who desired political rights commensurate with their economic power, and by intellectuals who no longer believed it possible to work for change within the Communist Party. While the students' calls for democracy were vague, the workers organized. For the first time since the Communist Revolution, they established an independent workers' organization, the Federation of Autonomous Workers.

The prodemocracy movement lasted for fifty-four days, from the death of Hu Yaobang on April 15, 1989, through its bloody suppression on June 4 of that year. Hu Yaobang's funeral meant citizens could assemble legally to mourn his passing. On April 17, prodemocracy demonstrators began congregating around the Monument to the Martyrs in Tiananmen Square. Some affixed wall posters lauding Hu as a people's hero, while others were highly critical of the Communists, making such comments as, "Seventy years have passed since the May Fourth Movement, and still we have no freedom and democracy!"[4] Students also presented a seven-point petition to the National People's Congress, demanding greater press freedom, the freedom to protest, and a renunciation of political campaigns to repress political dissidents.

At the height of the protests, in late April, over a million people gathered in Tiananmen Square, while on most days there were several thousand protesters. Even though the student leaders employed nonviolent tactics, in late April the government characterized the movement as a conspiracy. On April 19 and the morning of April 20, the first hint of violence appeared. Approximately 20,000 demonstrators gathered outside the compound where Premier Li Peng and the other major Communist leaders lived to demand that he personally address them. Under the guidance of Wuer Kaixi (Wu-erh K'ai-hsi), a young student of education from Xinjiang of Uighur descent, the crowd remained peaceful. Government spokesmen accused the demonstrators of being reactionaries. Soon, policemen appeared and began to beat the students. Those arrested became martyrs, and the movement quickly grew in size.

During the late evening of April 21, thousands gathered in Tiananmen Square in preparation for Hu Yaobang's funeral on the following day. As the ceremony was taking place in the Great Hall of the People, crowds outside again called for Premier Li Peng to come outside to receive their petition. In a gesture reminiscent of imperial times, three student representatives knelt before the doors, while one held a scroll intended for the emperor. The government leaders declined to accept the petition but could not escape the highly unfavorable symbolism of the moment. On April 26, the *People's Daily* attacked the students, hinting that military force might be necessary. The next day, students protested the editorial, while 150,000 demonstrators converged on Tiananmen Square.

Deng Xiaoping responded by visiting the regional military commanders and ordering their units to deploy to Beijing. On May 13, about four hundred students began a hunger strike that lasted for seven days, until May 19. Historically, China has been a country of terrible famines, and the hunger strike implied the moral bankruptcy of Communist rule. In the midst of these growing protests, Gorbachev was scheduled to arrive in Beijing on May 15, 1989, for a historic reconciliation to end the Sino–Soviet split. Deng intended the reconciliation to be one of the crowning achievements of his rule, but the presence of the famous Soviet reformer electrified the student protesters. By May 18, the PLA was in position to put down the demonstrations.

THE TIANANMEN MASSACRE

President Gorbachev's arrival to China on May 15 delayed military action against the prodemocracy activists. Not until after his May 18 departure did the government order the PLA to intervene. Many foreign correspondents originally sent to cover the Gorbachev visit remained in Beijing to continue reporting on the growing student demonstrations. By that time, over a million demonstrators were estimated to be in Tiananmen Square. On May 19, Li Peng announced that the PLA would be deployed in Beijing, and the next day martial law was declared.

During late May, PLA troops tried but failed to enter the capital. Local residents surrounded their trucks, refusing to let them pass. The soldiers did not want to fire on fellow citizens and so turned back instead. At

10:30 p.m. on the night of June 3, PLA troops were loaded into trucks and provided with live ammunition. A total of 25,000 troops converged on Tiananmen Square, while another 75,000 troops waited in reserve outside the city. PLA tanks slowly rolled into the square, crushing all in their path. By 3:00 a.m. on June 4, PLA troops and tanks approached the remaining demonstrators, who gathered around the statue of the Goddess of Democracy. Thirty minutes later, the square was empty. According to Beijing, no one died. Unofficial early estimates reported 4,000 dead and 6,500 wounded, while Russian sources reported 10,000 deaths.[5]

In the aftermath of the massacre, Beijing labeled the prodemocracy demonstrators counterrevolutionaries, described the massacre as a restoration of public order, and arrested and imprisoned the leaders of the movement. On June 9, Deng Xiaoping came out of retirement to hail the PLA as "a truly Great Wall of iron and steel around the Party and country."[6] Deng had lived through the Cultural Revolution and would not allow reckless youth to threaten social stability. Yet he underestimated the impact of the foreign-press coverage. Where tear gas would have sufficed to empty Tiananmen Square, Deng had authorized the use of live ammunition and tanks.

The Beijing Massacre undermined rose-tinted interpretations of China's political situation that were then popular in intellectual circles abroad. Television footage of the bloodshed at Tiananmen meant that certain pro-Communist positions were no longer tenable. Although the numbers killed or wounded were but a fraction of those who had perished in the earlier political campaigns, the televised images stood for the millions of deaths under Chinese Communist Party rule. The World Bank suspended loans to the PRC for a time. The United States, in particular, halted many types of exchanges. Thereafter, diplomatic relations remained tense. China's economy suffered a blow, as foreign tourists stopped coming and foreign companies were hesitant to invest. All of this sharply contrasted with Taiwan's generally peaceful transition to democracy.

THE INDEPENDENCE MOVEMENT IN TAIWAN

After 1989, comparisons of political freedoms in Taiwan versus the lack of freedoms in the PRC become increasingly unflattering. The Beijing Massacre caused a marked improvement in Taiwan's international standing. The international-trade sanctions applied to China meant investment money flowed into Taiwan instead. As a result, Taiwan's economy boomed. Taking advantage of Western squeamishness, Taiwanese investment into the PRC helped fill the vacuum, with billions of dollars of capital flowing from Taiwan to the mainland. Tiananmen also opened the door for greater Taiwanese political independence. Taiwan's growing democratization put it in the ranks among developed countries—now in political as well as economic terms. The stark contrast between the political freedoms of Taiwan and the massacre in Beijing generated much international sympathy for Taipei.

With Chiang Ching-kuo's death in 1988, the presidency had not gone to another politician with recent roots in mainland China but to Lee Teng-hui, whose family had lived in Taiwan for generations. In 1989 a new Law on Civic Organizations permitted the creation of new political parties, while the 1936 constitution was amended to phase out the old parliamentary incumbents originally elected on the mainland. By December 21, 1991, all were fully retired in time for the first general election since 1949. In preparation for the elections, a new parliament opened in 1990, and constitutional rule was established.

In 1996, Taiwan held its first direct presidential election, resulting in the reelection of President Lee. The proindependence candidate, Chen Shui-bian, almost won the 1996 election. Four years later, in 2000, the Democratic Progressive Party, composed mainly of those Han Chinese whose families had lived in Taiwan for many generations, won the election when the Nationalist Party gracefully relinquished office. It had monopolized power since the 1920s. This was the first peaceful and fully democratic change of power in Chinese history.

President Chen Shui-bian was outspoken in his opposition to reunification. The PRC had offered indisputable proof to many voters why independence was not a luxury but an imperative. From Beijing's point of view, the Nationalist Party of Lee Teng-hui was an enemy, but an enemy who accepted the general terms of engagement, meaning one China. After Chen served his two full terms in office, the 2008 presidential elections restored the Nationalists to power with the victory of Ma Ying-jeou.

A key motivation for the democratization under Chiang Ching-kuo and Lee Teng-hui was national security. Under Deng Xiaoping, the PRC had imitated the Taiwanese economic miracle. This meant that it would eventually overtake Taiwan economically. It was already channeling some of this wealth into military modernization programs that would soon make possible a cross-strait invasion. This drove Taiwan into a corner. It did not have international recognition, let alone a seat in the UN. It could not defeat the PRC militarily. And so Taiwan's new strategy became to defeat the PRC politically. Democratic changes strengthened the legitimacy of the Taiwanese government, which had done very well by its citizens in comparison to the Communist government of China.

The growing popular support in Taiwan for formal independence put the PRC in an awkward position. Reunification would require a bloody invasion, which might result in trade sanctions or even trigger military intervention by the United States, Japan, and other powers. There was also an economic element to the Taiwanese strategy. If foreign countries had investments throughout Taiwan and East Asia in general, and if

Taiwan had significant mainland investments from which China derived great economic benefits, an invasion would come at an enormous economic cost to the PRC. War would undermine the economy of all of Asia, which would grab the attention of the United States and Japan, raising the possibility of allies. Undoubtedly, many Taiwanese hoped that such potential costs might be sufficient to deter a PRC invasion.

Although Deng had officially retired from all official appointments by November 1989, he feared that a conservative backlash within the party leadership in response to the recent unrest would reverse his economic reforms. Behind the scenes, Deng negotiated a grand compromise that preserved his reforms: The central government would continue to promote economic reform, but in return provincial leaders would continue to funnel tax revenues to the central government necessary to sustain the reforms and a growing military budget. In addition, the central government would generously fund the continued modernization of the PLA, but in return the PLA would support the reforms and party leadership.

This arrangement met the most essential desires of three key constituencies: the military, the central government, and the provincial governments. This arrangement prevented the pro-Soviet-leaning faction from restoring centralized economic management. Deng hoped that this arrangement would endure beyond his death and become permanent. Unfortunately, in 1995 and 1996 another Taiwan Strait crisis—the fourth— threatened to mar Deng Xiaoping's good intentions.

THE FOURTH TAIWAN STRAIT CRISIS

The PRC observed the democratization in Taiwan with concern, because it believed that a democratic Taiwan was more likely to declare independence. In 1995 and 1996, the PRC attempted to influence the Taiwanese presidential election by firing missiles in the vicinity of the island: On July 21, 1995, the PRC began eight days of test-firing surface-to-surface missiles off Taiwan's northern coast. On March 8, 1996, China began another eight days of test-firing off Taiwan's major northeastern and southwestern ports. On March 12, it began nine days of naval and air exercises off of Jinmen Island and the Penghu Islands. And on March 18, it began eight days of joint war games also off Taiwan. While the missiles were not armed, the flurry of military activity sent the message that the PRC would use deadly force to prevent a formal Taiwanese declaration of independence.

The July 1995 missile tests by the PRC are often portrayed as a response to the granting of an American visa to Taiwan's president Lee Teng-hui for an unofficial visit to Cornell University in early June of that year. However, the real underlying concern for the PRC was over Taiwan's rapid democratization and the growing separatist claims by large numbers of Taiwanese. On July 18, 1995, China announced that ballistic-missile tests would take place between July 21 and 28. These dates corresponded with the fiftieth anniversary of the 1945 Potsdam treaty, which stated that China would regain all territories lost to Japan, including Taiwan, after the war ended.

The PRC missile tests were intended to create an exclusion zone—in this case a ten-nautical-mile circle in which ships and planes could not safely enter. This zone was located about eighty-five miles north of Taiwan, which was outside Taiwan's sovereign waters but actively interfered with flight paths and shipping lanes. Six DF-15 (CSS-6/M-9) short-range ballistic missiles (SRBMs) were fired, two each on July 21, 22, and 23, 1995. Beijing's announcement warned other states "against entering the said sea area and air space" during the firing period. Unlike similar Taiwanese tests during the mid-1960s, which had generally been ignored, these PRC missile tests diverted hundreds of commercial flights heading for Taipei.[7]

From August 15 to 25, 1995, PRC military exercises, including about twenty warships and forty aircraft, were held in a large area to the northwest of the SRBM splash zone. During this period, the PRC tested both antiship missiles and antiaircraft missiles. In November of that year, just prior to Taiwan's December parliamentary elections, the PLA staged further naval, amphibious, and air-assault operations near Dongshan Island. These exercises included conducting blockade exercises, which made it appear that the PRC was planning to mount a naval blockade against Taiwan.

The PRC's use of missiles in order to create exclusion zones around Taiwan was not new, since it essentially copied Taiwan's tests during the 1960s. However, due to the higher number of airplanes overflying these waters, it did put intense pressure on Taipei. This has been referred to as one of the first uses of a new form of "missile blockade."[8] By contrast, when Taiwan conducted similar Nike and Hawk tests in April of 1965 it did not elicit any public protests. Unlike this earlier period, the PRC's actions threatened the strategic sea-lanes running north to south through the Taiwan Strait. This prompted American naval intervention.

AMERICAN NAVAL INTERVENTION

The PRC strategy backfired. The United States increased its support for Taiwan, deploying two aircraft-carrier battle groups, including one led by the aircraft carrier USS *Independence*; although unintentional, the name of the aircraft carrier undoubtedly jarred PRC sensibilities. The fall of the USSR and the end of the Cold War in 1991 had greatly reduced the geostrategic importance of mainland China to the United States. Formerly, China had been the essential pressure point on the Soviet empire, but the USSR's collapse allowed the U.S. government to support democracy over dictatorship. Although Washington continued to recognize the PRC diplomatically, it backed Taiwan militarily.

In response to these heightened tensions, the U.S. Navy sailed the USS *Nimitz* (CVN 68) through the Taiwan Strait on December 19, 1995, on its way to the Indian Ocean. The stated reason for transiting the strait, rather than going east of Taiwan, was poor weather. The PRC did not seem to know about, or simply did not acknowledge, the transit. But on January 27, 1996, the *United Daily News* and the *New York Times* reported it. This was the first time an American aircraft carrier had transited the Taiwan Strait since the late 1970s. Whether intentional or not, it sent a sharp signal to Beijing to not interfere in Taiwan's domestic politics.

In many ways, the December 1995 transit by a U.S. aircraft carrier of the Taiwan Strait paralleled the visit by the aircraft carrier *Valley Forge* on June 29, 1950, which had helped signal the establishment of the Taiwan Patrol Force. Even if only by accident, the *Nimitz* transit sent a similar hands-off message to Beijing. In this regard, it has been described as "a carefully controlled and minimally provocative use of military power [that] allowed the United States to reemphasize the 'ambiguous' policy of previous U.S. presidents designed to maintain a balance in U.S. relations with both sides of the strait."[9]

Beijing warned the assistant secretary of defense, Charles ("Chas") Freeman, that the PRC would launch one missile per day against Taiwan for a period of thirty days if Taipei continued on its path toward formal independence. A Chinese official even warned Freeman that the United States should not intervene in a cross-strait crisis, because U.S. leaders "care more about Los Angeles than they do about Taiwan."[10] China's one-missile-per-day strategy and its implied nuclear threat against the United States were both reminiscent of similar PRC pressure tactics during the 1950s against Jinmen Island.

Sino–U.S. tensions remained high throughout this entire period. On March 5, 1996, the forty-third anniversary of the death of Stalin—one of the three major world leaders at Potsdam—Beijing announced that it would conduct a new series of ballistic missile exercises from March 8 through 15, which corresponded with the run-up to Taiwan's first presidential elections under universal suffrage. This time the northern missile zone was a square just thirty miles from Keelung, close to sea- and air lanes servicing Japan and Korea. The southern zone lay about forty-seven miles west of Kaohsiung and was close to air and sea-lanes to Hong Kong (see figure 9.1).

The tests were clearly intended to cut trade routes from Keelung in the north and Kaohsiung in the south. These two ports accounted for about 70 percent of Taiwan's commerce. Between March 8 and 13, four dummy missiles landed within the target areas. On March 9, the PRC also warned ships and aircraft to avoid a live-fire exercise from March 12 to 20 in the

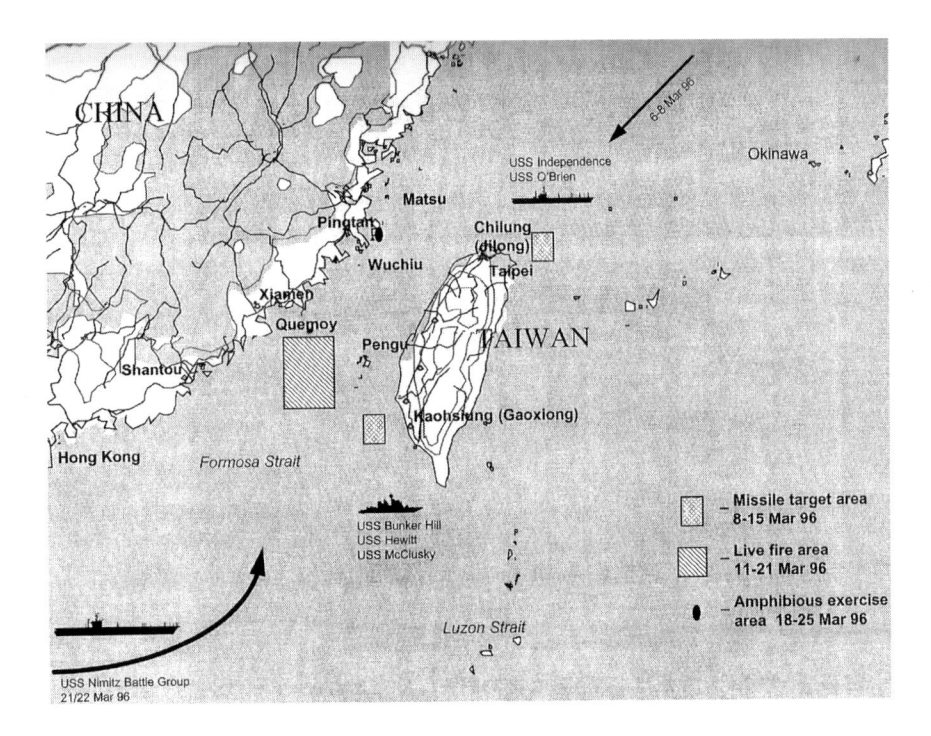

Figure 9.1. Location of PRC Missile Tests from 1995 to 1996. Source: Rick M. Gallagher, "The Taiwan Strait Crisis," SRD Report (Newport, RI: NWC Press, 1997)

southern part of the Taiwan Strait. The rectangular zone for these exercises was just south of Jinmen Island. A further exercise was announced on March 15, to be carried out from March 18 to 25, continuing the military pressure until after the presidential election. Although this zone was smaller, it was strategically located between the two small islands of Mazu and Wuchiu.[11]

The PRC tests were timed to put pressure on Taiwan's presidential elections, scheduled for March 23, so that the proindependence candidates would not win. In response to this action, the USN dispatched the USS *Independence* aircraft-carrier battle group to the area. Its aircraft were patrolling about 100 miles off of Taiwan. The USS *Nimitz* carrier group was also ordered to return from the Persian Gulf at high speed. Other naval assets included two Aegis guided-missile cruisers and U.S. Air Force RC-135 Rivet Joint electronic surveillance aircraft.[12]

CinCPac Admiral Joseph Prueher decided to put *Independence* east of Taiwan and to assign two Aegis cruisers north and south of Taiwan: "Got them there fast. Got them there quietly. But nobody knew that they were there, so we had to tell the media in Okinawa and Japan. Media switch is not vernier switch but on/off switch. Pictures in the press began to appear." As a result of Prueher's sending *Independence*, and later recalling *Nimitz* from the Persian Gulf, the Chinese only fired five missiles, three north and two south, instead of the much larger number that they had originally planned.[13] As noted by Admiral Lyle Bien, commander of Carrier Group 7, "ordering *Nimitz* to sail all the way from the Gulf at flank speed was an unmistakable signal to the PRC that we were serious, and it was noted by all onboard *Nimitz* that the missile firings stopped only when we approached on-station."[14]

The United States also sent official protests to the Chinese government, with Secretary of State Warren Christopher calling the PRC's actions "reckless" and a White House spokesman stating that Washington was "deeply disturbed by this provocative act."[15] The U.S. Congress resolved that in the face of overt threats by the PRC against Taiwan, and consistent with the commitment of the U.S. government under the Taiwan Relations Act, the United States would continue to supply Taiwan with defensive weapons systems, including "naval vessels, aircraft, and air defense, all of which are crucial to the security of Taiwan." The congressional resolution further stated that the "United States is committed to the military stability of the Taiwan Straits, and United States military forces should defend Taiwan in the event of invasion, missile attack, or blockade by the People's Republic of China."[16]

Not only was this reaction by the U.S. Congress closely parallel to congressional resolutions during the first Taiwan Strait crisis in 1954 and 1955, but the wording of the resolution matched almost exactly the stated goals of the long-gone Taiwan Patrol Force. The U.S. Navy's intervention gave the PRC pause. Washington's decision to send to the Taiwan Strait, not one, but two aircraft carriers—plus the two Aegis cruisers and other naval assets, including *O'Brien* (DD 975), the namesake of the 1950s destroyer that helped in the evacuation of the Dachen Islands and later rescued Nationalists sailors—constituted the largest demonstration of American naval diplomacy against China since the first two Taiwan Strait crises of the 1950s.[17]

The strategic rationale for sending ships to the Taiwan Strait, however, was much the same as it had been in 1950: to neutralize this region so as to not allow a cross-strait invasion. While perhaps not officially part of the Taiwan Patrol Force, therefore, *Independence* and *Nimitz* carried out a similar role. Seen in this larger historical context, Washington's decision to send in the U.S. Navy was a direct continuation in spirit of that naval operation. That spirit has largely continued to the present day.

CONCLUSIONS

Although the Taiwan Patrol Force officially ceased operations on January 1, 1979, the U.S. reaction to the PRC missile tests of 1995 and 1996 provoked a situation remarkably similar to the earlier Taiwan Strait crises. Even today the lingering effects of the Taiwan Patrol Force can still be felt. While fixed patrols have not been carried out in the Taiwan Strait since 1979, the USN's presence in the region remains strong. There is a compelling argument to be made—that the Taiwan Patrol Force never really disbanded. In fact, the 1995–1996 decision to send in aircraft carriers was part and parcel of the same 1950s buffer operation ensuring PRC–ROC tensions did not escalate into a larger war.

The U.S. Navy's reaction to the so-called "missile blockade" of 1995 and 1996 highlights not only the continuing strategic value of this region but also the importance of retaining the U.S. Navy's maritime presence to keep the peace in the Taiwan Strait. In this regard, all of these recent USN deployments to international waters near China have carried on the historical legacy of the Taiwan Patrol Force. It also shows the firm American resolve not to cede freedom of the seas to the PRC.

The most important outstanding territorial issue remains, as always, the security of Taiwan. Nationalists in the PRC accuse Washington of manipulating Taiwanese politics to prevent reunification. In particular, they condemn the U.S. arms sales mandated by the 1979 Taiwan Relations Act. There is widespread popular agreement in the PRC that Taiwan should rejoin the motherland. There also seems to be widespread public support for a coercive solution if Taiwan refuses. Little consideration is given in the PRC to the fact that the majority of Taiwanese reject reunification. However, in recent years the PRC and ROC have increased cooperation on a whole range of issues intended to increase trade, tourism, and communications.

NOTES

1. Michael S. Chase, "U.S.–Taiwan Security Cooperation: Enhancing an Unofficial Relationship," in *Dangerous Strait: The U.S.–Taiwan–China Crisis*, ed. Nancy Bernkopf Tucker, 164 (New York: Columbia University Press, 2005).

2. James C. Bussert and Bruce A. Elleman, *People's Liberation Army Navy (PLAN) Combat Systems Technology, 1949–2010* (Annapolis, MD: Naval Institute Press, 2011), 14–15, 101, 175.

3. Overlooking the 1962 crisis, Wikipedia incorrectly refers to these events as the "Third Taiwan Strait Crisis." See Wikipedia.org, "Third Taiwan Strait Crisis, http://en.wikipedia.org/wiki/Third_Taiwan_Strait_Crisis (accessed December 13, 2010).

4. Cited in Bruce A. Elleman, *Modern Chinese Warfare, 1795–1989* (London: Routledge, 2001), 303.

5. Ibid., 307.

6. Cited in Orville Schell, *Mandate of Heaven* (New York: Simon and Schuster, 1994), 167.

7. Richard D. Fisher, "China's Missiles over the Taiwan Strait: A Political and Military Assessment," in *Crisis in the Taiwan Strait*, ed. James R. Lilley and Chuck Downs, 170–71 (Ft. McNair, Washington, DC: National Defense University Press, 1997).

8. Chris Rahman, "Ballistic Missiles in China's Anti-Taiwan Blockade," in *Naval Blockades and Seapower: Strategies and Counter-Strategies, 1805–2005*, ed. Bruce A. Elleman and S. C. M. Paine, 215–24 (London: Routledge Press, 2006).

9. Rick M. Gallagher, *The Taiwan Strait Crisis* (Newport, RI: U.S. Naval War College, 1997), 2–3.

10. Patrick E. Tyler, "As China Threatens Taiwan, It Makes Sure U.S. Listens," *New York Times*, January 24, 1996, available online at http://www.nytimes.com/1996/01/24/world/as-china-threatens-taiwan-it-makes-sure-us-listens.html.

11. Patrick E. Tyler, "China Warns U.S. to Keep Away from Taiwan Strait," *New York Times*, March 18, 1996, available online at http://www.nytimes.com/1996/03/18/world/china-warns-us-to-keep-away-from-taiwan-strait.html.

12. Michael Richardson, "Asia Looks to U.S. to Protect Trade Routes around Taiwan," *New York Times*, March 14, 1996, available online at http://www.nytimes.com/1996/03/14/news/14iht-straits.t_0.html.

13. Bruce A. Elleman, "The Right Skill Set: Joseph Wilson Prueher (1941–)," in *Nineteen Gun Salute: Case Studies of Operational, Strategic, and Diplomatic Naval Leadership during the 20th and Early 21st Centuries*, ed. John B. Hattendorf and Bruce A. Elleman, 237 (Newport, RI: NWC Press, 2010).

14. E-mail communication with Vice Admiral Lyle Bien, U.S. Navy (Ret.), March 23, 2011.

15. Patrick E. Tyler, "China Signaling U.S. That It Will Not Invade Taiwan," *New York Times*, March 13, 1996, available online at http://www.nytimes.com/1996/03/13/world/china-signaling-us-that-it-will-not-invade-taiwan.html.

16. 104th Congress, 2d Session, H. Con. Res. 148, March 7, 1996, http://ftp.resource.org/gpo.gov/bills/104/hc148ih.txt (accessed December 15, 2010).

17. Fisher, "China's Missiles over the Taiwan Strait," 178.

TEN

Beijing–Taipei Cross-Strait Tensions and Cooperation

Tensions between the United States and the People's Republic of China continued after the fourth Taiwan Strait crisis. In 2001, Sino–U.S. tensions flared when a Chinese fighter bumped a U.S. EP-3 plane monitoring Chinese naval activities. The Chinese pilot died, while the U.S. plane barely managed to land safely on China's Hainan Island; ten days of tense negotiations followed before the PRC agreed to release the crew. Much later, it returned the plane in pieces, thoroughly studied. Relations between the two states have remained tense ever since. In 2009, Chinese ships harassed USN surveillance ship USNS *Victorious* (T-AGOS 19) and the civilian-manned U.S. submarine surveillance vessel USNS *Impeccable*.

Even though Beijing and Taipei dispute which government is the true government of China, they both agree that disputed islands in the East China Sea and the South China Sea are China's. Thus, Beijing and Taipei have cooperated with each other when conflicts erupt against another claimant, such as in 1988, when China fought with Vietnamese troops in the Spratlys. Disputed island territories includes the Diaoyu Islands (the Senkaku Islands, in Japanese) and the islands of the South China Sea. Since 1894 Japan has had de facto control over the Diaoyu Islands, really uninhabited rocks projecting out of the sea. Long considered worthless, these islands were included within Japan's Exclusive Economic Zone in July 1996, thus reigniting the dispute with Japan's assertion of the right to exploit any surrounding resources—such as gas, oil, and fish. The PRC immediately protested, sponsoring mass demonstrations aimed at Japan. Ever since, PRC activists have regularly slipped through Japanese coast guard patrols to land on these islands in a bid for Chinese sovereignty.

In June 1996, the book *China Can Still Say No* appeared on PRC bookshelves. It laid claim to all these disputed territories, blamed the United

States for organizing the rest of Asia against China, and portrayed China as the victim. It ignored the competing interests of the many other countries involved. The authors asserted that China should reclaim all territories lost since 1662, the year after the Ming loyalists retook Taiwan from the Dutch, thus implying that Taiwan is already part of greater China. If the two governments were ever to unify, either in reality or simply on paper—for example, in some kind of "united front"—then Taipei's greater territorial claims might even give Beijing an opportunity to reopen border negotiations with many of China's neighbors.

INCREASING SINO–U.S. NAVAL TENSIONS

U.S. Navy patrols have played a continuing and important role since the turn of the twenty-first century. After remaining fairly quiet for five years after the events of 1995 and 1996, U.S.–Chinese tensions exploded on April 1, 2001, following the collision between a Chinese and American plane. The standoff over the return of the EP-3 crew elicited discussion in Washington about whether or not to send yet another USN aircraft carrier to China. While in the end USN vessels were not sent into the area, the mere fact that it was proposed shows that the same rationale that led to the creation of the Taiwan Patrol Force still existed in 2001.

To resolve the EP-3 standoff, former U.S. admiral and then–U.S. ambassador to China Joseph Prueher worked closely with Annapolis classmates, including Richard Armitage, Secretary of State Colin L. Powell's deputy at the State Department, and Admiral Denny Blair, who was CinCPac. At one crucial stage of the negotiations, Admiral Blair offered to send an aircraft carrier to China. This would normally have been Prueher's favored solution, as shown by his actions in 1995 and 1996. But the ambassador declined this suggestion, fearing that too strong a signal might backfire and lead to the prolongation of the incident.[1]

Rather than turn to the U.S. Navy, Prueher urged the administration to ease tensions and instead focus on negotiations to find a way out of the impasse.[2] Early in the talks, Powell refused when the Chinese tried to get the U.S. to say it had invaded China's airspace: "We're not going to take that charge to the president, and we're not going to accept it." Prueher, however, in a substantial upgrade from offering to use the term *regret*, did agree to shift from using *sorry* for the airspace incursion to saying he was *very sorry*.[3] This change of terminology made it seem to the Chinese public that the United States was taking responsibility for the collision. After ten days of tense negotiations, this ambiguous apology helped break the diplomatic impasse.

After the two-sorrys letter was signed and delivered by Prueher, the EP-3's twenty-four crewmembers were released after exactly ten days. Resolving the EP-3 crisis peacefully was largely due to Prueher's qualifications as an aircraft-carrier pilot with actual combat experience in the region, as a test pilot cognizant of the capabilities of the airframes involved, and as a recent CinCPac with experience dealing with China. As Prueher later explained, the dispute was not about an airplane but about "face," and China needed a "signal that it is taken seriously."[4] Prueher wanted to find a graceful way for Beijing to back down from its untenable position. This eventually led to the two-sorrys letter, which the Chinese could interpret as a "formal apology," while the U.S. government could portray it as "merely a polite expression of regret."[5]

Even though a USN aircraft carrier was not sent into the region during 2001's tense standoff, the possibility had been seriously considered. This merely emphasizes the flexibility that is inherent in having USN forces within easy reach of the Taiwan Strait. During the following eight years, Sino–U.S. naval relations remained outwardly calm, with few publicly acknowledged maritime disputes. This situation changed beginning in March 2009, when two USN survey ships were accosted while conducting operations in international waters near China. At the time, PRC ships confronted the USNS *Impeccable* (T-AGOS 23) while it was conducting maritime research in international waters in the South China Sea. Two months later, in May, U.S. defense officials announced that Chinese vessels surrounded a second USN surveillance ship, USNS *Victorious* (T-AGOS 19), in the Yellow Sea. These two incidents prompted a strong USN response.

In the first instance, on March 8, 2009, five PRC ships harassed the civilian-manned U.S. submarine surveillance vessel USNS *Impeccable* while it was in international waters about seventy-five miles south of Hainan Island. Two of the Chinese vessels came within fifty feet of the U.S. vessel, and sailors onboard were observed "waving Chinese flags and telling the U.S. ship to leave the area." In addition to lodging a protest with China officials, State Department spokesman Robert Wood later told reporters that "We felt that our vessel was inappropriately harassed."[6]

The U.S. Navy's reaction to these Chinese provocations was rapid. Within days a guided-missile destroyer, the USS *Chung-Hoon* (DDG 93), "armed with torpedoes and missiles," was sent to the South China Sea to help *Impeccable*.[7] The Chinese government condemned this USN action as provocative. One Chinese scholar even acknowledged that "The '*Impeccable* Incident' constitutes the most serious friction between China and the United States since the collision of their military aircraft near Hainan Island in April 2001."[8]

Soon after the *Impeccable* incident, another USN surveillance ship, the USNS *Victorious*, operating 120 miles off China's coast in the Yellow Sea, was harassed several times between March 4 and 5, 2009, by Chinese patrol ships and aircraft. On May 1, 2009, U.S. defense officials announced that Chinese vessels had confronted the USNS *Victorious* in the

Yellow Sea.[9] Pentagon officials claimed that two Chinese ships came within thirty yards of the USNS *Victorious*, which was forced to use water hoses to warn them off. Once again protesting China's actions, the U.S. government reiterated that it would not "end its surveillance activities in the region."[10]

Both incidents took place in international waters. Due to the U.S. government's long-time support for freedom of the seas, U.S. Navy officials reiterated that it should not be necessary to send armed ships to protect USNS survey ships.[11] While the *Impeccable* incident took place in the South China Sea, to the south of Taiwan, the *Victorious* incident took place in the Yellow Sea, far to the north. These two incidents gave the outward appearance of testing the U.S. Navy's readiness and resolve at each geographic extreme of the Taiwan Strait. The USN's rapid responses to these PRC provocations were largely in line with operational procedures first adopted by the Taiwan Patrol Force beginning in late June 1950.

OVERLAPPING PRC–ROC MARITIME AND TERRITORIAL CLAIMS

Not surprisingly, Beijing and Taipei disagree on what territories they should control. Since 1949, the PRC and the ROC have each considered themselves to be the only legitimate government of China. While both Beijing and Taipei agree that Xinjiang, Tibet, and Inner Mongolia are part of China, for most of this period Taiwan has also claimed Mongolia (formerly called Outer Mongolia). The Taiwanese government recognized Mongolia as a separate country on October 3, 2002, even though the official borders of the Republic of China have apparently not yet been changed, nor have official ROC maps that include Mongolia as part of China been replaced.

The PRC claims not only the offshore islands garrisoned by Taiwan but all of the Penghu Islands, as well as Taiwan Island (also known as Formosa) and the much smaller Green Island, Orchid Island, and Lesser Orchid Island, right off Taiwan's east coast. Moreover, China and Taiwan both claim disputed territories in the South China Sea, which are likewise claimed in part or wholly by Vietnam, the Philippines, Brunei, and Malaysia. Additionally, while Indonesia holds uncontested sovereignty over the Natuna Islands, overlapping maritime claims may exist between Indonesia on behalf of these islands and China (and possibly other claimant states) generated from the disputed Spratly Islands.

Since the 1990s, to make good its territorial claims, China has invested heavily in naval ships, often bought from Russia. This has transformed the People's Liberation Army Navy from a coastal defense force to a blue-water navy potentially capable of projecting power and influencing events far from China's shores. In 1992, the Chinese government promulgated the Territorial Waters and Contiguous Areas Act, which claims as Chinese territory not only Taiwan but also the Penghu, Diaoyu, Pratas, Paracel, and Spratly islands and the Macclesfield Bank.

The Spratly Islands (Nansha in Chinese) consist of more than two hundred small islands, half-submerged rocks, and reefs scattered over a vast area. Estimates of natural gas and oil reserves range into the tens of billions of barrels, closely linking issues of sovereignty and future economic growth. Key shipping routes of East Asia traverse the South China Sea so that sovereignty over the many disputed islands also will determine whether these sea-lanes are international or national waters, with security implications for all. In particular, Chinese, Japanese, South Korean, and Taiwanese energy supplies all traverse this route.

Chinese historical records dating back to the second century a.d. predate any other historical claims. This does not mean that the islands were never explored or used by Vietnamese or Filipino fishermen, however, but that the Chinese were the first to document their early presence. One academic has concluded that "it is true that the weight of the evidence appears in the present case to be on the Chinese side, although this may reflect mainly the greater industry of traditional Chinese authors in keeping geographical and historical records."[12]

Beginning in the 1880s, France, Japan, and China became interested in dominating the South China Sea. As a result of the Sino–French conflict in 1884 and 1885, France made Annam (Vietnam) a protectorate and later a colony, and then during the first Sino–Japanese War of 1894 and 1895 Japan annexed Taiwan. Faced with what China considered to be illegal Japanese mining operations on several phosphorus- and guano-rich islands in the Pratas and Spratly islands, in 1907 Qing Admiral Sa Zhenbing led a naval expedition to reclaim these islands for China. In September of 1909 the Qing government renamed the Naval Reorganization Council as the Ministry of the Navy. China's newly modernized navy then conducted several naval operations in the South China Sea, and in 1909 and 1910 China formally annexed many of these islands—including the Paracel and Pratas islands—to Guangdong Province and also sent a ship every year to the South China Sea "to maintain contact with overseas Chinese on these islands."[13]

Following the collapse of the Qing dynasty in 1911, China fell into turmoil for many years. In 1926, the newly established Nationalist Navy built a radio station on the Pratas Islands. Taking advantage of China's comparative weakness, however, French Indochina occupied the Paracel Islands in 1932. But with Japan's invasion of China in 1937, the Japanese began to make their own claims to the Pratas, Paracel, and Spratly islands. In 1937, for example, as part of their occupation of China, Japan seized Pratas Island and captured and interrogated twenty-nine Nationalist soldiers. In response to the threat from Japan, France sent an expedition to the Paracels, officially claiming them as part of Annam (Vietnam) on July 4, 1938. Immediately, the Nationalist government-in-exile in Chongqing and the Japanese government protested France's action; Japan even stated in its own July 8, 1938, protest that France was violating Chinese sovereignty when occupying the Paracel Islands.

France next claimed the Paracel Islands as part of the French Union in 1939. In response, on March 31, 1939, Japan made a parallel claim on behalf of the governor-general of Taiwan, which was at that point an integral part of the Japanese empire. When France withdrew its forces the next year, however, Japan occupied the Paracels, this time not on behalf of Taiwan but as Japanese territory based on an earlier territorial claim dating back to 1917. Japan specified that its claim to the Spratly Islands included all of the islands 7°00' and 12°00' N and 111°30' and 117°00' E. From 1939 to 1945, the Japanese occupied Itu Aba, building a fuel depot, submarine base, and radio station there. Near the end of the war, the Japanese were forced to withdraw.

According to one view, only with the Japanese occupation of the islands in the late 1930s could valid claims of sovereignty be made through effective occupation. While Chinese historical interaction with these islands could establish the basis for a claim to sovereignty, therefore, such a right must be followed up with de facto occupation of the territory to establish legal sovereignty. This occupation was not attempted by the National government of China until after World War II.

POST–WORLD WAR II SOUTH CHINA SEA CLAIMS

Soon after World War II ended, the Nationalist government sent two destroyers to the South China Sea in November and December of 1946 to establish a garrison on Itu Aba (Taiping Island). Taiwan claims the Spratly Islands based on the fact that Nationalist troops were the first to occupy one of the Spratly Islands after the Japanese withdrawal in 1945. Beijing's parallel claim to the Spratlys agrees with this; plus, it is based directly on the 1947 eleven-dash map issued by the ROC, since Beijing claims to have inherited all ROC territory when the Chinese Communist Party took power in 1949. Accordingly, the PRC has claimed a nine-dash line from the early 1950s that includes most of the South China Sea.

However, there is disagreement over whether this Nationalist garrison was later removed, with some sources stating that all Chinese military forces left the Spratly Islands in May 1950 due to the ongoing civil war in China and that they only returned in July of 1956, possibly in response to exploratory activity in the area by Philippine nationals. During an interview in Taipei in March 1993, retired ROC Navy Vice Admiral Liu Dacai apparently confirmed that the island had lacked a Chinese military presence for several years. But other scholars argue that a "small contingent of Taiwanese troops remained on the largest island, Itu Aba (Taipingdao), in the Spratly group" during this period.[14]

On May 29, 1956, the PRC Foreign Ministry stated that "Taiping [Itu Aba] and Nanwei [Storm/Spratly] Island in the South China Sea, together with the small islands in their vicinity, are known in aggregate as the Nansha Islands. These islands have always been a part of Chinese territory. The People's Republic of China has indisputable, legitimate sovereignty over these islands."[15] On June 2, 1956, the American ambassador to Taipei reassured the ROC foreign minister that the United States had no intention of getting involved in the Spratly dispute. After receiving this assurance, the ROC also officially reclaimed Itu Aba.

Taiwan's action prompted Minister Cao Bai of South Vietnam (the Republic of Vietnam, or ROV) to state on June 5, 1956, that the Spratly and Paracel islands had been under the jurisdiction of the French colonial government and that Vietnam subsequently had jurisdiction by virtue of grant of sovereignty by France; soon afterward, South Vietnam landed naval units in the Spratlys. In response, Beijing insisted that an 1887 treaty with France, the Sino–French Convention, ceded to China the Paracel and Spratly groups. But other scholars argued that, despite the historical claims of the Chinese and Vietnamese, "only those events that took place since the 1930s are relevant to the analysis of the present dispute," which would make the 1887 treaty largely moot.[16]

From that time on, all subsequent claims and counterclaims to the Paracels and the Spratlys became even more complex. On September 4, 1958, the PRC issued its own "Declaration on Territorial Waters," which specifically stated that the Paracel (Xisha) and Spratly (Nansha) islands were Chinese territory.[17] The Communist government of North Vietnam, which sought aid from Communist China, appears to have accepted Chinese sovereignty over the Paracel and Spratly islands ten days later. On September 14, 1958, in a note to Chinese premier Zhou Enlai, North Vietnamese premier Pham Van Dong expressed his government's support for China's declaration, stating that "the Government of the Democratic Republic of Viet Nam recognizes and supports the Declaration of the Government of the People's Republic of China on China's territorial sea made on September 4, 1958."[18] These statements by the then–North Vietnamese government were later cited by the PRC as Vietnamese acceptance of China's sovereignty over the islands.[19]

With regard to the Paracels, both China and Taiwan agree that they were Chinese. In January 1974, the PLAN occupied these islands by force, taking them away from South Vietnam. The Chinese name for this expedition is *Xisha Ziwei Fanjizhan*—or "Counterattack in Self-Defense in the Paracel Islands."[20] Following Vietnam's reunification in 1975, Hanoi disputed China's possession, even though Hanoi had apparently recognized the PRC claim in 1958. On July 1, 1976, Vietnam restated its position that the Paracels were Vietnamese territory.

POTENTIAL PRC–ROC COOPERATION IN THE SOUTH CHINA SEA

For all of their political differences, the PRC and ROC might cooperate in furthering China's claims in the South China Sea. In 1988, the PRC incorporated the Paracels and the Spratlys into a new Chinese province called Hainan Province. Then, on December 4, 2007, China unilaterally announced it had created a new "city," called Sansha, in Hainan Province to administer the Paracels, Macclesfield Bank, and the Spratlys, even though China's sovereignty over these islands remains in dispute. According to news reports, "Shock waves were felt immediately throughout the region: both Vietnam and Indonesia formally protested China's unilateral and preemptive move."[21] In response to China's action, in February of 2008 Taiwanese president Chen Shui-bian flew to Itu Aba for an official visit. Chen's trip not only proved that the recently lengthened runway could handle C-130 cargo planes but was also perceived to reinforce Taiwan's claim to these disputed territories.[22] As recently as April of 2014, Taiwan held the largest military exercise ever on the island.

There is really no conflict between the sovereignty claims of China and Taiwan over the South China Sea. Both the PRC and the ROC feel that they are representing Chinese claims, and "historically, there is no question that the Paracels and Spratlys belong to China."[23] Other scholars disagree that they are of equal weight, however, arguing instead that the PRC's legal position on the islands, based on applicable international law, "is not only weak de jure but also de facto," principally because China had done nothing to exercise their jurisdiction over the Spratlys prior to establishing its own outposts in the area in 1988. By contrast, Taiwan has a more valid claim to Itu Aba, in particular since it has effectively held and developed it. However, "Taiwan cannot deduce from this any claim to the whole archipelago (which is, after all, an arbitrary definition in regard to insular affiliation and dimension) just because it occupies one feature of the group."[24]

Even though China and Taiwan dispute each other's claims, Taiwan's near-continuous occupation of Itu Aba since the end of World War II, which is arguably the "main island" in the Spratlys group, could be considered to underpin the claims made by mainland China. Thus, any assertion that Beijing has the ability to alone settle the territorial disputes in the South China Sea is debatable, since complete resolution of sovereignty, and delimitation of maritime boundaries, over these disputed territories really hinges on the final resolution of the PRC–ROC political dispute.

While the ROC and the PRC disagree over the ownership of particular islands in the Spratlys, they would appear to back a single Chinese claim against any other. For example, the PRC and Taiwan dispute Vietnam's claim to sovereignty over the Paracels. In the Spratlys, the PRC, Taiwan, and Vietnam all claim the entire group, while the Philippines, Brunei, and Malaysia have more limited claims. Except for Brunei, all these nations have at one time or another supported military actions—there were almost a dozen reported incidents during the 1990s alone. However, of all the countries that have an interest in these waters, the PRC has arguably spent the most time and money building a comprehensive military-support infrastructure in the South China Sea that might allow it to one day obtain its strategic goals through force.

In the past, the PRC and ROC have each shown a willingness to cooperate against other claimants in the South China Sea dispute. For example, when Sino–Vietnamese tensions led to military conflict in 1988, Taiwan appears to have supported the PRC. Taiwan's defense minister Cheng Wei-yuan reportedly stated that, if Taiwan was asked, it would help defend PLA forces in the Spratlys against a third party. Although this did not happen, there have been credible claims "that PRC garrisons received freshwater supplies from the ROC troops on Itu Aba in that year."[25] There is no guarantee, however, that similar cooperation will occur in future conflicts in the South China Sea.

Beijing's and Taipei's opposing territorial claims make the PRC–ROC situation one of the most complex of any of the ongoing maritime and territorial disputes between neighbors. Both governments agree on their territorial claims against Japan, including the Diaoyu/Senkaku dispute, and they also agree that China's sovereign territory includes the South China Sea. But Taiwan currently occupies some of the largest islands there, including the Pratas Islands and Itu Aba, or Taiping Island, even while the PRC occupies the Paracels and ten small islands in the Spratlys. In general, Taiwan supports the PLAN activities against all other South China Sea claimants, even though the PRC's official policy is that only Beijing has the right to claim sovereignty over the entire South China Sea, including all Taiwan-controlled islands.

SIGNS OF INCREASED PRC–ROC COOPERATION

Since 1992, the PRC and ROC have conducted a series of informal talks designed to clarify their positions on a wide range of issues, including Taiwan's support for the "one China" principle. These talks broke down in 1998, due to the increasing strength of the Taiwanese proindependence movement, as indicated by Chen Shui-bian's presidential victories in 2000 and 2004, but resumed again during June 2008 following the Nationalist return to power. To date, twenty-one agreements have been signed by the two governments. Since 2008, PRC–ROC relations have improved dramatically, including increased travel, cross-strait investment, and direct shipping. Taiwanese investment in the PRC rose sharply, hitting $13.3 billion in 2010 alone.[26]

The May 20, 2008, election of Nationalist candidate Ma Ying-jeou could presage greater ROC–PRC cooperation in the South China Sea, and perhaps other disputed areas as well, such as over the Diaoyu/Senkaku Islands, where the PRC and Taiwan agree that the islands should be China's. While there is still relatively little support on Taiwan for reunifying with the PRC, fully half of Taiwanese agree with continuing economic integration. But the possibility that the Taiwanese government will back down before PRC pressure already concerns some scholars who fear that "Ma may wittingly sell Taiwan out or inadvertently give away too much, with results that will be harmful to the U.S. and potentially ruinous for Taiwan."[27]

In 2010, China and Taiwan signed the Cross-Straits Economic Cooperation Framework Agreement (see appendix 10). As Taiwan's economy moves more toward service industries, which account for 70 percent of the nation's GDP, it is important that Taiwan be able to provide services to the mainland. This has led to PRC–ROC negotiations on the Cross-Strait Trade in Services Agreement. According to President Ma Ying-jeou, the services agreement "underscores Taiwan's commitment to trade liberalization and regional economic integration," and, when signed, Taiwan's service industry should see "an increase of 37 percent." This will "present great opportunities for local [Taiwanese] industries such as banking, e-commerce, food, and gaming software."[28]

Deepening PRC–ROC cooperation could result in other benefits for Beijing as well. It is often overlooked that the Nationalist government on Taiwan still claims territory from its neighbors that equals—and in many cases exceeds—those lands claimed by the PRC. For example, the ROC constitution apparently still lists all of Mongolia as being part of China, and perhaps all of Tuva (formerly Tannu Tuva), which was annexed by the USSR outright during World War II. Taiwan also potentially has a large number of outstanding territorial disputes with countries that do not currently recognize it, including Afghanistan, Bhutan, Myanmar, India, North Korea, Pakistan, Russia, and Tajikistan.

In 1927, the Nationalist government even published a map showing the largest extent of China's former borders (see figure 10.1).[29] In May of 2012, the PRC government appeared to support these Nationalist borders when Foreign Ministry officials stated that Beijing's claim to the South China Sea could be dated to a 1279 survey "commissioned by Emperor Kublai Khan," a Mongol leader from China's Yuan dynasty who controlled most of Eurasia at that time.[30] Notably, Beijing announced on July 26, 2012, that Senior Colonel Cai Xihong would command a newly created Sansha garrison, located on Woody Island in the disputed Paracel chain, to help defend China's South China Sea claims.

Reunification of Taiwan and the mainland might cause further opportunities to extend China's territory. For example, during negotiations leading to the unification of East and West Germany, Poland was very

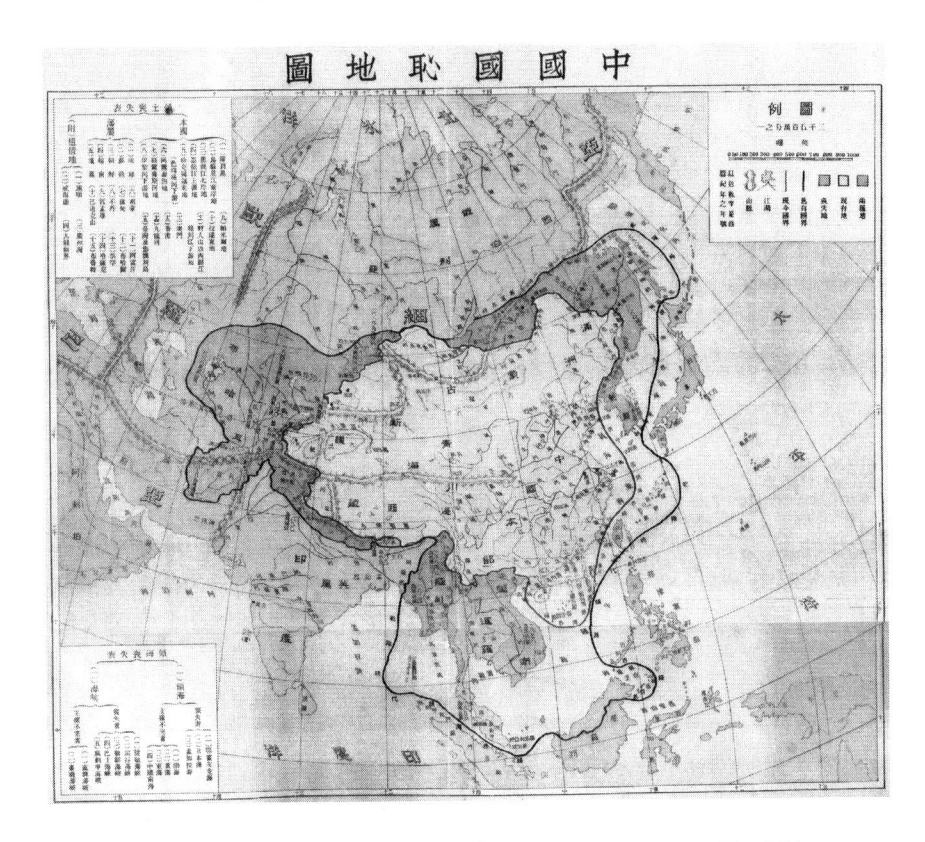

Figure 10.1. 1927 Nationalist Map with "Former Borders" Outer Black Line.
Source: William A. Callahan

concerned when German Chancellor Helmut Kohl indicated that the border with Poland might need to be renegotiated. During the ensuing two-plus-four talks, only the intervention of the United States, France, Great Britain, and the USSR convinced Germany to declare that the current borders would be maintained unchanged: "The treaty which finally came out of these talks, and paved the way for reuniting Germany, calls for the current borders to be maintained."[31] Unlike Kohl's decision to respect the status quo, it is highly doubtful that a newly unified China would back down so quickly before foreign pressure.

This history of Cold War division and eventual reunification raises the possibility that if China and Taiwan ever unify peacefully then a whole host of border disputes that appear to be settled today could be reopened for further discussion and negotiation. Taiwan's territorial claims are most likely larger than those of the PRC, so unification might give Beijing a "second chance" to reopen talks with various bordering countries, based on the Taiwanese claims, where border negotiations have already been completed by the PRC. This, in turn, could open Pandora's box on a whole host of border conflicts.

CONCLUSIONS

The PRC and the United States have faced off many times since the 2001 EP-3 incident. Amid Sino–U.S. tensions in 2009, there was even a "touch of irony" assigning *Chung-Hoon* to guard *Impeccable*, since this vessel was "named for a Chinese-American naval officer awarded the Navy Cross, the nation's second-highest combat decoration, for heroic action against Japanese kamikaze pilots during World War II."[32] Assigning this particular ship to patrol duty could not help but remind the PRC that the two countries had been close allies in World War II against Japan.

The PRC has repeatedly stated that it will not interfere with freedom of navigation in the South China Sea, but it refuses to clarify exactly what areas it claims. Beijing's submission of the infamous nine-dash map of the South China Sea to the Commission on the Limit of the Continental Shelf in May 2009 suggests that the PRC continues to treat this entire region as "historic waters." In the unlikely event that the PRC would be able to persuade the international community as to the validity of its historic waters claim, this could exempt all or part of the South China Sea from freedom of navigation and overflight principles. According to one scholar, "Beijing could be intent on transferring large areas of the South China Sea from a regime in which warships have immunity from its jurisdiction to one in which permission is required for entry. Of course, China cannot now enforce such a regime. But when it is strong enough, it may try to do so."[33]

Taking into account the historical examples of the PRC's maritime disputes—including over the Pratas, Paracel, and Spratly islands—repeated assertions by Beijing beginning in 2002 that it will work with the Association of Southeast Asian Nations (ASEAN) countries to limit frictions over these islands and to resolve their differences peacefully should be met with healthy skepticism. Such doubts are supported by the minimal progress that has been made in the implementation of the confidence-building measures outlined in the 2002 China–ASEAN Declaration on the Conduct of Parties in the South China Sea. In particular, Taiwan is excluded from this agreement, even though Taipei is a major claimant of these disputed territories and actually occupies several of the larger disputed islands in the South China Sea. Conversely, if the PRC and ROC were to one day unify, or create a political united front, then new border claims could perhaps be made based on Taiwanese maps; this might give Beijing a golden opportunity to renegotiate borders that it was already not completely satisfied with.

NOTES

1. David E. Sanger and Steven Lee Myers, "Collision with China: The Negotiations; How Bush Had to Calm Hawks in Devising a Response to China," *New York Times*, April 13, 2001, available online at http://www.nytimes.com/2001/04/13/world/collision-with-china-negotiations-bush-had-calm-hawks-devising-response-china.html.

2. Steven Mufson and Dana Milbank, "Diplomats Resurgent in Bush's 1st Test," *Washington Post*, April 13, 2001.

3. Johanna McGeary, reported by Jay Branegan, James Carney, John F. Dickerson, and Mark Thompson/Washington, Massimo Calabresi with Jeff Powell and Jeffrey Ressner/Whidbey Island "Safe Landing: A Carefully Engineered Game Plan Helped Bush Bring the U.S. Flight Crew Home; An Inside Look," CNN: Inside Politics, April 23, 2001, available online at http://www.cnn.com/ALLPOLITICS/time/2001/04/23/landing.html.

4. Elisabeth Rosenthal, "News Analysis: China Gets White House's Attention, and Some Respect," *New York Times*, April 12, 2001, available online at http://www.nytimes.com/2001/04/12/world/12RESP.html.

5. Bruce A. Elleman, "The Right Skill Set: Joseph Wilson Prueher (1941–)," in *Nineteen Gun Salute: Case Studies of Operational, Strategic, and Diplomatic Naval Leadership during the 20th and Early 21st Centuries*, ed. John B. Hattendorf and Bruce A. Elleman, 242 (Newport, RI: NWC Press, 2010).

6. Tony Capaccio, "Chinese Vessels Harass U.S. Navy Ship, Pentagon Says," Bloomberg.com, March 9, 2009, http://www.bloomberg.com/apps/news?pid=newsarchive&sid=aUMS9YLJ2OmM (accessed March 24, 2011).

7. Ann Scott Tyson, "Navy Sends Destroyer to Protect Surveillance Ship after Incident in South China Sea," *Washington Post*, March 13, 2009, available online at http://www.washingtonpost.com/wp-dyn/content/article/2009/03/12/AR2009031203264.html.

8. Ji Guoxing, "The Legality of the '*Impeccable* Incident,'" *China Security* 5, no. 2 (Spring 2009): 16–21.

9. Jane Macartney, "Chinese and American Ships Clash Again in the Yellow Sea," *Times*, May 6, 2009, http://www.timesonline.co.uk/tol/news/world/asia/article6233796.ece (accessed March 17, 2011).

10. Voice of America, "Pentagon Reports Naval Incident in Yellow Sea," May 5, 2009, available online at http://www.voafanti.com/gate/big5/www.voanews.com/articleprintview/359961.html.

11. Barbara Starr, "Chinese Boats Harassed U.S. Ships, Officials Say," CNN, May 5, 2009, http://articles.cnn.com/2009-05-05/world/china.maritime.harassment_1_chinese-ships-chinese-vessels-yellow-sea?_s=PM:WORLD (accessed March 24, 2011).

12. John K. T. Chao, "South China Sea: Boundary Problems Relating to the Nansha and Hsisha Islands," in *Chinese Yearbook of International Law and Affairs*, vol. 9, *1989–1990*, ed. Hungdah Chiu, 113 (Taipei: Chinese Society of International Law, 1991).

13. Bruce Swanson, *Eighth Voyage of the Dragon: A History of China's Quest for Seapower* (Annapolis, MD: Naval Institute Press, 1982), 117–20.

14. Pao-Min Chang, *Sino–Vietnamese Territorial Dispute* (New York: Praeger, 1986), 18.

15. Jianming Shen, "China's Sovereignty over the South China Sea Islands: A Historical Perspective," *Chinese JIL* (2002): 146, available online at http://chinesejil.oxfordjournals.org/content/1/1/94.full.pdf.

16. Hungdah Chiu and Choon-Ho Park, "Legal Status of the Paracel and Spratly Islands," *Ocean Development and International Law*, 3, no. 1 (1975): 19, text available online at http://colp.sjtu.edu.cn/image/20130227/20130227112060586058.pdf.

17. Government of the People's Republic of China, "Declaration on China's Territorial Sea," *Peking [Beijing] Review*, no. 1 (September 9, 1958): 21, English text available online at http://www.state.gov/documents/organization/58832.pdf.

18. Ibid. A photographic image of this letter can be found at Wikipedia.org, "File: 1958 Diplomatic Note from Phamvandong to Zhouenlai," http://en.wikipedia.org /wiki/File:1958_diplomatic_note_from_phamvandong_to_zhouenlai.jpg (accessed January 11, 2012).

19. Ministry of Foreign Affairs of China, "China's Indisputable Sovereignty Over the Xisha and Nansha islands," *Beijing Review* 23, no. 7 (February 18, 1980): 21.

20. Yang Zhiben 杨志本, ed., 中国海军百科全书 [*China Navy Encyclopedia*], vol. 2 (Beijing: 海潮出版社 [Sea Tide Press], 1998), 1,747.

21. Vu-Duc Vuong, "Between a Sea and a Hard Rock," *AsianWeek*, January 8, 2008, http://www.asianweek.com/2008/01/08/between-a-sea-and-a-hard-rock/.

22. Brian McCartan, "Roiling the Waters in the Spratlys," *Asia Sentinel*, February 4, 2008, http://www.asiasentinel.com/politics/roiling-the-waters-in-the-spratlys/.

23. Peter Kien-hong Yu, *The Four Archipelagoes in the South China Sea* (Taipei: Council for Advanced Policy Studies, 1991), 10–18.

24. R. Haller-Trost, *Occasional Paper No. 14: The Spratly Islands; a Study on the Limitations of International Law* (Canterbury: University of Kent Centre of South-East Asian Studies, 1990), 61.

25. Kristen Nordhaug, "Taiwan and the South China Sea Conflict: The 'China Connection' Revisited," paper presented at the Workshop on the Conflict in the South China Sea, Oslo, Norway, April 24–26, 1999. http://www.southchinasea.org/docs/Nordhaug.pdf; Mark Valencia, personal communication with the author, March 29, 1999.

26. "Taiwan Investment in China Rises Sharply in 2010," *Straits Times*, December 31, 2010.

27. Jacques deLisle, "Taiwan under President Ma Ying-jeou: Changing Horses in the Middle of the Strait? Taiwan's External Relations," *Foreign Policy Research Institute*, June 5, 2008, text available online at http://www.isn.ethz.ch/Digital-Library/Articles/Detail/?id=88435.

28. *Taiwan Today*, "Ma Touts Cross-Strait Trade in Services Agreement," June 27, 2014, http://www.taiwantoday.tw/ct.asp?xItem=219021&ctNode=445.

29. *Zhonghua guochi ditu, zaiban* [Map of China's National Humiliation, Reprint] (Shanghai: Zhonghua Shuju, 1927); reprinted with permission from William A. Callahan, "The Cartography of National Humiliation and the Emergence of China's Geobody," *Public Culture* 21, no. 1 (2009): 154–55.

30. Jane Perlez, "Beijing Exhibiting New Assertiveness in South China Sea," *New York Times*, May 31, 2012, http://www.nytimes.com/2012/06/01/world/asia/beijing-projects-power-in-strategic-south-china-sea.html.

31. David Petina, "Unified Germany: Friend or Foe?" *Res Publica* 2, no. 1 (January 1991), http://www.ashbrook.org/publicat/respub/v2n1/petina1.html (accessed on October 27, 2011).

32. Richard Halloran, "US–Chinese Contacts Are Imperative for Military," *Taipei Times*, March 17, 2009, http://www.taipeitimes.com/News/editorials/archives/2009/03/17/2003438702.

33. Mark J. Valencia, "Tension Increasing in South China Sea," *Honolulu Advertiser*, April 5, 2001, http://the.honoluluadvertiser.com/article/2001/Apr/05/op/op05a.html.

Conclusion

The Taiwan Strait Challenge

The Taiwan Strait acts as a maritime buffer, keeping two belligerents from attacking each other and thereby precipitating a larger war, perhaps even a global war. But the regular and intermittent patrols of the U.S. Navy's Taiwan Patrol Force in the Taiwan Strait from 1950 to 1979 did more than simply buffer the two Chinas. Acting as moving trip wires, which, if provoked, could quickly call in massive reinforcements from the Seventh Fleet, these USN patrols also exerted varying degrees of military pressure on the PRC along the highly strategic Taiwan Strait. When needed, tensions could be ramped up along the strait to divert China's attention from other theaters, as happened during the summer of 1953 when Beijing agreed to an armistice ending the Korean War. In helping attain this goal, the Taiwan Patrol Force achieved an enormously important military objective.

The U.S. policies in the Taiwan Strait produced valuable economic effects as well. The combination of the ten-year Nationalist naval blockade, plus the twenty-one-year-long U.S. strategic embargo, limited the PRC's foreign maritime trade, which forced Beijing to rely more heavily on the USSR, both as a trade partner and a conduit—by way of the Trans-Siberian Railroad—with other trade partners in Eastern Europe. Over time, China's economic overreliance on the USSR exacerbated underlying political tensions that eventually resulted in the collapse of the Sino–Soviet monolith. The split met with Washington's expectations: forcing the two Communist countries to work together meant that increasingly bitter tensions eventually ripped them apart. By 1960, therefore, the U.S. goal of using an economic weapon to break up the Sino–Soviet alliance was achieved, even while Taiwan was well on its ways to creating its own economic miracle. Both outcomes were to a large degree aided, and in some measure were a direct result, of the presence of the Taiwan Patrol Force.

Finally, Washington's political signal in 1969 changing the Taiwan Patrol Force from a constant to an intermittent patrol helped bring about the decades-long diplomatic realignment of the PRC leaders toward the United States. By June of 1971, the U.S. strategic embargo of China ended, ushering in President Richard Nixon's historic visit in 1972, the gradual opening of U.S. diplomatic relations with the PRC, and finally President

Jimmy Carter's recognition of the PRC in 1979. Arguably, this political reorientation allowed China and the United States to cooperate to exert pressure on the USSR from both East and West—exploiting Russia's historically most-dreaded fear of a two-front war. This policy deepened the Soviet Union's domestic and international problems and eventually helped lead to the collapse of its empire, the end of the Cold War, and the demise of the USSR.

MILITARY IMPACT OF U.S. POLICIES IN THE TAIWAN STRAIT

The U.S. government's decision to establish the Taiwan Patrol Force in 1950 meant that neither the PRC nor the ROC ever mounted a major attack across the Taiwan Strait. This neutralized the Taiwan Strait and prevented a regional conflict's ever escalating into a new Hot War in Asia. This objective remained valid during most of the duration of the patrol's existence, since all attempts to urge a peace agreement on the PRC and Taiwan failed. In April of 1955, during the first Taiwan Strait crisis, the U.S. government even proposed that the Nationalists would evacuate all disputed offshore islands if the PRC would promise to not liberate Taiwan by force. Zhou Enlai flatly rejected this proposal, instead insisting that Chiang Kai-shek and his military forces first "leave the island" of Taiwan.[1]

Given the PRC's refusal to guarantee Taiwan's security, an ongoing and robust U.S. Navy presence in the Taiwan Strait was essential. The presence of the Taiwan Patrol Force not only undermined any PRC plans to invade Taiwan during the early 1950s but also allowed the U.S. government to exert military pressure on the PRC—by means of threats of unleashing Chiang Kai-shek—to reallocate military units away from the north and to the south. In this regard, the Taiwan Patrol Force acted much like a vernier switch, allowing the USN to increase or decrease cross-strait tensions to suit the U.S. government's larger policy objectives.

In March of 1956, British intelligence services gave the Taiwan Patrol Force credit for keeping the peace throughout the region. Their report concluded that, although the Communists were capable of launching a full-scale attack on the offshore islands, it is "highly improbable that they will conduct military operations of this magnitude as long as the Seventh Fleet remains in the area." Instead of trying to stage an invasion, therefore, the PRC falsely assumed that time was on its side and that "it would be pointless to fight for areas which they hope to acquire in due course through subversion and propaganda."[2]

An equally important military goal of the Taiwan Patrol Force was to reassure America's East Asian allies—including Japan, South Korea, the Philippines, and Australia—that the PRC could not invade the first island chain. The Japanese were especially worried about Chinese expansionism. In 1955, a Japanese official in Taipei clarified that it was the physical location of Taiwan, dominating the sea-lanes from Japan to the south, that mattered most to Tokyo: "for the future the real problem of Taiwan was the strategic value of the island itself and the importance of keeping it from the Chinese Communists rather than the Chiang Kai-shek government."[3] In 1958, when discussing his upcoming talks with Chiang, Dulles emphasized that the Japanese were watching to see whether the United States would give way to China on the issue of the disputed offshore islands. Dulles even expressed concern that if the Japanese thought the United States was weaker than the PRC "they would go over to the Chinese Communists just as quickly as they could."[4]

The Taiwan Patrol Force supported America's Asian alliances and coalition partners by making it more difficult for the PRC to invade Taiwan. One method to dissuade the PRC from attacking was to provide the Nationalists with a dependable source of military equipment and training to defend themselves, even while not giving them sufficiently advanced equipment to allow Taiwan to attack the PRC of its own volition. According to a U.S. intelligence advisory committee report from April 1957, in the near term the "Nationalists are very unlikely to launch an invasion or, in the absence of Chinese Communist provocation, to initiate other major military action."[5] On June 25, 1962, Rusk even reminded the British foreign secretary, Lord Home, that Chiang Kai-shek would not have U.S. support if he attempted to attack the mainland, and it was agreed that the British chargé d'affaires would tell PRC leaders that the "United States had done and were doing everything possible to restrain the Nationalists from provocative action."[6]

Meanwhile, the Taiwan Patrol Force also contributed to high morale in Taiwan. In February of 1955, a report from the British consulate in Tamsui, Taiwan, concluded that the morale of the Nationalist troops was excellent and that there was no chance of the PRC winning Taiwan by "subversion alone."[7] For the overseas Chinese community, a strong Taiwan acted as a viable alternative to aligning with the PRC. In October of 1956, a U.S. intelligence advisory committee correctly predicted that "morale on Taiwan probably will not weaken critically so long as the people there remain confident of firm U.S. support for the defense of Taiwan."[8]

The Taiwan Patrol Force was truly a maritime buffer between the PRC and Taiwan, which succeeded in neutralizing both sides of the Taiwan Strait. While constant patrols were replaced with intermittent patrols in 1969, USN vessels continued to transit the Taiwan Strait on a regular basis through the mid- to late 1970s. Following Nixon's 1972 visit to China, however, it became clear to many USN officers that the patrol would eventually be terminated. In preparation for this day, U.S. military advisors redoubled their efforts to assist the Nationalist Navy. According to Admiral Philip Beshany, "I believe that there was a very deep feeling there—and there's no question about the Chinese Military and the

American counterparts on the island—that was a very strong bond and a desire to work together. I think all of us, and I don't know of any of my officers who didn't have a strong and motivated feeling to help these people to be able to defend themselves."[9]

That a war never broke out between the PRC and Taiwan was directly due to the certainty of military intervention by the Seventh Fleet. Maintaining the military balance between the PRC and Taiwan successfully kept the peace for the past sixty-five years even while making the PRC and Taiwan's economic development the most important measure of success. From the earliest days of the Taiwan Patrol Force, its goals included exerting economic pressure on the PRC.

U.S. ECONOMIC IMPACT ON THE ROC AND THE PRC

The Korean War may have been the initial catalyst for the U.S. government's decision to neutralize the Taiwan Strait, but the U.S. policy of isolating the PRC economically had arguably already started during the summer of 1949 and then increased in January 1950 with the adoption of an embargo on strategic goods. Beijing's decision to intervene in the Korean War resulted in China's further economic isolation, as the U.S. government adopted a full strategic embargo. Faced with the Nationalist naval blockade on the one hand and a U.S.-led embargo on the other, the PRC had to make up its trade losses by turning to the Soviet Union. Before World War II, only 1 percent of China's foreign trade was with the USSR; by 1957, this figure skyrocketed to over 50 percent.[10]

Following the June 1950 creation of the Taiwan Patrol Force, the PRC immediately condemned the U.S. neutralization policy as an aggressive action and demanded that the Seventh Fleet withdraw from the Taiwan Strait. Beijing claimed the U.S. policy favored Taipei. But, according to British statistics covering the first nine months of 1950, the value of PRC imports from Hong Kong were three and a half times the value of goods imported in 1949. Therefore, prior to China's decision to intervene in Korea in November of 1950, the U.S. neutralization plan actually stabilized cross-strait relations, which helped promote international trade with China. As reported by British officials, Anglo–Chinese trade was booming during most of 1950, since there was active trade between Hong Kong and the major PRC coastal ports, at first through the Nationalist blockade but even more freely since "President Truman's declaration neutralizing Formosa."[11]

After the PLA's intervention in the Korean War, the JCS considered adopting a total naval blockade against the PRC. However, Hong Kong's strategic vulnerability had to be considered, so instead of a blockade the U.S. government tightened the embargo on strategic goods. The ongoing Nationalist blockade was secretly used to help enforce the U.S. embargo.

Washington's long-range goal was to deny the PRC a wider range of trade partners. Over time, it was hoped that this would add additional friction to the already tense Sino–Soviet relations.

This plan worked perfectly. By the mid-1950s, the PRC was forced to turn more and more to the Soviet bloc countries. It signed over one hundred trade treaties and agreements with the USSR and Eastern European countries, as compared to only twenty to thirty treaties with the rest of the world. The Nationalist blockade and the U.S. strategic embargo had their intended impact. On July 18, 1955, the U.S. consulate general in Hong Kong reported that Chinese officials were admitting that the U.S. embargo had slowed down their industrial program, causing the sudden loss of an estimated 75 percent of their foreign trade. As a result, China was "forced to turn to the USSR as a source of supply and as their prime market, which resulted in highly adverse terms of trade and required an increase in the overall volume of trade in order to maintain the desired pace of industrialization."[12] Due to these economic factors, by the late 1950s China's debts to the USSR had grown to almost $2 billion, roughly equal to the U.S. government's economic aid to Taiwan between 1950 and 1969.

While an extremely long-term policy—taking well over two decades to complete and therefore not one that brought immediate benefits to Washington—the Nationalist blockade and the U.S. strategic embargo were highly successful in furthering the Sino–Soviet rift. One Dutch official confirmed in 1957 that there had been a profound deterioration in the PRC's economic situation and in living conditions since he had arrived in China eighteen months before. This sharp decline could not help but create tensions between China and its Soviet advisors, and "the Russians he met while traveling in China were very frank about their contempt for the Chinese, their dislike of their assignments in China, and their eagerness to return to the USSR as soon as possible."[13]

By the late 1950s, tensions between the PRC and the Soviet Union had worsened dramatically. In order to try to begin to pay off China's enormous foreign debt to the USSR, Mao Zedong adopted economic policies, including the Great Leap Forward, which produced a nationwide famine.[14] Some historians have argued that the resulting Sino–Soviet rift took Washington by surprise and that the U.S. government did not adopt policies to widen the rift.[15] But others have confirmed that Secretary of State Dulles actively sought to split the Chinese and Russians by driving them closer together.[16] Washington had to be careful that their plan would not backfire, so Eisenhower refused to even talk about Sino–Soviet tensions so as to avoid saying something that might undermine the development of the Sino–Soviet split.[17] In fact, the Sino–Soviet monolith's collapse in 1960 was fully in line with Washington's strategic objectives.

Meanwhile, with U.S. assistance, Taiwan took a completely different development path. British officials reported in 1955 that Taiwan was prosperous due to U.S. aid and that the local standard of living was higher than that of most other Asian countries. While political rights in Taiwan were negligible, the British consulate found no large-scale corruption, so the average person on Taiwan could "enjoy considerable freedom otherwise."[18] Eschewing a simple military solution to China's unification, Chiang Kai-shek prophetically told an Australian newspaper that Taiwan would focus on economic development: "We shall continue to build up Taiwan as an example of what free men can do."[19]

When the Nationalists took power, Taiwan had an annual per capita income of less that $100, putting it on a par with India. It had no industrial base beyond some small textile factories, a few modern sugar refineries, and other food-processing plants, and 60 percent of the work force was employed in agriculture. War left the island suffering from acute inflation, supply shortages, and a massive population influx from the mainland. The Nationalists, acutely aware of their many failings during the Chinese Civil War, focused on land reform and inflation control to solidify their rule. These proved to be highly successful and were completed by 1953.

Foreign education proved essential to Taiwan's survival. A high percentage of those in charge of Taiwan's economic planning had advanced degrees from the United States. Taiwanese planners concluded that they should emulate the Japanese model for economic development. Initially they focused on an import-substitution strategy. This entailed import restrictions to enable Taiwanese infant industries to become established. In contrast to the PRC's economic-growth policies, which focused on heavy industry, Taiwanese planners emphasized light industry, particularly textiles. Soon they also developed their capacity to produce bicycles, flour, cement, and other goods for the domestic consumer market. Production was not aimed specifically at military production, the focus that the PRC continued to follow.

By 1960, Taiwanese planners shifted from import substitution to export promotion. They introduced economic reforms to remove tariff walls, foreign-exchange controls, and restrictions on direct foreign investment. They also provided tax incentives for targeted export industries, made massive infrastructure investments, and turned to the development of heavy industry. By 1965, U.S. aid was down to 2 percent of Taiwan's GNP, and a generation of political and technological leaders, particularly engineers and scientists, had received U.S. advanced degrees and returned home with their expertise. Taiwan's economy also benefited from all the U.S. procurements necessary to prosecute the Korean and Vietnam wars.

In the 1970s and 1980s, Taipei targeted Ten Major Projects to improve the island's infrastructure, including a superhighway system, an international airport, two state-of-the-art port facilities, modernization of the railway system, construction of two nuclear power plants, an integrated steel mill, and shipbuilding facilities. These investments provided economic efficiencies that helped counteract the dramatic rise in oil prices resulting from the 1973 international oil embargo by the Organization of Petroleum Exporting Countries. From 1974 to 1984, Taiwan had the second-highest economic-growth rate in the world after Singapore.

The rapidly growing economies of Taiwan, Singapore, Hong Kong, and South Korea collectively became known as Asia's "Little Tigers." During the 1950s, real GNP growth in Taiwan exceeded 7 percent per year, while in the 1960s and 1970s it reached almost 10 percent. The ratio of agricultural production dropped quickly, from about a third in the 1950s to only 3 percent in the 1970s. During the same period, the share of industry in the economy increased from about 25 percent to 35 percent. Taiwanese businesses were among the first in Asia to emphasize developing high-tech industries and soon became third behind the United States and Japan in computer-hardware manufacturing. In particular, Taiwan took advantage of the East Asian sea-lanes along its shores to create a globalized domestic economy; its Evergreen Shipping Company soon become one of the largest container companies in the world.

In order to work efficiently in the global economy, Taiwan has adopted international law wholesale. Conformity to international law had been the key issue bedeviling Sino–Western relations since the Qing dynasty. While business contacts remain important, the ultimate arbiter of business relations is contract law before a duly appointed judiciary. In contrast, the PRC did not reform its legal system until after its application in 1984 to join the General Agreement on Tariff and Trade (GATT), the predecessor organization to the World Trade Organization (WTO). It would take China fifteen years to implement the required legal reforms allowing it to become a full member of the WTO on November 10, 2001. Taiwan secured its membership one day later, not because of long-standing deficiencies in its own legal system, but because the PRC had used its international influence to make sure that it was admitted first.

The most spectacular change in Taiwanese society has been the rapidly growing prosperity of the general population, to the point where the International Monetary Fund reclassified Taiwan in 1997 as an advanced economy. Fully half the population considers itself to be part of the middle class. In 2000, Taiwan's twenty-two million people had created a GNP over one-quarter that of the PRC with its 1.2 billion people. This translated into a GNP per capita in China of $1,000 versus $16,000 for Taiwan, putting Taiwan on a par with Spain. Even accounting for the greater purchasing power of $1,000 in the PRC than in Taiwan, the difference in standards of living remains dramatic. Taiwan's foreign-exchange reserves became so large in the late 1980s (hitting $70 billion) that they approximated half the GNP of the PRC at that time. Some joked that Taiwan could soon buy back the PRC piece by piece.

These successes became known as the Taiwanese economic miracle. A small island nation with few natural resources and a tenuous international standing had catapulted itself in two generations from poverty into the ranks of the most-developed nations. The miracle was a hybrid of Han culture, primarily originating from South China and Fujian Province; Meiji Japanese agricultural and business models; technical expertise from U.S. higher education; and Nationalist Party leadership. Although the Nationalists had lost the civil war, they seemed to have won the peace. It remains unclear how many decades it will take the PRC to match the current Taiwanese standard of living.

U.S. support for Taiwan was absolutely crucial to its success. It has been largely overlooked that Taiwan's GNP grew 72.7 percent between 1953 and 1961, which was an average increase of 7.1 percent per year, with a high of 8.4 percent in 1954. Even more importantly, Taiwan's industrial-growth rates between 1953 and 1978 averaged 15.9 percent annually, with a 25.4 percent increase in 1978 alone. Without a doubt, Taiwan's enormous growth rates were made possible by the security provided by the U.S. Navy, backed up by a large infusion of American economic aid and scientific expertise.[20] In large measure, the PRC's huge growth rates since the adoption of the open door in the 1980s have merely replicated Taiwan's earlier economic growth from 1950 to 1978.

In the final analysis, Beijing's overwhelming reliance on Moscow restricted China's economic options, thereby exacerbating friction within the international Communist movement. The end result was the shift of the PRC away from the Soviet bloc and closer to the West. Following the 1960 split, the PRC's army and naval forces became focused not just on a domestic foe—Taiwan—but on a foreign one as well—China's former ally, the Soviet Union. During the mid- to late 1960s, Sino–Soviet tensions erupted into open fighting along the Amur River to the north. There were even valid concerns that this conflict might grow into a nuclear war. These border conflicts helped prompt the PRC government's political decision to begin the process of opening diplomatic relations with the United States.

THE TAIWAN STRAIT POLICY'S POLITICAL IMPACT

Ever since the U.S. government established its Taiwan Strait policy in 1950, the U.S. Navy's defense of the offshore islands denied the PRC the opportunity to invade Taiwan and politically unify all of China.[21] By ensuring that any PRC invasion could not succeed, even while intensifying the PRC's increasingly tense relations with the USSR, the Taiwan Patrol Force contributed to bringing about a seminal political shift in the PRC's foreign diplomacy. Within little more than a decade after the Sino–Soviet split, the PRC moved from being a Soviet ally to opening diplomatic relations with the United States. President Nixon's visit to Beijing in 1972 eventually led to full U.S. recognition of the PRC under President Carter in 1979, which was an essential step leading to a two-front strategy against the USSR.

The Taiwan Patrol Force was a necessary compromise underpinning the U.S. Cold War alliance with the United Kingdom. On the surface, U.S. and UK economic policies with the PRC differed dramatically. But they both sought the same goal: bringing the PRC into the Western camp. Rather than cutting China off from international trade, the British thought that it was better to leave the door open. This difference caused friction in Anglo–U.S. relations. In 1962, Rusk told Harold Macmillan that "it was not comfortable for the United States when the United Kingdom traded with China and the United States provided the gendarmes to keep the Chinese in their place."[22] In private, however, Foreign Secretary Selwyn Lloyd reassured Dulles that "Your troubles are our troubles," and he even asked Dulles, "is there any way in which we can help?"[23]

Over time, this carrot-and-stick approach contributed to Beijing's political decision to move closer to the West. In late 1959, the U.S. State Department felt compelled to remind the Department of Defense of the Taiwan Patrol Force's political role. After a September 14, 1959, shift in the patrol pattern in the Taiwan Strait that had been authorized by the U.S. Seventh Fleet without first consulting the Department of State, a memorandum was prepared by State, criticizing the DOD. After emphasizing that the Free World had confidence that the United States would adhere strictly to a "posture of restraint vis-à-vis the Chinese Communists" and "eschew unnecessary actions that could lead to, or give a plausible pretext for, Communist counteraction," the memorandum concluded that "It is therefore requested that in the future, the Department of Defense inform the Department of State of any contemplated change in the Taiwan Strait patrol pattern in an inshore direction sufficiently in advance that its political implications may be fully assessed and given due weight in the final decision."[24]

Clearly, the Taiwan Patrol Force was being used by the U.S. State Department as a political tool to impact the PRC's behavior. Due to the Vietnam War, Sino–U.S. relations remained particularly unfriendly throughout the 1960s. However, in March of 1969 a series of border incidents along the Ussuri and Amur rivers pitted the Chinese PLA against the Soviet Red Army.[25] There were real concerns that a Sino–Soviet conflict might even escalate into a nuclear war.[26] Although neither side was victorious, the 1969 clashes gave the PLA confidence that it could counter the Red Army. This set the political stage for China's leaders to adopt a new foreign-policy initiative by promoting the opening of diplomatic relations with the United States.

The Nixon administration's 1969 decision to change the Taiwan Patrol Force from a permanent to an intermittent patrol sent a potent signal to

Beijing. Although Taiwan was told that this change was due to economic necessity, it was in fact a political decision. This first small step in opening relations with the PRC eventually led to Nixon's historic trip to Beijing from February 21 to 28, 1972. Following this much-publicized visit, Mao Zedong endorsed a major military-modernization program that called for developing an oceangoing navy. The PRC's naval modernization, which started in the 1950s with Soviet assistance, had ground to a halt in the early 1960s. Without foreign help, China's domestic production of naval vessels slowed almost to a standstill. Beginning in the early 1980s the PLAN began to grow again, largely with U.S. assistance.[27] Rather than opposing Taiwan, however, the PRC's military forces were now almost entirely focused on the USSR and its allies, including the recently reunified Vietnam, which was a firm supporter of the Soviet Union.

On January 1, 1979, Jimmy Carter and Deng Xiaoping brought this lengthy political process to its ultimate conclusion when they exchanged mutual recognition. As a result of this Sino–U.S. rapprochement, the USSR suddenly had to be concerned about war with American-led NATO forces in the West and Chinese forces in the East. Throughout the 1980s, the United States and China cooperated in their efforts to undermine the Soviet Union. By 1989, these policies had helped precipitate the collapse of the Berlin Wall and the end of the Cold War, followed two years later in 1991 by the breakup of the Soviet Union.

While the USN's impact on these seminal political events was largely outside the public eye, China's gradual political reorientation from a member of the Soviet bloc to cooperation with the United States against the USSR was just one result of the constant political pressure put on Beijing by the United States' containment policy and by U.S. allies; to a large degree, it was the Taiwan Patrol Force that was America's tip of the spear in this larger effort, as best shown by its 1969 role in signaling Beijing of Washington's desire to open talks. Thus, a relatively obscure naval operation helped produce enormous political consequences far beyond the scope of its daily activities. Using similar methods, the U.S. Navy has continued to shape the military, economic, and political environment in East Asia.

THE FUTURE OF THE TAIWAN STRAIT

The U.S. government's buffer operation was conducted from 1950 through 1979, but the neutralization of the Taiwan Strait arguably continues unchanged to this day. The U.S. Navy may not operate ships on a daily basis in the Taiwan Strait, but in 1995 and 1996, a number of USN vessels, including the aircraft carriers *Nimitz* and *Independence*, conducted patrons near the island.[28] It is widely acknowledged that U.S. intervention may have "closed out the option" of PLA escalation.[29]

The U.S. Navy also signaled its opposition to PRC missile tests. The Chinese certainly interpreted the U.S. decision to send *Independence* to be a political signal that Washington supported Taiwan's independence from China. According to Admiral Prueher, *Independence* just happened to be in the Philippines, and so it was the logical choice to be sent. As he later recalled, it just "happened to be that ship. I tell the Chinese, you give us better credit for planning" than we deserve. "It was just there in the Philippines."[30] The *Nimitz* carrier group also did not reappear in the vicinity of Taiwan until the Chinese missile tests were almost over, arriving in the South China Sea on March 21, 1996.[31] The U.S. government even reportedly slowed the *Nimitz* arrival once the PLA began to deescalate the missile campaign.[32]

Similar to the Taiwan Strait crises during the 1950s, the U.S. decision in 1995 and 1996 to send in aircraft carriers clearly had a profound effect on Chinese strategic thinking. According to Vice Admiral Lyle Bien, USN (Ret.), Commander of Carrier Group 7, who was embarked in USS *Nimitz* throughout 1996, the Chinese were "very embarrassed by their inability to respond to our presence, and so much of their antiaccess capability developed since 1996 is precisely in response to this event."[33] Rear Admiral James P. Wisecup, Captain of the USS *Callaghan* (DDG 994) in 1996 and later the president of the U.S. Naval War College, said he could imagine—had the shoe been on the other foot—the type of meeting that might have occurred after such an incident, with China's leaders demanding of the PLAN, "I want to know what you are doing to make sure that never happens again."[34]

The PRC's failure to halt American intervention in the Taiwan Strait in 1995 and 1996 has almost certainly contributed to PLAN efforts to buy and build a formidable arsenal of area denial capabilities. These include ballistic missiles, conventional submarines, modern combat aircraft, and guided-missile destroyers equipped with supersonic antiship missiles. The PLAN also purchased a Soviet-era aircraft carrier from the Ukraine, rebuilt it, and renamed it *Liaoning*.

The PRC acquisition of such high-tech sea denial weapons has increased the risk to USN forces, so the U.S. Navy has arguably been used more selectively since the mid-1990s. On purpose, an aircraft carrier was not called in during the 2001 EP-3 standoff, since there were legitimate fears that this action might backfire. Prueher concluded after achieving a successful outcome that negotiating with the PRC is really a job of "building ladders for Chinese to climb down," and he wanted to be careful not to make China "lose face."[35] Later, in March of 2009, the U.S. Navy responded more forcefully to the *Impeccable* incident by deploying *Chung-Hoon*, named after a famous Chinese-American.

The Taiwan Patrol Force has enjoyed a sporadic existence, in spirit if not in name, ever since the mid-1990s. So long as the PRC's goals include reunification with Taiwan by force, then the underlying conditions for the patrol's existence remain.[36] It is mainly the presence of the U.S. Navy that reminds Beijing of Washington's commitment to defend Taiwan.[37] With the recent "pivot to Asia" in U.S. foreign policy, the U.S. Navy remains the primary tool for crafting U.S. military, economic, and political goals of retaining manageable military relations with the PRC, even while promoting China's continued economic integration with the rest of the world, acceptance of international law, and hopefully its gradual transition to Western-style democracy. Sixty-five years after the Taiwan Patrol Force's 1950 creation, these goals are equally important to U.S. national security. Considering the large number of times USN vessels have either been sent to the Taiwan Strait or to adjacent East Asian waters since the mid-1990s, it could well be argued that Taiwan Patrol Force activity has continued uninterrupted to this day.

NOTES

1. John Foster Dulles Papers, Princeton University, Reel 210/211, April 25, 1955, 93219.
2. John Foster Dulles Papers, Princeton University, Reel 212/213, March 6, 1956, 94964.
3. John Foster Dulles Papers, Princeton University, Reel 212/213, November 22, 1955, 94355.
4. Telegram from Foreign Office to UK Embassy, Washington, DC, October 22, 1958, TNA/UK, PREM 11/3738.
5. John Foster Dulles Papers, Princeton University, Reel 216, April 5, 1957, 97367.
6. "Record of a Conversation between the Foreign Secretary and Mr. Dean Rusk on Monday, June 25, 1962," TNA/UK, PREM 11/3738.
7. Report from UK Consulate, Tamsui, to Foreign Office (confidential), February 24, 1955, PREM 11/879.
8. John Foster Dulles Papers, Princeton University, Reel 214/215, October 11, 1956, 96227.
9. Philip A. Beshany, *The Reminiscences of Vice Admiral Philip A. Beshany, U.S. Navy (Retired)*, Oral History 45 (Annapolis, MD: U.S. Naval Institute, 1983), 944–45.
10. "Notes on Sino–Soviet Relations," 1958, TNA/UK, FO 371/133366.
11. Effect on British shipping of stoppage of trade with China, January 16, 1951, TNA/UK, FO 371/ 92273, 2–3.
12. John Foster Dulles Papers, Princeton University, Reel 210/211, July 18, 1953, 93678.
13. John Foster Dulles Papers, Princeton University, Reel 216, April 5, 1957, 97310.
14. Lawrence C. Reardon, *The Reluctant Dragon: Crisis Cycles in Chinese Foreign Economic Policy* (Seattle: University of Washington Press, 2002), 103–4.
15. Shu Guang Zhang, *Economic Cold War: America's Embargo against China and the Sino–Soviet Alliance, 1949–1963* (Stanford, CA: Stanford University Press, 2001), 237.
16. Marilyn B. Young, *The Vietnam Wars, 1945–1990* (New York: HarperCollins, 1991), 309–10.
17. Gordan H. Chang, *Friends and Enemies: The United States, China, and the Soviet Union, 1948–1972* (Stanford, CA: Stanford University Press, 1990), 331, note 24.

18. Report from the UK Consulate, Tamsui, to the Foreign Office (confidential), February 24, 1955, PREM 11/879.

19. John Foster Dulles Papers, Princeton University, Reel 214/215, August 29, 1956, 96035.

20. Sheppard Glass, "Some Aspects of Formosa's Economic Growth," in *Formosa Today*, ed. Mark Mancall, 70 (New York: Frederick A. Praeger, 1964). Edwin K. Snyder, A. James Gregor, and Maria Hsia Chang, *The Taiwan Relations Act and the Defense of the Republic of China* (Berkeley: University of California Press, 1980), 3.

21. Piers M. Wood and Charles D. Ferguson, "How China Might Invade Taiwan," *Naval War College Review* 54, no. 4 (Autumn 2001): 55–68, https://www.usnwc.edu/getattachment/cee1306d-0372-47cb-8261-1c7d1a5f0422/How-China-Might-Invade-Taiwan---Wood,-Piers-M-,-Fe.aspx.

22. "Record of a Conversation after Dinner at 1 Carlton Gardens on June 24, 1962," TNA/UK, PREM 11/3738.

23. Letter from Selwyn Lloyd to John Foster Dulles (top secret), September 11, 1958, TNA/UK, CAB 21/3272.

24. "Memorandum Prepared in the Department of State," undated, in *Foreign Relations of the United States, 1958–1960*, vol. 19, *China*, ed. Harriet Dashiell Schwar and gen. ed. Glen W. LaFantasie, 627–28 (Washington, DC: United States Government Printing Office, 1996).

25. Bruce A. Elleman, *Modern Chinese Warfare, 1795–1989* (London: Routledge Press, 2001), 280.

26. Andrew Osborn, Peter Foster, "USSR Planned nuclear attack on China in 1969," *Telegraph*, May 13, 2010, http://www.telegraph.co.uk/news/worldnews/asia/china/7720461/USSR-planned-nuclear-attack-on-China-in-1969.html (accessed December 16, 2010).

27. James C. Bussert and Bruce A. Elleman, *People's Liberation Army Navy (PLAN): Combat Systems Technology, 1949–2010* (Annapolis, MD: Naval Institute Press, 2011), 12–14.

28. Nicholas D. Kristof, "Off Taiwan, U.S. Sailors Are Unworried," *New York Times*, March 19, 1996, http://www.nytimes.com/1996/03/19/world/off-taiwan-us-sailors-are-unworried.html.

29. Douglas Porch, "The Taiwan Strait Crisis of 1996: Strategic Implications for the United States Navy," *Naval War College Review* 52, no. 3 (Summer 1999): 21–23, original edition downloadable from https://www.usnwc.edu/Publications/Naval-War-College-Review/Archivedissues/1990s/1999-Summer.aspx.

30. Bruce A. Elleman, "The Right Skill Set: Joseph Wilson Prueher (1941–)," in *Nineteen Gun Salute: Case Studies of Operational, Strategic, and Diplomatic Naval Leadership during the 20th and Early 21st Centuries*, ed. John B. Hattendorf and Bruce A. Elleman, 237 (Newport, RI: NWC Press, 2010).

31. Jonathan Drake, "Nimitz Battle Group Ploughs Past Singapore," *Reuters*, March 21, 1996.

32. Wan-chin Tai, "U.S. Intervention in March 1996 Taiwan Strait Crisis: Interpretation from the Model of Coercive Diplomacy," *Tamkang Journal of International Affairs* 2, no. 1 (March 1998): 13–14.

33. E-mail communication with Vice Admiral Lyle Bien, U.S. Navy (Ret.), March 23, 2011.

34. Interview with Rear Admiral James P. Wisecup, March 8, 2011.

35. Elleman, "The Right Skill Set," 242.

36. Chen Ming-tong, *The China Threat Crosses the Strait: Challenges and Strategies for Taiwan's National Security*, trans. Kiel Downey (Taipei: Dong Fan Color Printing Co., 2007), 39.

37. Ralph N. Clough, *Island China* (Cambridge, MA: Harvard University Press, 1978), 99.

Appendix 1
Further Reading

Alagappa, Muthiah, ed. *Taiwan's Presidential Politics: Democratization and Cross-Strait Relations in the Twenty-first Century*. Armonk, NY: M. E. Sharpe, 2001.
Barnett, A. Doak, et al., eds. *Modernizing China: Post-Mao Reform and Development*. Boulder, CO: Westview, 1986.
Brady, Anne-Marie, ed. *Looking North, Looking South: China, Taiwan, and the South Pacific*. New Jersey: World Scientific, 2010.
Bramall, Chris. *Sources of Chinese Economic Growth, 1978–1996*. Oxford: Oxford University Press, 2001.
Brown, Melissa J. *Is Taiwan Chinese: The Impact of Culture, Power, and Migration on Changing Identities*. Berkeley: University of California Press, 2004.
Chang, Gordon. *Friends, Enemies: The United States, China, and the Soviet Union, 1948–1972*. Stanford, CA: Stanford University Press, 1990.
Chang, Jung, and Jon Halliday. *Mao: The Unknown Story*. New York: Alfred A. Knopf, 2005.
Chang, Maria Hsia. *Return of the Dragon: China's Wounded Nationalism*. Boulder, CO: Westview, 2001.
Chassin, Lionel Max. *The Communist Conquest of China: A History of the Civil War, 1945–1949*. Trans. Timothy Osato and Louis Gelas. Cambridge: Harvard University Press, 1965.
Cheng, Siwei. *Studies on Economic Reforms and Development in China*. Oxford: Oxford University Press, 2001.
Chin, Ko-lin. *Heijin: Organized Crime, Business, and Politics in Taiwan*. Armonk, NY: M. E. Sharpe, 2003.
Christensen, Thomas J. *Useful Adversaries: Grand Strategy, Domestic Mobilization, and Sino-American Conflict, 1947–1958*. Princeton: Princeton University Press, 1996.
Cohen, Warren. *East Asia at the Center: Four Thousand Years of Engagement with the World*. New York: Columbia University Press, 2000.
Copper, John F. *Taiwan: Nation-State or Province?* 4th ed. Boulder, CO: Westview, 2003.
Diamond, Larry, et al. *Elections and Democracy in Greater China*. Oxford: Oxford University Press, 2001.
Dickson, Bruce J., et al., eds. *Assessing the Lee Teng-hui Legacy in Taiwan's Politics*. Armonk, NY: M. E. Sharpe, 2002.
Dreyer, Edward L. *China at War, 1901–1949*. London: Longman, 1995.
Dreyer, June Teufel. *China's Forty Millions: Minority Nationalities and National Integration in the People's Republic of China*. Cambridge: Harvard University Press, 1976.
Eastman, Lloyd E. *Seeds of Destruction: Nationalist China in War and Revolution, 1937–1949*. Stanford, CA: Stanford University Press, 1984.
———. *Throne and Mandarins: China's Search for a Policy during the Sino–French Controversy, 1880–1885*. Cambridge: Harvard University Press, 1967.
Elleman, Bruce A. *Modern Chinese Warfare, 1795–1989*. London: Routledge, 2001.

Elvin, Mark. *The Retreat of the Elephants: An Environmental History of China*. New Haven: Yale University Press, 2004.
Feigenbaum, Eva. *China's Techno-Warriors: National Security and Strategic Competition from the Nuclear to the Information Age*. Stanford: Stanford University Press, 2003.
Furuya, Keiji. *Chiang Kai-shek: His Life and Times*. Trans. and abridg. Chun-ming Chang. New York: St. John's University, 1981.
Gries, Peter Hays. *China's New Nationalism: Price, Politics, and Diplomacy*. Berkeley: University of California Press, 2004.
Han Minzhu, ed. *Cries for Democracy: Writings and Speeches from the 1989 Chinese Democracy Movement*. Princeton: Princeton University Press, 1990.
Ho, Samuel P. S. *Economic Development of Taiwan, 1860–1970*. New Haven: Yale University Press, 1978.
Hsü, Immanuel C. Y. *China's Entrance into the Family of Nations: The Diplomatic Phase, 1858–1880*. Cambridge: Harvard University Press, 1960.
Huang, Jing, and Xiaoting Li. *Inseparable Separation: The Making of China's Taiwan Policy*. New Jersey: World Scientific, 2010.
Hutchings, Graham. *Modern China: A Guide to a Century of Change*. Cambridge: Harvard University Press, 2001.
Jian, Chen. *Mao's China and the Cold War*. Chapel Hill: University of North Carolina Press, 2001.
Kleinberg, Robert. *China's "Opening" to the Outside World: The Experiment with Foreign Capitalism*. Boulder, CO: Westview, 1990.
Lampton, David M. *The Making of Chinese Foreign and Security Policy in the Era of Reform, 1978–2000*. Stanford: Stanford University Press, 2001.
Lardy, Nicholas R. *Foreign Trade and Economic Reform in China, 1978–1990*. Cambridge: Cambridge University Press, 1991.
Lewis, John Wilson, and Xue Litai. *Imagined Enemies: China Prepares for Uncertain War*. Stanford: Stanford University Press, 2006.
Li, Zhisui. *The Private Life of Chairman Mao*. Trans. Tai Hung-chao. New York: Random House, 1994.
Liu, Ta-chung. *The Economy of the Chinese Mainland: National Income and Economic Development, 1933–1959*. Princeton: Princeton University Press, 1965.
Lone, Stewart. *Japan's First Modern War: Army and Society in the Conflict with China, 1894–95*. London: St. Martin's Press, 1994.
Marti, Michael E. *China and the Legacy of Deng Xiaoping: From Communist Revolution to Capitalist Evolution*. Washington, DC: Brassey's, 2002.
Paine, S. C. M. *Imperial Rivals: China, Russia, and Their Disputed Frontier*. Armonk, NY: M. E. Sharpe, 1996.
———. *The Sino-Japanese War of 1894–1895: Perceptions, Power, and Primacy*. Cambridge: Cambridge University Press, 2003.
Powell, Ralph L. *The Rise of Chinese Military Power, 1895–1912*. Princeton: Princeton University Press, 1955.
Rubinstein, Murray A., ed. *Taiwan: A New History*. Armonk, NY: M. E. Sharpe, 1999.
Rummel, R. J. *China's Bloody Century: Genocide and Mass Murder since 1900*. New Brunswick, NJ: Transaction Publishers, 1991.
Schiffrin, Harold. *Sun Yat-sen and the Origins of the Chinese Revolution*. Berkeley: University of California Press, 1968.
Sharman, Lyon. *Sun Yat-sen: His Life and Its Meaning*. Stanford: Stanford University Press, 1968.
Sheng, Lijun. *China's Dilemma: The Taiwan Issue*. New York: I. B. Tauris, 2001.
Sheridan, James E. *China in Disintegration: The Republican Era in Chinese History, 1912–1949*. New York: Free Press, 1975.
Taylor, Jay. *The Generalissimo's Son: Chiang Ching-kuo and the Revolutions in China and Taiwan*. Cambridge: Harvard University Press, 2000.
Tsou, Tang. *Embroilment over Quemoy: Mao, Chiang, and Dulles*. Salt Lake City: University of Utah, 1959.

Vogel, Ezra. *The Four Little Dragons: The Spread of Industrialization in Asia*. Cambridge: Harvard University Press, 1991.

Wang, Gabe T. *China and the Taiwan Issue: Impending War at Taiwan Strait*. Lanham, MD: University Press of America, 2006.

Whiting, Allen S. *China Crosses the Yalu: The Decision to Enter the Korean War*. New York: Macmillan, 1960.

Wilbur, C. Martin, and Julie Lien-ying How. *Missionaries of Revolution: Soviet Advisers and Nationalist China, 1920–1927*. Cambridge: Harvard University Press, 1989.

Xiang, Lanxin. *Recasting the Imperial Far East: Britain and America in China, 1945–1950*. Armonk, NY: M. E. Sharpe, 1995.

Appendix 2
Time Line of Major Events in the Taiwan Strait

1514	Portuguese discover maritime route to China
1624	Dutch found town of Zeelandia on Taiwan
1644	Fall of Beijing to Qing army and enthronement of Shunzhi emperor
1645	Qing occupation of Nanjing, the capital of the Southern Ming dynasty
1650	Fall of Xiamen (Amoy) and Jinmen (Quemoy) to Zheng Chenggong
1662	Ming loyalists expel Dutch from Taiwan
1683	Qing conquest of Taiwan
1721	Failed revolt in Taiwan
1787–1798	Taiwan uprising put down by Qing fleet
1874	Japan sends punitive mission against Taiwan
1879	Japanese annexation of Ryukyu (Okinawa) Islands
1883–1885	Sino–French War over Vietnam
1885	Taiwan becomes a province
1894–1895	Sino–Japanese War; Japan takes Taiwan
1895–1898	Scramble for concessions
August 15, 1945	Japanese surrenders; Taiwan returned to China
July 1946	Resumption of full-scale civil war
February 28, 1947	So-called February 28 (in Mandarin, *er-er-ba*) Incident

Appendix 2

September 2, 1948	Founding of the Democratic People's Republic of Korea
January 31, 1949	PLA enters Beijing
February 25, 1949	Mutiny of Nationalist flagship, *Chongqing*
April 12, 1949	Rent reduction for tenant farmers on Taiwan
April 20, 1949	PLA crosses Yangzi River
April 23, 1949	PLA enters Nanjing
May 27, 1949	PLA enters Shanghai
October 1, 1949	Establishment of People's Republic of China
October 1, 1949	Creation of the PRC with Mao Zedong as chairman and Zhou Enlai as premier
October 2, 1949	United States continues to recognize Nationalist government
December 8, 1949	Final Nationalist troops flee to Taiwan
January 6, 1950	Great Britain recognizes PRC
February 14, 1950	Sino–Soviet Friendship Treaty
March 3–April 23, 1950	Campaign to take Hainan
June 25, 1950	North Korean invasion of South Korea
June 27, 1950	United States sends Seventh Fleet to Taiwan Strait
January 10, 1953	Land redistribution on Taiwan, compensated with stocks and bonds
March 5, 1953	Stalin dies
September 3, 1954	PRC shells Jinmen Island, touching off first Taiwan Strait crisis (1954–1955)
December 2, 1954	U.S.–Taiwan Mutual Defense Treaty
January 25, 1955	House approves Formosa Resolution (1955)
January 28, 1955	Senate approves Formosa Resolution (1955)
August 23, 1958	China increases shelling of Jinmen Island, creating second Taiwan Strait crisis (late August to early October)
June 27, 1962	Kennedy announcement during Third Taiwan Strait Crisis
October 16, 1964	China tests first atomic bomb
June 17, 1967	China tests first nuclear bomb

March 2, 1969	Sino–Soviet fighting on Zhenbao Island
June–Aug. 1969	Sino–Soviet fighting in Xinjiang
July 8, 1969	Sino–Soviet fighting near Khabarovsk
April 14, 1971	U.S. announces loosening of trade restrictions for PRC
July 9–11, 1971	Kissinger secretly visits Beijing
October 25, 1971	PRC to replace Taiwan at the United Nations
February 21–27, 1972	Richard Nixon visits China
February 28, 1972	Shanghai Communiqué
January 8, 1975	Deng Xiaoping becomes party vice-chairman
April 5, 1975	Chiang Kai-shek dies; Chiang Ching-kuo becomes president
April 7, 1976	Deng Xiaoping fired; Hua Guofeng becomes premier
September 9, 1976	Mao Zedong dies
July 21, 1977	Deng Xiaoping reinstated
August 12–18, 1977	End of Cultural Revolution and adoption of Four Modernizations proclaimed at 11th Party Congress
November 19, 1978	First Democracy Wall posters appear
December 16, 1978	Joint Communiqué on the Establishment of Diplomatic Relations between the People's Republic of China and the United States of America
January 1, 1979	Normalization of Sino–U.S. relations
March 29, 1979	Suppression of Democracy Wall
April 10, 1979	Taiwan Relations Act provides U.S. military support
December 10, 1979	Kaohsiung Incident
August 26, 1980	Opening of Special Economic Zones
January 11, 1982	Deng Xiaoping announces One Country, Two Systems doctrine
August 17, 1982	Joint Communiqué on the Question of Arms Sales to Taiwan
December 19, 1984	Anglo–Chinese declaration on the return of Hong Kong

March 11, 1985	Mikhail Gorbachev comes to power
September 28, 1986	End of Nationalist one-party monopoly in Taiwan
December 5, 1986	Prodemocracy student movement in PRC becomes nationwide
April 13, 1987	Sino–Portuguese agreement on the return of Macao
July 15, 1987	End of martial law in Taiwan after thirty-eight years
November 2, 1987	Taiwan allows citizens to visit relatives on the mainland
January 13, 1988	Chiang Ching-kuo dies; replaced by Lee Teng-hui
January 20, 1989	Law on Civic Organizations permits creation of new political parties in Taiwan
January 26, 1989	Taiwan law on retirement of senior parliamentarians
April 15, 1989	Hu Yaobang dies
May 15–18, 1989	Mikhail Gorbachev visits China to normalize relations
May 17, 1989	Prodemocracy demonstration at Tiananmen
May 20, 1989	Martial law proclaimed in Beijing
May 31, 1989	Large sympathy demonstration in Taipei
June 4, 1989	Tiananmen massacre
June 10, 1989	Direct phone links opened between China and Taiwan
July 4, 1990	Conference concluded in Taiwan on government reforms
April 30, 1991	Lee Teng-hui recognizes PRC government
December 21, 1991	Legislative elections in Taiwan
February 25, 1992	Territorial Waters and Contiguous Areas Act
December 19, 1992	Legislative elections in Taiwan
July 21, 1995	PRC begins test-firing missiles off Taiwan, creating fourth Taiwan Strait crisis
March 8, 1996	PRC begins test-firing missiles off Taiwan

March 12, 1996	PRC begins military exercises off Jinmen Island
March 18, 1996	PRC begins joint war games off Taiwan
March 23, 1996	Presidential elections in Taiwan
February 19, 1997	Deng Xiaoping dies
July 1, 1997	Return of Hong Kong to Chinese sovereignty
June 30, 1998	Clinton's Three No's Policy
December 20, 1999	Return of Macao to Chinese sovereignty
February 21, 2000	PRC issues white paper on Taiwan
March 18, 2000	Democratic Progressive Party wins Taiwan presidency
April 1, 2001	Downing of the U.S. EP-3 plane on Hainan
March 14, 2005	PRC Anti-Secession Law
December 4, 2007	PRC announces Sansha "city" in Hainan Province to administer the Paracels, Macclesfield Bank, and the Spratlys
February 4, 2008	Taiwanese president Chen Shui-bian flies to Itu Aba, South China Sea
May 20, 2008	Nationalist candidate Ma Ying-jeou elected Taiwan's president
March 8, 2009	PRC ships harass civilian-manned U.S. submarine surveillance vessel USNS *Impeccable*
June 29, 2010	Cross-Straits Economic Cooperation Framework Agreement
July 26, 2012	Senior Colonel Cai Xihong assumes command of a newly created Sansha garrison, located on Woody Island in disputed Paracel Islands

Appendix 3

U.S.–ROC Mutual Defense Treaty, 2 December 1954 (Ratified 3 March 1955; terminated by the United States in 1980)

MUTUAL DEFENSE TREATY BETWEEN THE UNITED STATES OF AMERICA AND THE REPUBLIC OF CHINA

The Parties to this Treaty,

Reaffirming their faith in the purposes and principles of the Charter of the United Nations and their desire to live in peace with all peoples and all Governments, and desiring to strengthen the fabric of peace in the West Pacific Area,

Recalling with mutual pride the relationship which brought their two peoples together in a common bond of sympathy and mutual ideals to fight side by side against imperialist aggression during the last war,

Desiring to declare publicly and formally their sense of unity and their common determination to defend themselves against external armed attack, so that no potential aggressor could be under the illusion that either of them stands alone in the West Pacific Area, and

Desiring further to strengthen their present efforts for collective defense for the preservation of peace and security pending the development of a more comprehensive system of regional security in the West Pacific Area,

Have agreed as follows:

Article 1

The Parties undertake, as set forth in the Charter of the United Nations, to settle any international dispute in which they may be involved by peaceful means in such a manner that international peace, security and justice are not endangered and to refrain in their international relations from the threat or use of force in any manner inconsistent with the purposes of the United Nations.

Article 2

In order more effectively to achieve the objective of this Treaty, the Parties separately and jointly by self-help and mutual aid will maintain and develop their individual and collective capacity to resist armed attack and communist subversive activities directed from without against their territorial integrity and political stability.

Article 3

The Parties undertake to strengthen their free institutions and to cooperate with each other in the development of economic progress and social well-being and to further their individual and collective efforts toward these ends.

Article 4

The Parties, through their Foreign Ministers or their deputies, will consult together from time to time regarding the implementation of this Treaty.

Article 5

Each Party recognizes that an armed attack in the West Pacific Area directed against the territories of either of the Parties would be dangerous to its own peace and safety and declares that it would act to meet the common danger in accordance with its constitutional processes.

Any such armed attack and all measures taken as a result thereof shall be immediately reported to the Security Council of the United Nations. Such measures shall be terminated when the Security Council has taken the measures necessary to restore and maintain international peace and security.

Article 6

For the purposes of Articles 2 and 5, the terms "territorial" and "territories" shall mean in respect of the Republic of China, Taiwan and the Pescadores; and in respect of the United States of America, the island territories in the West Pacific under its jurisdiction. The provisions of Articles 2 and 5 will be applicable to such other territories as may be determined by mutual agreement.

Article 7

The Government of the Republic of China grants, and the Government of the United States of America accepts, the right to dispose such United States land, air, and sea forces in and about Taiwan and the Pescadores as may be required for their defense, as determined by mutual agreement.

Article 8

This Treaty does not affect and shall not be interpreted as affecting in any way the rights and obligations of the Parties under the Charter of the United Nations or the responsibility of the United Nations for the maintenance of international peace and security.

Article 9

This Treaty shall be ratified by the Republic of China and the United States of America in accordance with their respective constitutional processes and will come into force when instruments of ratification thereof have been exchanged by them at Taipei.

Article 10

This Treaty shall remain in force indefinitely. Either Party may terminate it one year after notice has been given to the other party.

IN WITNESS whereof, The undersigned Plenipotentiaries have signed this Treaty.
done in duplicate, in the Chinese and English languages, at Washington on this Second day of the Twelfth month of the Forty-third Year of the Republic of China, corresponding to the Second day of December of the Year One Thousand Nine Hundred and Fifty-four.

For the Republic of China:
GEORGE K. C. YEH
For the United States of America:
JOHN FOSTER DULLES

NOTE

United States of America and the Republic of China, "Mutual Defense Treaty between the United States of America and the Republic of China," December 2, 1954, available online at http://www.taiwandocuments.org/mutual01.htm.

Appendix 4
The U.S. Congress Formosa Resolution (1955)

1955

U.S. Congressional Authorization for the President to Employ the Armed Forces of the United States to Protect Formosa, the Pescadores, and Related Positions and Territories of That Area

Whereas the primary purpose of the United States, in its relations with all other nations, is to develop and sustain a just and enduring peace for all; and Whereas certain territories in the West Pacific under the jurisdiction of the Republic of China are now under armed attack, and threats and declarations have been and are being made by the Chinese Communists that such armed attack is in aid of and in preparation for armed attack on Formosa and the Pescadores,

Whereas such armed attack if continued would gravely endanger the peace and security of the West Pacific Area and particularly of Formosa and the Pescadores; and

Whereas the secure possession by friendly governments of the Western Pacific Island chain, of which Formosa is a part, is essential to the vital interests of the United States and all friendly nations in or bordering upon the Pacific Ocean; and

Whereas the President of the United States on January 6, 1955, submitted to the Senate for its advice and consent to ratification a Mutual Defense Treaty between the United States of America and the Republic of China, which recognizes that an armed attack in the West Pacific Area directed against territories, therein described, in the region of Formosa and the Pescadores, would be dangerous to the peace and safety of the parties to the treaty:

Therefore be it Resolved by the Senate and House of Representatives of the United States of America in Congress assembled, That the President of the United States be and he hereby is authorized to employ the

Armed Forces of the United States as he deems necessary for the specific purpose of securing and protecting Formosa and the Pescadores against armed attack, this authority to include the securing and protection of such related positions and territories of that area now in friendly hands and the taking of such other measures as he judges to be required or appropriate in assuring the defense of Formosa and the Pescadores.

This resolution shall expire when the President shall determine that the peace and security of the area is reasonably assured by international conditions created by action of the United Nations or otherwise, and shall so report to the Congress.

NOTE

Approved by U.S. Congress House vote 409–3 on January 25, 1955, and by Senate vote 85–3 on January 28, 1955, the act appears in U.S. Congress, *United States Statutes at Large*, vol. 69 (Washington, DC: U.S. Government Printing Office, 1955), 7. The resolution was repealed on October 26, 1974; see U.S. Congress, *United States Statutes at Large*, vol. 88, part 2 (Washington, DC: U.S. Government Printing Office, 1974), 1,439.

Appendix 5
Shanghai Communiqué, February 28, 1972

JOINT COMMUNIQUÉ BETWEEN THE PEOPLE'S REPUBLIC OF CHINA AND THE UNITED STATES OF AMERICA ISSUED IN SHANGHAI, FEBRUARY 28, 1972

President Richard Nixon of the United States of America visited the People's Republic of China at the invitation of Premier Chou En-lai of the People's Republic of China from February 21 to February 28, 1972.

Accompanying the President were Mrs. Nixon, U.S. Secretary of State William Rogers, Assistant to the President Dr. Henry Kissinger, and other American officials.

President Nixon met with Chairman Mao Tsetung of the Communist Party of China on February 21. The two leaders had a serious and frank exchange of views on Sino–U.S. relations and world affairs.

During the visit, extensive, earnest and frank discussions were held between President Nixon and Premier Chou En-lai on the normalization of relations between the United States of America and the People's Republic of China, as well as on other matters of interest to both sides. In addition, Secretary of State William Rogers and Foreign Minister Chi Peng-fei held talks in the same spirit.

President Nixon and his party visited Peking and viewed cultural, industrial and agricultural sites, and they also toured Hangchow and Shanghai where, continuing discussions with Chinese leaders, they viewed similar places of interest.

The leaders of the People's Republic of China and the United States of America found it beneficial to have this opportunity, after so many years without contact, to present candidly to one another their views on a variety of issues. They reviewed the international situation in which important changes and great upheavals are taking place and expounded their respective positions and attitudes.

[Note: Two versions of the Shanghai Communiqué were signed, one in English and one in Chinese. The American version had the U.S. position first, whereas the Chinese version had the Chinese position at top. The translated Chinese version is presented here.]

The Chinese side stated: Wherever there is oppression there is resistance. Countries want independence, nations want liberation and the people want revolution—this has become the irresistible trend of history. All nations, big or small, should be equal; big nations should not bully the small and strong nations should not bully the weak. China will never be a superpower and it opposes hegemony and power politics of any kind. The Chinese side stated that it firmly supports the struggles of all the oppressed people and nations for freedom and liberation and that the people of all countries have the right to choose their social systems according to their own wishes and the right to safeguard the independence, sovereignty and territorial integrity of their own countries and oppose foreign aggression, interference, control and subversion. All foreign troops should be withdrawn to their own countries. The Chinese side expressed its firm support to the peoples of Viet Nam, Laos and Cambodia in their efforts for the attainment of their goal and its firm support to the seven-point proposal of the Provisional Revolutionary Government of the Republic of South Viet Nam and the elaboration of February this year on the two key problems in the proposal, and to the Joint Declaration of the Summit Conference of the Indochinese Peoples. It firmly supports the eight-point program for the peaceful unification of Korea put forward by the Government of the Democratic People's Republic of Korea on April 12, 1971, and the stand for the abolition of the "U.N. Commission for the Unification and Rehabilitation of Korea." It firmly opposes the revival and outward expansion of Japanese militarism and firmly supports the Japanese people's desire to build an independent, democratic, peaceful and neutral Japan. It firmly maintains that India and Pakistan should, in accordance with the United Nations resolutions on the India-Pakistan question, immediately withdraw all their forces to their respective territories and to their own sides of the ceasefire line in Jammu and Kashmir and firmly supports the Pakistan Government and people in their struggle to preserve their independence and sovereignty and the people of Jammu and Kashmir in their struggle for the right of self-determination.

The U.S. side stated: Peace in Asia and peace in the world requires efforts both to reduce immediate tensions and to eliminate the basic causes of conflict. The United States will work for a just and secure peace; just, because it fulfills the aspirations of peoples and nations for freedom and progress; secure, because it removes the danger of foreign aggression. The United States supports individual freedom and social progress for all the peoples of the world, free of outside pressure or intervention. The United States believes that the effort to reduce tensions is served by improving communication between countries that have different ideologies so as to lessen the risks of confrontation through accident, miscalculation or misunderstanding. Countries should treat each other with mutual respect and be willing to compete peacefully, letting performance be the ultimate judge. No country should claim infallibility and each country should be prepared to reexamine its own attitudes for the common good. The United States stressed that the peoples of Indochina should be allowed to determine their destiny without outside intervention; its constant primary objective has been a negotiated solution; the eight-point proposal put forward by the Republic of Viet Nam and the United States on January 27, 1972, represents a basis for the attainment of that objective; in the absence of a negotiated settlement, the United States envisages the ultimate withdrawal of all U.S. forces from the region consistent with the aim of self-determination for each country of Indochina. The United States will maintain its close ties with and support for the Republic of Korea; the United States will support efforts of the Republic of Korea to seek a relaxation of tension and increased communication in the Korean peninsula. The United States places the highest value on its friendly relations with Japan; it will continue to develop the existing close bonds. Consistent with the United Nations Security Council Resolution of December 21, 1971, the United States favors the continuation of the ceasefire between India and Pakistan and the withdrawal of all military forces to within their own territories and to their own sides of the ceasefire line in Jammu and Kashmir; the United States supports the right of the peoples of South Asia to shape their own future in peace, free of military threat, and without having the area become the subject of great power rivalry.

There are essential differences between China and the United States in their social systems and foreign policies. However, the two sides agreed that countries, regardless of their social systems, should conduct their relations on the principles of respect for the sovereignty and territorial integrity of all states, non-aggression against other states, non-interference in the internal affairs of other states, equality and mutual benefit, and peaceful coexistence. International disputes should be settled on this basis, without resorting to the use or threat of force. The United States and the People's Republic of China are prepared to apply these principles to their mutual relations.

With these principles of international relations in mind the two sides stated that:

- progress toward the normalization of relations between China and the United States is in the interests of all countries;
- both wish to reduce the danger of international military conflict;

- neither should seek hegemony in the Asia-Pacific region and each is opposed to efforts by any other country or group of countries to establish such hegemony; and
- neither is prepared to negotiate on behalf of any third party or to enter into agreements or understandings with the other directed at other states.

Both sides are of the view that it would be against the interests of the peoples of the world for any major country to collude with another against other countries, or for major countries to divide up the world into spheres of interest.

The two sides reviewed the long-standing serious disputes between China and the United States.

The Chinese side reaffirmed its position: The Taiwan question is the crucial question obstructing the normalization of relations between China and the United States; the Government of the People's Republic of China is the sole legal government of China; Taiwan is a province of China which has long been returned to the motherland; the liberation of Taiwan is China's internal affair in which no other country has the right to interfere; and all U.S. forces and military installations must be withdrawn from Taiwan. The Chinese Government firmly opposes any activities which aim at the creation of "one China, one Taiwan," "one China two governments," "two Chinas," an "independent Taiwan" or advocate that "the status of Taiwan remains to be determined."

The U.S. side declared: The United States acknowledges that all Chinese on either side of the Taiwan Strait maintain there is but one China and that Taiwan is a part of China. The United States Government does not challenge that position. It reaffirms its interest in a peaceful settlement of the Taiwan question by the Chinese themselves. With this prospect in mind, it affirms the ultimate objective of the withdrawal of all U.S. forces and military installations from Taiwan. In the meantime, it will progressively reduce its forces and military installations on Taiwan as the tension in the area diminishes.

The two sides agreed that it is desirable to broaden the understanding between the two peoples. To this end, they discussed specific areas in such fields as science, technology, culture, sports and journalism, in which people-to-people contacts and exchanges would be mutually beneficial. Each side undertakes to facilitate the further development of such contacts and exchanges.

Both sides view bilateral trade as another area from which mutual benefit can be derived, and agreed that economic relations based on equality and mutual benefit are in the interest of the peoples of the two countries. They agree to facilitate the progressive development of trade between their two countries.

The two sides agreed that they will stay in contact through various channels, including the sending of a senior U.S. representative to Peking from time to time for concrete consultations to further the normalization of relations between the two countries and continue to exchange views on issues of common interest.

The two sides expressed the hope that the gains achieved during this visit would open up new prospects for the relations between the two countries. They believe that the normalization of relations between the two countries is not only in the interest of the Chinese and American peoples but also contributes to the relaxation of tension in Asia and the world.

President Nixon, Mrs. Nixon and the American party expressed their appreciation for the gracious hospitality shown them by the Government and people of the People's Republic of China.

NOTE

People's Republic of China and the United States of America, "Joint Communiqué between the People's Republic of China and the United States of America Issued in Shanghai, February 28, 1972," February 28, 1972, available online at http://www.sinomania.com/CHINANEWS/shanghai_communique_30th_anniversary.htm.

Appendix 6

Joint Communiqué on the Establishment of Diplomatic Relations between the People's Republic of China and the United States of America, December 16, 1978

December 16, 1978

The People's Republic of China and the United States of America have agreed to recognize each other and to establish diplomatic relations as of January 1, 1979.

The United States of America recognizes the Government of the People's Republic of China as the sole legal Government of China. Within this context, the people of the United States will maintain cultural, commercial, and other unofficial relations with the people of Taiwan.

The People's Republic of China and the United States of America reaffirm the principles agreed on by the two sides in the Shanghai Communique and emphasize once again that:

- Both wish to reduce the danger of international military conflict.
- Neither should seek hegemony in the Asia-Pacific region or in any other region of the world and each is opposed to efforts by any other country or group of countries to establish such hegemony.
- Neither is prepared to negotiate on behalf of any third party or to enter into agreements or understandings with the other directed at other states.
- The Government of the United States of America acknowledges the Chinese position that there is but one China and Taiwan is part of China.

- Both believe that normalization of Sino-American relations is not only in the interest of the Chinese and American peoples but also contributes to the cause of peace in Asia and the world.

The People's Republic of China and the United States of America will exchange Ambassadors and establish Embassies on March 1, 1979.

NOTE

People's Republic of China and the United States of America, "Joint Communiqué on the Establishment of Diplomatic Relations between the People's Republic of China and the United States of America (December 16, 1978)," December 16, 1978, available on-line at http://www.china-embassy.org/eng/zmgx/doc/ctc/t36256.htm.

Appendix 7
Taiwan Relations Act, April 10, 1979

January 1, 1979

TAIWAN RELATIONS ACT

Public Law 96-8, 96th Congress

An Act

To help maintain peace, security, and stability in the Western Pacific and to promote the foreign policy of the United States by authorizing the continuation of commercial, cultural, and other relations between the people of the United States and the people on Taiwan, and for other purposes.

Be it enacted by the Senate and House of Representatives of the United States of America in Congress assembled,

Short Title

Section 1. This Act may be cited as the "Taiwan Relations Act."

Findings and Declaration of Policy

Section 2.

1. The President—having terminated governmental relations between the United States and the governing authorities on Taiwan recognized by the United States as the Republic of China prior to January 1, 1979, the Congress finds that the enactment of this Act is necessary—

    a. to help maintain peace, security, and stability in the Western Pacific; and

b. to promote the foreign policy of the United States by authorizing the continuation of commercial, cultural, and other relations between the people of the United States and the people on Taiwan.
2. It is the policy of the United States—
   a. to preserve and promote extensive, close, and friendly commercial, cultural, and other relations between the people of the United States and the people on Taiwan, as well as the people on the China mainland and all other peoples of the Western Pacific area;
   b. to declare that peace and stability in the area are in the political, security, and economic interests of the United States, and are matters of international concern;
   c. to make clear that the United States decision to establish diplomatic relations with the People's Republic of China rests upon the expectation that the future of Taiwan will be determined by peaceful means;
   d. to consider any effort to determine the future of Taiwan by other than peaceful means, including by boycotts or embargoes, a threat to the peace and security of the Western Pacific area and of grave concern to the United States;
   e. to provide Taiwan with arms of a defensive character; and
   f. to maintain the capacity of the United States to resist any resort to force or other forms of coercion that would jeopardize the security, or the social or economic system, of the people on Taiwan.
3. Nothing contained in this Act shall contravene the interest of the United States in human rights, especially with respect to the human rights of all the approximately eighteen million inhabitants of Taiwan. The preservation and enhancement of the human rights of all the people on Taiwan are hereby reaffirmed as objectives of the United States.

Implementation of United States Policy with Regard to Taiwan

Section 3.

1. In furtherance of the policy set forth in section 2 of this Act, the United States will make available to Taiwan such defense articles and defense services in such quantity as may be necessary to enable Taiwan to maintain a sufficient self-defense capability.
2. The President and the Congress shall determine the nature and quantity of such defense articles and services based solely upon their judgment of the needs of Taiwan, in accordance with proce-

dures established by law. Such determination of Taiwan's defense needs shall include review by United States military authorities in connection with recommendations to the President and the Congress.
3. The President is directed to inform the Congress promptly of any threat to the security or the social or economic system of the people on Taiwan and any danger to the interests of the United States arising therefrom. The President and the Congress shall determine, in accordance with constitutional processes, appropriate action by the United States in response to any such danger.

Application of Laws; International Agreements

Section 4.

1. The absence of diplomatic relations or recognition shall not affect the application of the laws of the United States with respect to Taiwan, and the laws of the United States shall apply with respect to Taiwan in the manner that the laws of the United States applied with respect to Taiwan prior to January 1, 1979.
2. The application of subsection (a) of this section shall include, but shall not be limited to, the following:
    a. Whenever the laws of the United States refer or relate to foreign countries, nations, states, governments, or similar entities, such terms shall include and such laws shall apply with such respect to Taiwan.
    b. Whenever authorized by or pursuant to the laws of the United States to conduct or carry out programs, transactions, or other relations with respect to foreign countries, nations, states, governments, or similar entities, the President or any agency of the United States Government is authorized to conduct and carry out, in accordance with section 6 of this Act, such programs, transactions, and other relations with respect to Taiwan (including, but not limited to, the performance of services for the United States through contracts with commercial entities on Taiwan), in accordance with the applicable laws of the United States.
1. The absence of diplomatic relations and recognition with respect to Taiwan shall not abrogate, infringe, modify, deny, or otherwise affect in any way any rights or obligations (including but not limited to those involving contracts, debts, or property interests of any kind) under the laws of the United States heretofore or hereafter acquired by or with respect to Taiwan.
2. For all purposes under the laws of the United States, including actions in any court in the United States, recognition of the Peo-

ple's Republic of China shall not affect in any way the ownership of or other rights or interests in properties, tangible and intangible, and other things of value, owned or held on or prior to December 31, 1978, or thereafter acquired or earned by the governing authorities on Taiwan.

    a. Whenever the application of the laws of the United States depends upon the law that is or was applicable on Taiwan or compliance therewith, the law applied by the people on Taiwan shall be considered the applicable law for that purpose.

    b. Nothing in this Act, nor the facts of the President's action in extending diplomatic recognition to the People's Republic of China, the absence of diplomatic relations between the people on Taiwan and the United States, or the lack of recognition by the United States, and attendant circumstances thereto, shall be construed in any administrative or judicial proceeding as a basis for any United States Government agency, commission, or department to make a finding of fact or determination of law, under the Atomic Energy Act of 1954 and the Nuclear Non-Proliferation Act of 1978, to deny an export license application or to revoke an existing export license for nuclear exports to Taiwan.

    c. For purposes of the Immigration and Nationality Act, Taiwan may be treated in the manner specified in the first sentence of section 202(b) of that Act.

    d. The capacity of Taiwan to sue and be sued in courts in the United States, in accordance with the laws of the United States, shall not be abrogated, infringed, modified, denied, or otherwise affected in any way by the absence of diplomatic relations or recognition.

    e. No requirement, whether expressed or implied, under the laws of the United States with respect to maintenance of diplomatic relations or recognition shall be applicable with respect to Taiwan.

3. For all purposes, including actions in any court in the United States, the Congress approves the continuation in force of all treaties and other international agreements, including multilateral conventions, entered into by the United States and the governing authorities on Taiwan recognized by the United States as the Republic of China prior to January 1, 1979, and in force between them on December 31, 1978, unless and until terminated in accordance with law.

4. Nothing in this Act may be construed as a basis for supporting the exclusion or expulsion of Taiwan from continued membership in

any international financial institution or any other international organization.

Overseas Private Investment Corporation

Section 5.
1. During the three-year period beginning on the date of enactment of this Act, the $1,000 per capita income restriction in insurance, clause (2) of the second undesignated paragraph of section 231 of the reinsurance, Foreign Assistance Act of 1961 shall not restrict the activities of the Overseas Private Investment Corporation in determining whether to provide any insurance, reinsurance, loans, or guaranties with respect to investment projects on Taiwan.
2. Except as provided in subsection (a) of this section, in issuing insurance, reinsurance, loans, or guaranties with respect to investment projects on Taiwan, the Overseas Private Insurance Corporation shall apply the same criteria as those applicable in other parts of the world.

The American Institute of Taiwan

Section 6.
1. Programs, transactions, and other relations conducted or carried out by the President or any agency of the United States Government with respect to Taiwan shall, in the manner and to the extent directed by the President, be conducted and carried out by or through—
    a. The American Institute in Taiwan, a nonprofit corporation incorporated under the laws of the District of Columbia, or
    b. such comparable successor nongovermental entity as the President may designate, (hereafter in this Act referred to as the "Institute").
    c. Whenever the President or any agency of the United States Government is authorized or required by or pursuant to the laws of the United States to enter into, perform, enforce, or have in force an agreement or transaction relative to Taiwan, such agreement or transaction shall be entered into, performed, and enforced, in the manner and to the extent directed by the President, by or through the Institute.
2. To the extent that any law, rule, regulation, or ordinance of the District of Columbia, or of any State or political subdivision thereof in which the Institute is incorporated or doing business, impedes or otherwise interferes with the performance of the functions of the

Institute pursuant to this Act; such law, rule, regulation, or ordinance shall be deemed to be preempted by this Act.

Services by the Institute to United States Citizens on Taiwan

Section 7.
1. The Institute may authorize any of its employees on Taiwan—
    a. to administer to or take from any person an oath, affirmation, affidavit, or deposition, and to perform any notarial act which any notary public is required or authorized by law to perform within the United States;
    b. To act as provisional conservator of the personal estates of deceased United States citizens; and
    c. to assist and protect the interests of United States persons by performing other acts such as are authorized to be performed outside the United States for consular purposes by such laws of the United States as the President may specify.
2. Acts performed by authorized employees of the Institute under this section shall be valid, and of like force and effect within the United States, as if performed by any other person authorized under the laws of the United States to perform such acts.

Tax Exempt Status of the Institute

Section 8.
1. The Institute, its property, and its income are exempt from all taxation now or hereafter imposed by the United States (except to the extent that section 11(a)(3) of this Act requires the imposition of taxes imposed under chapter 21 of the Internal Revenue Code of 1954, relating to the Federal Insurance Contributions Act) or by State or local taxing authority of the United States.
2. For purposes of the Internal Revenue Code of 1954, the Institute shall be treated as an organization described in sections 170(b)(1)(A), 170(c), 2055(a), 2106(a)(2)(A), 2522(a), and 2522(b).

Furnishing property and services to and obtaining services from the institute

Section 9.
1. Any agency of the United States Government is authorized to sell, loan, or lease property (including interests therein) to, and to perform administrative and technical support functions and services for the operations of, the Institute upon such terms and conditions as the President may direct. Reimbursements to agencies under

this subsection shall be credited to the current applicable appropriation of the agency concerned.
2. Any agency of the United States Government is authorized to acquire and accept services from the Institute upon such terms and conditions as the President may direct. Whenever the President determines it to be in furtherance of the purposes of this Act, the procurement of services by such agencies from the Institute may be effected without regard to such laws of the United States normally applicable to the acquisition of services by such agencies as the President may specify by Executive order.
3. Any agency of the United States Government making funds available to the Institute in accordance with this Act shall make arrangements with the Institute for the Comptroller General of the United States to have access to the; books and records of the Institute and the opportunity to audit the operations of the Institute.

Taiwan Instrumentality

Section 10.

1. Whenever the President or any agency of the United States Government is authorized or required by or pursuant to the laws of the United States to render or provide to or to receive or accept from Taiwan, any performance, communication, assurance, undertaking, or other action, such action shall, in the manner and to the. extent directed by the President, be rendered or Provided to, or received or accepted from, an instrumentality established by Taiwan which the President determines has the necessary authority under the laws applied by the people on Taiwan to provide assurances and take other actions on behalf of Taiwan in accordance with this Act.
2. The President is requested to extend to the instrumentality established by Taiwan the same number of offices and complement of personnel as were previously operated in the United States by the governing authorities on Taiwan recognized as the Republic of China prior to January 1, 1979.
3. Upon the granting by Taiwan of comparable privileges and immunities with respect to the Institute and its appropriate personnel, the President is authorized to extend with respect to the Taiwan instrumentality and its appropriate; personnel, such privileges and immunities (subject to appropriate conditions and obligations) as may be necessary for the effective performance of their functions.

Separation of Government Personnel for Employment with the Institute

Section 11.

1. Under such terms and conditions as the President may direct, any agency of the United States Government may separate from Government service for a specified period any officer or employee of that agency who accepts employment with the Institute.
2. An officer or employee separated by an agency under paragraph (1) of this subsection for employment with the Institute shall be entitled upon termination of such employment to reemployment or reinstatement with such agency (or a successor agency) in an appropriate position with the attendant rights, privileges, and benefits with the officer or employee would have had or acquired had he or she not been so separated, subject to such time period and other conditions as the President may prescribe.
3. An officer or employee entitled to reemployment or reinstatement rights under paragraph (2) of this subsection shall, while continuously employed by the Institute with no break in continuity of service, continue to participate in any benefit program in which such officer or employee was participating prior to employment by the Institute, including programs for compensation for job-related death, injury, or illness; programs for health and life insurance; programs for annual, sick, and other statutory leave; and programs for retirement under any system established by the laws of the United States; except that employment with the Institute shall be the basis for participation in such programs only to the extent that employee deductions and employer contributions, as required, in payment for such participation for the period of employment with the Institute, are currently deposited in the program's or system's fund or depository. Death or retirement of any such officer or employee during approved service with the Institute and prior to reemployment or reinstatement shall be considered a death in or retirement from Government service for purposes of any employee or survivor benefits acquired by reason of service with an agency of the United States Government.
4. Any officer or employee of an agency of the United States Government who entered into service with the Institute on approved leave of absence without pay prior to the enactment of this Act shall receive the benefits of this section for the period of such service.
5. Any agency of the United States Government employing alien personnel on Taiwan may transfer such personnel, with accrued allowances, benefits, and rights, to the Institute without a break in service for purposes of retirement and other benefits, including continued participation in any system established by the laws of

the United States for the retirement of employees in which the alien was participating prior to the transfer to the Institute, except that employment with the Institute shall be creditable for retirement purposes only to the extent that employee deductions and employer contributions as required, in payment for such participation for the period of employment with the Institute, are currently deposited in the system's fund or depository.
6. Employees of the Institute shall not be employees of the United States and, in representing the Institute, shall be exempt from section 207 of title 18, United States Code.

   a. For purposes of sections 911 and 913 of the Internal Revenue Code of 1954, amounts paid by the Institute to its employees shall not be treated as earned income. Amounts received by employees of the Institute shall not be included in gross income, and shall be exempt from taxation, to the extent that they are equivalent to amounts received by civilian officers and employees of the Government of the United States as allowances and benefits which are exempt from taxation under section 912 of such Code.
   b. Except to the extent required by subsection (a)(3) of this section, service performed in the employ of the Institute shall not constitute employment for purposes of chapter 21 of such Code and title II of the Social Security Act.

Reporting Requirement

Section 12.

1. The Secretary of State shall transmit to the Congress the text of any agreement to which the Institute is a party. However, any such agreement the immediate public disclosure of which would, in the opinion of the President, be prejudicial to the national security of the United States shall not be so transmitted to the Congress but shall be transmitted to the Committee on Foreign Relations of the Senate and the Committee on Foreign Affairs of the House of Representatives under an appropriate injunction of secrecy to be removed only upon due notice from the President.
2. For purposes of subsection (a), the term "agreement" includes—

   a. any agreement entered into between the Institute and the governing authorities on Taiwan or the instrumentality established by Taiwan; and
   b. any agreement entered into between the Institute and an agency of the United States Government.
   c. Agreements and transactions made or to be made by or through the Institute shall be subject to the same congres-

sional notification, review, and approval requirements and procedures as if such agreements and transactions were made by or through the agency of the United States Government on behalf of which the Institute is acting.

3. During the two-year period beginning on the effective date of this Act, the Secretary of State shall transmit to the Speaker of the House and Senate House of Representatives and the Committee on Foreign Relations of Foreign Relations the Senate, every six months, a report describing and reviewing economic relations between the United States and Taiwan, noting any interference with normal commercial relations.

Rules and Regulations

Section 13.

The President is authorized to prescribe such rules and regulations as he may deem appropriate to carry out the purposes of this Act. During the three-year period beginning on the effective date speaker of this Act, such rules and regulations shall be transmitted promptly to the Speaker of the House of Representatives and to the Committee on Foreign Relations of the Senate. Such action shall.not, however, relieve the Institute of the responsibilities placed upon it by this Act.'

Congressional Oversight

Section 14.

1. The Committee on Foreign Affairs of the House of Representatives, the Committee on Foreign Relations of the Senate, and other appropriate committees of the Congress shall monitor—

    a. the implementation of the provisions of this Act;
    b. the operation and procedures of the Institute;
    c. the legal and technical aspects of the continuing relationship between the United States and Taiwan; and
    d. the implementation of the policies of the United States concerning security and cooperation in East Asia.

2. Such committees shall report, as appropriate, to their respective Houses on the results of their monitoring.

Definitions

Section 15. For purposes of this Act—

1. the term "laws of the United States" includes any statute, rule, regulation, ordinance, order, or judicial rule of decision of the United States or any political subdivision thereof; and
2. the term "Taiwan" includes, as the context may require, the islands of Taiwan and the Pescadores, the people on those islands, corporations and other entities and associations created or organized under the laws applied on those islands, and the governing authorities on Taiwan recognized by the United States as the Republic of China prior to January 1, 1979, and any successor governing authorities (including political subdivisions, agencies, and instrumentalities thereof).

Authorization of Appropriations

Section 16.

In addition to funds otherwise available to carry out the provisions of this Act, there are authorized to be appropriated to the Secretary of State for the fiscal year 1980 such funds as may be necessary to carry out such provisions. Such funds are authorized to remain available until expended.

Severability of Provisions

Section 17.

If any provision of this Act or the application thereof to any person or circumstance is held invalid, the remainder of the Act and the application of such provision to any other person or circumstance shall not be affected thereby.

Effective Date

Section 18.

This Act shall be effective as of January 1, 1979. Approved April 10, 1979.

NOTE

U.S. Congress, *Taiwan Relations Act*, Public Law 96-8, 96th Cong., January 1, 1979, available online at http://www.ait.org.tw/en/taiwan-relations-act.html.

Appendix 8

Joint Communiqué of the United States of America and the People's Republic of China, August 17, 1982

August 17, 1982

In the Joint Communiqué on the Establishment of Diplomatic Relations on January 1, 1979, issued by the Government of the United States of America and the People's Republic of China, the United States of America recognized the Government of the People's Republic of China as the sole legal Government of China, and it acknowledged the Chinese position that there is but one China and Taiwan is part of China. Within that context, the two sides agreed that the people of the United States would continue to maintain cultural, commercial, and other unofficial relations with the people of Taiwan. On this basis, relations between the United States and China were normalized.

The question of United States arms sales to Taiwan was not settled in the course of negotiations between the two countries on establishing diplomatic relations. The two sides held differing positions, and the Chinese side stated that it would raise the issue again following normalization. Recognizing that this issue would seriously hamper the development of United States–China relations, they have held further discussions on it, during and since the meetings between President Ronald Reagan and Premier Zhao Ziyang and between Secretary of State Alexander M. Haig, Jr. and Vice Premier and Foreign Minister Huang Hua in October 1981.

Respect for each other's sovereignty and territorial integrity and non-interference in each other's internal affairs constitute the fundamental principles guiding United States China relations. These principles were confirmed in the Shanghai Communiqué of February 28, 1972 and reaffirmed in the Joint Communiqué on the Establishment Of Diplomatic Relations which came into effect on January 1, 1979. Both sides emphatically state that these principles continue to govern all aspects of their relations.

The Chinese Government reiterates that the question of Taiwan is China's internal affair. The Message to Compatriots in Taiwan issued by China on January 1, 1979 promulgated a fundamental policy of striving for peaceful reunification of the motherland. The Nine-Point Proposal put forward by China on September 30, 1981 represented a further major effort under this fundamental policy to strive for a peaceful solution to the Taiwan question.

The United States Government attaches great importance to its relations with China, and reiterates that it has no intention of infringing on Chinese sovereignty and territorial integrity, or interfering in China's internal affairs, or pursuing a policy of "two Chinas" or "one China, one Taiwan." The United States Government understands and appreciates the Chinese policy of striving for a peaceful resolution of the Taiwan question as indicated in China's Message to Compatriots in Taiwan issued on January 1, 1979 and the Nine-Point Proposal put forward by China on September 30, 1981. The new situation which has emerged with regard to the Taiwan question also provides favorable conditions for the settlement of United States–China differences over United States arms sales to Taiwan.

Having in mind the foregoing statements of both sides, the United States Government states that it does not seek to carry out a long-term policy of arms sales to Taiwan, that its arms sales to Taiwan will not exceed, either in qualitative or in quantitative terms, the level of those supplied in recent years since the establishment of diplomatic relations between the United States and China, and that it intends gradually to reduce its sale of arms to Taiwan, leading, over a period of time, to a final resolution. In so stating, the United States acknowledges China's consistent position regarding the thorough settlement of this issue.

In order to bring about, over a period of time, a final settlement of the question of United States arms sales to Taiwan, which is an issue rooted in history, the two Governments will make every effort to adopt measures and create conditions conducive to the thorough settlement of this issue.

The development of United States—China relations is not only in the interests of the two peoples but also conducive to peace and stability in the world. The two sides are determined, on the principle of equality and mutual benefit, to strengthen their ties in the economic, cultural, educational, scientific, technological and other fields and make strong, joint efforts for the continued development of relations between the Governments and peoples of the United States and China.

In order to bring about the healthy development of United States–China relations, maintain world peace and oppose aggression and expansion, the two Governments reaffirm the principles agreed on by the two sides in the Shanghai Communiqué and the Joint Communiqué on the Establishment of Diplomatic Relations. The two sides will maintain contact and hold appropriate consultations on bilateral and international issues of common interest.

NOTE

Government of the United States of America and the People's Republic of China, "Joint Communiqué of the United States of America and the People's Republic of China," August 17, 1982, available online at http://www.fapa.org/generalinfo/shanghai1982.html.

Appendix 9
Anti-Secession Law adopted by NPC, March 14, 2005

ORDER OF THE PRESIDENT OF THE PEOPLE'S REPUBLIC OF CHINA, NO. 34

The Anti-Secession Law, adopted at the Third Session of the Tenth National People's Congress of the People's Republic of China on March 14, 2005, is hereby promulgated and shall go into effect as of the date of promulgation.
Hu Jintao
President of the People's Republic of China
March 14, 2005

The following is the full text of the Anti-Secession Law adopted at the Third Session of the Tenth National People's Congress Monday:

Anti-Secession Law

(Adopted at the Third Session of the Tenth National People's Congress on March 14, 2005)

Article 1

This Law is formulated, in accordance with the Constitution, for the purpose of opposing and checking Taiwan's secession from China by secessionists in the name of "Taiwan independence," promoting peaceful national reunification, maintaining peace and stability in the Taiwan Straits, preserving China's sovereignty and territorial integrity, and safeguarding the fundamental interests of the Chinese nation.

Article 2

There is only one China in the world. Both the mainland and Taiwan belong to one China. China's sovereignty and territorial integrity brook no division. Safeguarding China's sovereignty and territorial integrity is the common obligation of all Chinese people, the Taiwan compatriots included.

Taiwan is part of China. The state shall never allow the "Taiwan independence" secessionist forces to make Taiwan secede from China under any name or by any means.

Article 3

The Taiwan question is one that is left over from China's civil war of the late 1940s.

Solving the Taiwan question and achieving national reunification is China's internal affair, which subjects to no interference by any outside forces.

Article 4

Accomplishing the great task of reunifying the motherland is the sacred duty of all Chinese people, the Taiwan compatriots included.

Article 5

Upholding the principle of one China is the basis of peaceful reunification of the country.

To reunify the country through peaceful means best serves the fundamental interests of the compatriots on both sides of the Taiwan Straits. The state shall do its utmost with maximum sincerity to achieve a peaceful reunification.

After the country is reunified peacefully, Taiwan may practice systems different from those on the mainland and enjoy a high degree of autonomy.

Article 6

The state shall take the following measures to maintain peace and stability in the Taiwan Straits and promote cross-Straits relations:

1. to encourage and facilitate personnel exchanges across the Straits for greater mutual understanding and mutual trust;
2. to encourage and facilitate economic exchanges and cooperation, realize direct links of trade, mail and air and shipping services, and bring about closer economic ties between the two sides of the Straits to their mutual benefit;

3. to encourage and facilitate cross-Straits exchanges in education, science, technology, culture, health and sports, and work together to carry forward the proud Chinese cultural traditions;
4. to encourage and facilitate cross-Straits cooperation in combating crimes; and
5. to encourage and facilitate other activities that are conducive to peace and stability in the Taiwan Straits and stronger cross-Straits relations.

The state protects the rights and interests of the Taiwan compatriots in accordance with law.

Article 7

The state stands for the achievement of peaceful reunification through consultations and negotiations on an equal footing between the two sides of the Taiwan Straits. These consultations and negotiations may be conducted in steps and phases and with flexible and varied modalities.

The two sides of the Taiwan Straits may consult and negotiate on the following matters:
1. officially ending the state of hostility between the two sides;
2. mapping out the development of cross-Straits relations;
3. steps and arrangements for peaceful national reunification;
4. the political status of the Taiwan authorities;
5. the Taiwan region's room of international operation that is compatible with its status; and
6. other matters concerning the achievement of peaceful national reunification.

Article 8

In the event that the "Taiwan independence" secessionist forces should act under any name or by any means to cause the fact of Taiwan's secession from China, or that major incidents entailing Taiwan's secession from China should occur, or that possibilities for a peaceful reunification should be completely exhausted, the state shall employ non-peaceful means and other necessary measures to protect China's sovereignty and territorial integrity.

The State Council and the Central Military Commission shall decide on and execute the non-peaceful means and other necessary measures as provided for in the preceding paragraph and shall promptly report to the Standing Committee of the National People's Congress.

Article 9

In the event of employing and executing non-peaceful means and other necessary measures as provided for in this Law, the state shall exert its utmost to protect the lives, property and other legitimate rights and interests of Taiwan civilians and foreign nationals in Taiwan, and to minimize losses. At the same time, the state shall protect the rights and interests of the Taiwan compatriots in other parts of China in accordance with law.

Article 10

This Law shall come into force on the day of its promulgation.

NOTE

Hu Jintao, "Anti-Secession Law adopted by NPC (full text)," March 14, 2005, available online at http://www.chinadaily.com.cn/english/doc/2005-03/14/content_424643.htm.

Appendix 10

Cross-Straits Economic Cooperation Framework Agreement, June 29, 2010

PREAMBLE

The Straits Exchange Foundation and the Association for Relations Across the Taiwan Straits, adhering to the principles of equality, reciprocity and progressiveness and with a view to strengthening cross-Straits trade and economic relations.

Have agreed, in line with the basic principles of the World Trade Organization (WTO) and in consideration of the economic conditions of the two Parties, to gradually reduce or eliminate barriers to trade and investment for each other, create a fair trade and investment environment, further advance cross-Straits trade and investment relations by signing the Cross-Straits Economic Cooperation Framework Agreement (hereinafter referred to as this Agreement), and establish a cooperation mechanism beneficial to economic prosperity and development across the Straits.

The two Parties have agreed through consultations to the following:

CHAPTER 1: GENERAL PRINCIPLES

Article 1: Objectives

The objectives of this Agreement are:

1. To strengthen and advance the economic, trade and investment cooperation between the two Parties;
2. To promote further liberalization of trade in goods and services between the two Parties and gradually establish fair, transparent and facilitative investment and investment protection mechanisms;
3. To expand areas of economic cooperation and establish a cooperation mechanism.

Article 2: Cooperation Measures

The two Parties have agreed, in consideration of their economic conditions, to take measures including but not limited to the following, in order to strengthen cross-Straits economic exchange and cooperation:

1. Gradually reducing or eliminating tariff and non-tariff barriers to trade in a substantial majority of goods between the two Parties;
2. Gradually reducing or eliminating restrictions on a large number of sectors in trade in services between the two Parties;
3. Providing investment protection and promoting two-way investment;
4. Promoting trade and investment facilitation and industry exchanges and cooperation.

CHAPTER 2: TRADE AND INVESTMENT

Article 3: Trade in Goods

1. The two Parties have agreed, on the basis of the Early Harvest for Trade in Goods as stipulated in Article 7 of this Agreement, to conduct consultations on an agreement on trade in goods no later than six months after the entry into force of this Agreement, and expeditiously conclude such consultations.
2. The consultations on the agreement on trade in goods shall include, but not be limited to:
    a. modalities for tariff reduction or elimination;
    b. rules of origin;
    c. customs procedures;
    d. non-tariff measures, including but not limited to technical barriers to trade (TBT) and sanitary and phytosanitary (SPS) measures;
    e. trade remedy measures, including measures set forth in the Agreement on Implementation of Article VI of the General Agreement on Tariffs and Trade 1994, the Agreement on Subsidies and Countervailing Measures and the Agreement on Safeguards of the World Trade Organization, and the safeguard measures between the two Parties applicable to the trade in goods between the two Parties.
3. Goods included in the agreement on trade in goods pursuant to this Article shall be divided into three categories: goods subject to immediate tariff elimination, goods subject to phased tariff reduction, and exceptions or others.

4. Either Party may accelerate the implementation of tariff reduction at its discretion on the basis of the commitments to tariff concessions in the agreement on trade in goods.

Article 4: Trade in Services

1. The two Parties have agreed, on the basis of the Early Harvest for Trade in Services as stipulated in Article 8, to conduct consultations on an agreement on trade in services no later than six months after the entry into force of this Agreement, and expeditiously conclude such consultations.
2. The consultations on the agreement on trade in services shall seek to:
    a. gradually reduce or eliminate restrictions on a large number of sectors in trade in services between the two Parties;
    b. further increase the breadth and depth of trade in services;
    c. enhance cooperation in trade in services between the two Parties.
    d. Either Party may accelerate the liberalization or elimination of restrictive measures at its discretion on the basis of the commitments to liberalization in the agreement on trade in services.

Article 5: Investment

1. The two Parties have agreed to conduct consultations on the matters referred to in paragraph 2 of this Article within six months after the entry into force of this Agreement, and expeditiously reach an agreement.
2. Such an agreement shall include, but not be limited to, the following:
    a. establishing an investment protection mechanism;
    b. increasing transparency on investment-related regulations;
    c. gradually reducing restrictions on mutual investments between the two Parties;
    d. promoting investment facilitation.

CHAPTER 3: ECONOMIC COOPERATION

Article 6: Economic Cooperation

1. To enhance and expand the benefits of this Agreement, the two Parties have agreed to strengthen cooperation in areas including, but not limited to, the following:

a. intellectual property rights protection and cooperation;
   b. financial cooperation;
   c. trade promotion and facilitation;
   d. customs cooperation;
   e. e-commerce cooperation;
   f. discussion on the overall arrangements and key areas for industrial cooperation, promotion of cooperation in major projects, and coordination of the resolution of issues that may arise in the course of industrial cooperation between the two Parties;
   g. promotion of small and medium-sized enterprises cooperation between the two Parties, and enhancement of the competitiveness of these enterprises;
   h. promotion of the mutual establishment of offices by economic and trade bodies of the two Parties.
2. The two Parties shall expeditiously conduct consultations on the specific programs and contents of the cooperation matters listed in this Article.

CHAPTER 4: EARLY HARVEST

Article 7: Early Harvest for Trade in Goods

1. To accelerate the realization of the objectives of this Agreement, the two Parties have agreed to implement the Early Harvest Program with respect to the goods listed in Annex I. The Early Harvest Program shall start to be implemented within six months after the entry into force of this Agreement.
2. The Early Harvest Program for trade in goods shall be implemented in accordance with the following rules:
   a. the two Parties shall implement the tariff reductions in accordance with the product list and tariff reduction arrangements under the Early Harvest stipulated in Annex I, unless their respective non-interim tariff rates generally applied on imports from all other WTO members are lower, in which case such rates shall apply;
   b. the products listed in Annex I of this Agreement shall be subject to the Provisional Rules of Origin stipulated in Annex II. Each Party shall accord preferential tariff treatment to the above-mentioned products that are determined, pursuant to such Rules, as originating in the other Party upon importation;

    c. the provisional trade remedy measures applicable to the products listed in Annex I of this Agreement refer to measures provided for in subparagraph (5) of paragraph 2 of Article 3 of this Agreement. The safeguard measures between the two Parties are specified in Annex III of this Agreement.

3. As of the date of the entry into force of the agreement on trade in goods to be reached by the two Parties pursuant to Article 3 of this Agreement, the Provisional Rules of Origin stipulated in Annex II and the provisional trade remedy measures provided for in subparagraph (3) of paragraph 2 of this Article shall cease to apply.

Article 8: Early Harvest for Trade in Services

1. To accelerate the realization of the objectives of this Agreement, the two Parties have agreed to implement the Early Harvest Program on the sectors and liberalization measures listed in Annex IV. The Early Harvest Program shall be implemented expeditiously after the entry into force of this Agreement.
2. The Early Harvest Program for Trade in Services shall be implemented in accordance with the following rules:

    a. each Party shall, in accordance with the Sectors and Liberalization Measures Under the Early Harvest for Trade in Services in Annex IV, reduce or eliminate the restrictive measures in force affecting the services and service suppliers of the other Party;

    b. the definition of service suppliers stipulated in Annex V applies to the sectors and liberalization measures with respect to trade in services in Annex IV of this Agreement;

    c. as of the date of the entry into force of the agreement on trade in services to be reached by the two Parties pursuant to Article 4 of this Agreement, the definitions of service suppliers stipulated in Annex V of this Agreement shall cease to apply;

    d. in the event that the implementation of the Early Harvest Program for Trade in Services has caused a material adverse impact on the services sectors of one Party, the affected Party may request consultations with the other Party to seek a solution.

CHAPTER 5: OTHER PROVISIONS

Article 9: Exceptions

No provision in this Agreement shall be interpreted to prevent either Party from adopting or maintaining exception measures consistent with the rules of the World Trade Organization.

Article 10: Dispute Settlement

1. The two Parties shall engage in consultations on the establishment of appropriate dispute settlement procedures no later than six months after the entry into force of this Agreement, and expeditiously reach an agreement in order to settle any dispute arising from the interpretation, implementation and application of this Agreement.
2. Any dispute over the interpretation, implementation and application of this Agreement prior to the date the dispute settlement agreement mentioned in paragraph 1 of this Article enters into force shall be resolved through consultations by the two Parties or in an appropriate manner by the Cross-Straits Economic Cooperation Committee to be established in accordance with Article 11 of this Agreement.

Article 11: Institutional Arrangements

1. The two Parties shall establish a Cross-Straits Economic Cooperation Committee (hereinafter referred to as the Committee), which consists of representatives designated by the two Parties. The Committee shall be responsible for handling matters relating to this Agreement, including but not limited to:
    a. concluding consultations necessary for the attainment of the objectives of this Agreement;
    b. monitoring and evaluating the implementation of this Agreement;
    c. interpreting the provisions of this Agreement;
    d. notifying important economic and trade information;
    e. settling any dispute over the interpretation, implementation and application of this Agreement in accordance with Article 10 of this Agreement.
2. The Committee may set up working group(s) as needed to handle matters in specific areas pertaining to this Agreement, under the supervision of the Committee.

3. The Committee will convene a regular meeting on a semi-annual basis and may call ad hoc meeting(s) when necessary with consent of the two Parties.
4. Matters related to this Agreement shall be communicated through contact persons designated by the competent authorities of the two Parties.

Article 12: Documentation Formats

The two Parties shall use the agreed documentation formats for communication of matters arising from this Agreement.

Article 13: Annexes and Subsequent Agreements

All annexes to this Agreement and subsequent agreements signed in accordance with this Agreement shall be parts of this Agreement.

Article 14: Amendments

Amendments to this Agreement shall be subject to consent through consultations between, and confirmation in writing by, the two Parties.

Article 15: Entry into Force

After the signing of this Agreement, the two Parties shall complete the relevant procedures respectively and notify each other in writing. This Agreement shall enter into force as of the day following the date that both Parties have received such notification from each other.

Article 16: Termination

1. The Party terminating this Agreement shall notify the other Party in writing. The two Parties shall start consultations within 30 days from the date the termination notice is issued. In case the consultations fail to reach a consensus, this Agreement shall be terminated on the 180th day from the date the termination notice is issued by the notifying Party.
2. Within 30 days from the date of termination of this Agreement, the two Parties shall engage in consultations on issues arising from the termination.

This Agreement is signed in quadruplicate on this 29th day of June [2010] with each Party retaining two copies. The different wording of the corresponding text of this Agreement shall carry the same meaning, and all four copies are equally authentic.

Annex I: Product List and Tariff Reduction Arrangements Under the Early Harvest for Trade in Goods
Annex II: Provisional Rules of Origin Applicable to Products Under the Early Harvest for Trade in Goods
Annex III: Safeguard Measures Between the Two Parties Applicable to Products Under the Early Harvest for Trade in Goods
Annex IV: Sectors and Liberalization Measures Under the Early Harvest for Trade in Services
Annex V: Definitions of Service Suppliers Applicable to Sectors and Liberalization Measures Under the Early Harvest for Trade in Services

Chairman	President
Straits Exchange Foundation	Association for Relations Across the Taiwan Straits

NOTE

Chairman of the Straits Exchange Foundation and President of the Association for Relations Across the Taiwan Straits, "China–Taiwan Economic Cooperation Framework Agreement (ECFA), June 29, 2010," English translation, published October 28, 2010, available online at http://china.usc.edu/ShowArticle.aspx?articleID=2273&AspxAutoDetectCookieSupport=1.

Acronyms

AA	anti-aircraft
ARIES	airborne-reconnaissance integrated electronic system
ARL	landing-craft repair ship
ASEAN	Association of Southeast Asian Nations
ASW	antisubmarine warfare
CCK	Ching Chuan Kang Air Base (Taiwan)
CHINATS	Chinese Nationalists
CHINCOM	China Committee, Chinese communists
CIA	Central Intelligence Agency
CIC	Combat Information Center
CinCPac	Commander-in-Chief, U.S. Pacific Command
CinCPacFlt	commander in chief of the Pacific Fleet
CLCS	Commission on the Limit of the Continental Shelf
CNAF	Chinese Nationalist Air Force
CNO	chief of naval operations
CO	commanding officer
COCOM	Coordinating Committee for Multilateral Export Controls
ComNavFE	commander of naval forces in the Far East
ComSeventhFlt	Commander of the Seventh Fleet
CommOff	communication officer
CTG	commander of the task group
CVA	attack aircraft carrier
CVS	antisubmarine-aircraft carrier
DER	destroyer radar picket escort ship
DE	destroyer escort
DFC	Distinguished Flying Cross
DOD	Department of Defense

DPP	(Taiwanese) Democratic Progressive Party
ECM	electronic countermeasures
EEZ	exclusive economic zone
ELINT	electronic intelligence
EMCON	emission control
FAW	fleet air wing
GATT	General Agreement on Tariff and Trade
GCA	ground-controlled approach
GNP	gross national product
HUK	hunter-killer
JATO	jet-assisted takeoff
JCS	Joint Chiefs of Staff
LCM	landing-craft mechanized
LCVD	landing-craft vehicle personnel
LSD	Dock Landing Ship
LSM	Landing Ship Medium
LST	landing ship, tank
MAAG	military-assistance advisory group
NDB	nuclear depth bomb
NGRC	Nationalist Government of the Republic of China
NSC	National Security Council
ONI	(U.S. Navy's) Office of Naval Intelligence
OpOrders	operations orders
OpPlans	operations plans
OTC	officer in tactical command
PBM	patrol-bomber mariner
PLA	People's Liberation Army
PLAAF	People's Liberation Army Air Force
PLAN	People's Liberation Army Navy
POW	prisoner of war
PRC	People's Republic of China
R & D	research and development
R & R	rest and recreation

RCN	Republic of China Navy
ROC	Republic of China on Taiwan
ROE	rule(s) of engagement
ROV	Republic of Vietnam
SAR	search and rescue
SLOC	sea line of communication
SRBM	short-range ballistic missile
TBT	technical barriers to trade
TG	task group
TDCAT	Tachen Defense Command Advisory Team
UN	United Nations
USN	U.S. Navy
USSR	Union of Soviet Socialist Republics
USTDC	United States Taiwan Defense Command
VFW	Veterans of Foreign Wars
VP	U.S. Navy patrol squadron
WEI	Western Enterprises Incorporated
WTO	World Trade Organization
XO	executive officer

Bibliography

ARCHIVES AND MANUSCRIPT COLLECTIONS

John Foster Dulles Papers. Princeton University.
The National Archives. Ministry of Justice of the United Kingdom. Kew, England.
Naval History and Heritage Command Archives. U.S. Navy. Washington, DC.
The National Archives and Records Administration. Federal Government of the United States. Washington, DC.
U.S. Army Center of Military History. Ft. McNair. Washington, DC.

ORAL HISTORIES

Anderson, George W. *Reminiscences of Admiral George W. Anderson, Jr., U.S. Navy (Retired)*. Oral History 42. Annapolis, MD: U.S. Naval Institute, 1983.
Ansel, Walter. *The Reminiscences of Rear Admiral Walter C. W. Ansel, U.S. Navy (Retired)*. Oral History 74. Annapolis, MD: U.S. Naval Institute, 1972.
Beshany, Philip A. *The Reminiscences of Vice Admiral Philip A. Beshany, U.S. Navy (Retired)*. Oral History 45. Annapolis, MD: U.S. Naval Institute, 1983.
Bucklew, Phil H. *Reminiscences of Captain Phil H. Bucklew, U.S. Navy (Retired)*. Oral History 34. Annapolis, MD: U.S. Naval Institute, 1982.
Burke, Arleigh A. *Recollections of Admiral Arleigh A. Burke, U.S. Navy (Retired)*. Oral History 64. Annapolis, MD: U.S. Naval Institute, 1973.
Felt, Harry Donald. *Reminiscences of Admiral Harry Donald Felt, U.S. Navy (Retired)*. Oral History 138. Annapolis, MD: U.S. Naval Institute, 1974.
Frankel, Samuel B. *The Reminiscences of Rear Admiral Samuel B. Frankel, U.S. Navy (Retired)*. Oral History 325. Annapolis, MD: U.S. Naval Institute, 1972.
Smoot, Vice Admiral Roland N. "As I Recall . . . The U.S. Taiwan Defense Command." *Proceedings* 110/9/979 (September 1984): 56–59.
Stroop, Paul David. *The Reminiscences of Vice Admiral Paul D. Stroop, U.S. Navy (Retired)*. Oral History 139. Annapolis, MD: U.S. Naval Institute, 1970.

PUBLISHED DOCUMENTS

"Study on the Problems Involved in Military Aid to China." In *Foreign Relations of the United States*, vol. 9, *The Far East: China, 1949*. Washington, DC: United States Government Printing Office, 1974.
Chairman of the Straits Exchange Foundation and President of the Association for Relations across the Taiwan Straits. "China–Taiwan Economic Cooperation Framework Agreement (ECFA), June 29, 2010." English translation. Published October 28, 2010. Available online at http://china.usc.edu/ShowArticle.aspx?articleID=2273&AspxAutoDetectCookieSupport=1.
Government of the United States of America and the People's Republic of China. "Joint Communiqué of the United States of America and the People's Republic of

China." August 17, 1982. Available online at http://www.fapa.org/generalinfo/shanghai1982.html.
Jintao, Hu. "Anti-Secession Law adopted by NPC (full text)." March 14, 2005. Available online at http://www.chinadaily.com.cn/english/doc/2005-03/14/content_424643.htm.
People's Republic of China and the United States of America. "Joint Communiqué between the People's Republic of China and the United States of America Issued in Shanghai, February 28, 1972." February 28, 1972. Available online at http://www.sinomania.com/CHINANEWS/shanghai_communique_30th_anniversary.htm.
———. "Joint Communiqué on the Establishment of Diplomatic Relations between the People's Republic of China and the United States of America (December 16, 1978)." December 16, 1978. Available online at http://www.china-embassy.org/eng/zmgx/doc/ctc/t36256.htm.
Philips, Steven E., ed., and Edward C. Keefer, gen. ed. *Foreign Relations of the United States, 1969–1976*. Vol. 17, *China, 1969–1972*. Washington, DC: United States Government Printing Office, 2006.
Schwar, Harriet Dashiell, ed., and Glen W. LaFantasie, gen. ed. "Memorandum of Conversation," September 2, 1958. In *Foreign Relations of the United States, 1958–1960*. Vol. 19, *China*. Washington, DC: United States Government Printing Office, 1996.
———. "Memorandum of Conversation," September 16, 1958. In *Foreign Relations of the United States, 1958–1960*. Vol. 19, *China*. Washington, DC: United States Government Printing Office, 1996.
———. "Memorandum Prepared in the Department of State," undated. In *Foreign Relations of the United States, 1958–1960*. Vol. 19, *China*. Washington, DC: United States Government Printing Office, 1996.
Schwar, Harriet D., and Louis J. Smith, eds., and John P. Glennon, gen. ed., "Memorandum for the Record, by the Ambassador in the Republic of China (Rankin)," April 29, 1955, 529–31. In *Foreign Relations of the United States, 1955–1957*. Vol. 3, *China*. Washington, DC: U.S. Government Printing Office, 1986.
United States of America and the Republic of China. "Mutual Defense Treaty between the United States of America and the Republic of China." December 2, 1954. Available online at http://www.taiwandocuments.org/mutual01.htm.
U.S. Congress, Taiwan Relations Act, Public Law 96-8, 96th Cong., January 1, 1979, available online at http://www.ait.org.tw/en/taiwan-relations-act.html.
———. *United States Statutes at Large*, vol. 69. Washington, DC: U.S. Government Printing Office, 1955.
———. *United States Statutes at Large*, vol. 88, part 2. Washington, DC: U.S. Government Printing Office, 1974.

BOOKS AND ARTICLES

Accinelli, Robert. *Crisis and Commitment: United States Policy toward Taiwan, 1950–1955*. Chapel Hill: The University of North Carolina Press, 1996.
Ballantine, Joseph W. *Formosa: A Problem for United States Foreign Policy*. Washington, DC: The Brookings Institution, 1952.
Barlow, Jeffrey G. *From Hot War to Cold: The U.S. Navy and National Security Affairs, 1945–1955*. Stanford, CA: Stanford University Press, 2009.
Bate, H. Maclear. *Report from Formosa*. New York: E. P. Dutton & Co., Inc., 1952.
Bell, Christopher, and Bruce A. Elleman, eds. *Naval Mutinies of the Twentieth Century: An International Perspective*. London: Frank Cass, 2003.
Black, Jeremy, ed. *The Seventy Great Battles of All Time*. London: Thames and Hudson, 2005.
Bouchard, Joseph F. *Command in Crisis: Four Case Studies*. New York: Columbia University Press, 1991.

Bush, Richard C. *At Cross Purposes: U.S.–Taiwan Relations since 1942.* Armonk, NY: M. E. Sharpe Press, 2004.
Bussert, James and Bruce A. Elleman. *People's Liberation Army Navy (PLAN): Combat Systems Technology, 1949–2010.* Annapolis, MD: Naval Institute Press, 2011.
"Central People's Government Formed; KMT Seizes U.S. Ships," *China Weekly Review,* October 8, 1949.
Chao, John K. T. "South China Sea: Boundary Problems Relating to the Nansha and Hsisha Islands." In *Chinese Yearbook of International Law and Affairs,* vol. 9, 1989–1990, edited by Hungdah Chiu, 66–156. Taipei: Chinese Society of International Law, 1991.
Chase, Michael S. "U.S.–Taiwan Security Cooperation: Enhancing an Unofficial Relationship." In *Dangerous Strait: The U.S.–Taiwan–China Crisis,* edited by Nancy Bernkopf Tucker (New York: Columbia University Press, 2005).
Chang, Gordan H. *Friends and Enemies: The United States, China, and the Soviet Union, 1948–1972.* Stanford, CA: Stanford University Press, 1990.
Chang, Jung. *Wild Swans.* New York: Simon and Schuster, 1991.
Chang, Jung, and Jon Halliday. *Mao: The Unknown Story.* New York: Alfred A. Knopf, 2005.
Chang, Pao-Min. *Sino–Vietnamese Territorial Dispute.* New York: Praeger, 1986.
Chen, Jian. *Mao's China and the Cold War.* Chapel Hill: University of North Carolina Press, 2001.
Chen, Ming-tong. *The China Threat Crosses the Strait: Challenges and Strategies for Taiwan's National Security.* Translated by Kiel Downey. Taipei: Dong Fan Color Printing Co., 2007.
Chiu, Hungdah. *China and the Taiwan Issue.* New York: Praeger Publishers, 1979.
Chiu, Hungdah, and Choon-Ho Park. "Legal Status of the Paracel and Spratly Islands," *Ocean Development and International Law,* 3, no. 1 (1975): 1–28. Text available online at http://colp.sjtu.edu.cn/image/20130227/20130227112060586058.pdf.
Christensen, Thomas J. *Useful Adversaries: Grand Strategy, Domestic Mobilization, and Sino–American Conflict, 1947–1958.* Princeton, NJ: Princeton University Press, 1996.
Clough, Ralph N. *Island China.* Cambridge, MA: Harvard University Press, 1978.
Cohen, Warren I., ed. *New Frontiers in American–East Asian Relations.* New York: Columbia University Press, 1983.
Copper, John F. "The Origins of Conflict across the Taiwan Strait: The Problem of Differences in Perceptions." In *Across the Taiwan Strait: Mainland China, Taiwan, and the 1995–1996 Crisis,* edited by Suisheng Zhao. New York: Routledge Press, 1999.
Daugherty, Leo J., III, *The Marine Corps and the State Department: Enduring Partners in United States Foreign Policy, 1798–2007.* Jefferson, NC: Macfarland and Co., 2009.
Di, He. "The Last Campaign to Unify China." In *Chinese Warfighting: The PLA Experience since 1949,* ed. Mark A. Ryan, David M. Finkelstein, and Michael A. McDevitt, 73–90. Armonk, NY: M. E. Sharpe Publishers, 2003.
Dikötter, Frank. *Mao's Great Famine: The History of China's Most Devastating Catastrophe, 1958–1962.* New York: Walker and Co., 2010.
Dulles, Foster Rhea. *American Policy toward Communist China, 1949–1969.* New York: Thomas Y. Crowell Company, 1972.
Durkin, Michael F. *Naval Quarantine: A New Addition to the Role of Sea Power.* Maxwell Air Force Base, AL: Air University, Air War College, 1964.
Eisenhower, Dwight D. *The White House Years: Mandate for Change, 1953–1956.* Garden City, NY: Doubleday and Co., 1963.
———. *The White House Years: Waging Peace, 1956–1961.* Garden City, NY: Doubleday and Co., 1965.
Elleman, Bruce A. "The *Chongqing* Mutiny and the Chinese Civil War, 1949." In *Naval Mutinies of the Twentieth Century: An International Perspective,* edited by Christopher Bell and Bruce A. Elleman, 232–45. London: Frank Cass, 2003.
———. "Huai-Hai." In *The Seventy Great Battles of All Time,* edited by Jeremy Black, 279–81. London: Thames and Hudson, 2005.

———. *Modern Chinese Warfare, 1795–1989*. London: Routledge Press, 2001.

———. *Moscow and the Emergence of Communist Power in China, 1925–30: The Nanchang Uprising and the Birth of the Red Army*. London: Routledge, 2009.

———. "The Nationalists' Blockade of the PRC, 1949–58." In *Naval Blockades and Seapower; Strategies and Counter-Strategies, 1805–2005*, edited by Bruce A. Elleman and S. C. M. Paine, 133–44. London: Routledge Press, 2006.

———. "The Right Skill Set: Joseph Wilson Prueher (1941–)." In *Nineteen Gun Salute: Case Studies of Operational, Strategic, and Diplomatic Naval Leadership during the 20th and Early 21st Centuries*, edited by John B. Hattendorf and Bruce A. Elleman. Newport, RI: NWC Press, 2010.

Elleman, Bruce A., and S. C. M. Paine. *Modern China: Continuity and Change, 1644 to the Present*. Upper Saddle River, NJ: Prentice-Hall, 2010.

———, eds. *Naval Blockades and Seapower: Strategies and Counter-strategies, 1805–2005*. London: Routledge Press, 2006.

———, eds., *Naval Power and Expeditionary Warfare: Peripheral Campaigns and New Theatres of Naval Warfare*. London: Routledge Press, 2011.

Elleman, Bruce A., and Stephen Kotkin, eds. *Manchurian Railways and the Opening of China: An International History*. Armonk, NY: M. E. Sharpe, 2010.

Fisher, Richard D. "China's Missiles over the Taiwan Strait: A Political and Military Assessment." In *Crisis in the Taiwan Strait*, ed. James R. Lilley and Chuck Downs (Ft. McNair, Washington, DC: National Defense University Press, 1997).

Gallagher, Rick M. *The Taiwan Strait Crisis*. Newport, RI: U.S. Naval War College, 1997.

Garver, John W. *China's Decision for Rapprochement with the United States, 1968–1971*. Boulder, CO: Westview Press, 1982.

———. *The Sino–American Alliance: Nationalist China and American Cold War Strategy in Asia*. Armonk, NY: M. E. Sharpe, 1997.

Gibert, Stephen P., and William M. Carpenter. *America and Island China: A Documentary History*. Lanham, MD: University Press of America, 1989.

Gittings, John. *The Role of the Chinese Army*. New York: Oxford University Press, 1967.

Glass, Sheppard. "Some Aspects of Formosa's Economic Growth." In *Formosa Today*, edited by Mark Mancall, 68–90. New York: Frederick A. Praeger, 1964.

Government of the People's Republic of China. "Declaration on China's Territorial Sea," *Peking [Beijing] Review*, no. 1 (September 9, 1958): 21. English text available online at http://www.state.gov/documents/organization/58832.pdf.

Gu, Weigun. *Conflicts of Divided Nations: The Case of China and Korea*. Westport, CT: Praeger, 1995.

Guoxing, Ji. "The Legality of the '*Impeccable* Incident.'" *China Security* 5, no. 2 (Spring 2009): 16–21.

Haller-Trost, R. *Occasional Paper No. 14: The Spratly Islands; a Study on the Limitations of International Law*. Canterbury: University of Kent Centre of South-East Asian Studies, 1990.

Hickey, Dennis Van Vranken. *United States–Taiwan Security Ties: From Cold War to Beyond Containment*. Westport, CT: Praeger, 1994.

Hinton, Harold C. *China's Turbulent Quest*. New York: The Macmillan Company, 1972.

Holober, Frank. *Raiders of the China Coast: CIA Covert Operations during the Korean War*. Annapolis, MD: Naval Institute Press, 1999.

Hugill, Paul D. *The Continuing Utility of Naval Blockades in the Twenty-First Century*. Fort Leavenworth, KS: U.S. Army Command and General Staff College, 1998.

"The Illegal Blockade," *China Weekly Review*, December 31, 1949.

Kerr, George H. *Formosa Betrayed*. Boston: Houghton Mifflin Company, 1965.

Khrushchev, Sergei, ed. *Memoirs of Nikita Khrushchev: Statesman, 1953–1964*. Translated by George Shriver. University Park: Pennsylvania State University, 2007.

Kierman, Frank A., Jr., and John K. Fairbank, eds. *Chinese Ways in Warfare*. Cambridge, MA: Harvard University Press, 1974.

Kissinger, Henry. *White House Years*. Boston: Little, Brown, 1979.

Kondapalli, Srikanth. *China's Naval Power*. New Delhi: Knowledge World, 2001.

Lasater, Martin L., ed. *Beijing's Blockade Threat to Taiwan: A Heritage Roundtable.* Washington, DC: Heritage Foundation, 1986.

Li, Xiaobing. *A History of the Modern Chinese Army.* Lexington: The University of Kentucky, 2007.

———. "PLA Attacks and Amphibious Operations during the Taiwan Strait Crises of 1954–55 and 1958." In *Chinese Warfighting*, edited by Mark A. Ryan, David Finkelstein, and Michael Devitt, 143–172. Armonk, NY: M. E. Sharpe, 2003.

Liu, Ta Jen. *U.S.–China Relations, 1784–1992.* Lanham, MD: University Press of America, 1997.

Love, Robert W., Jr., Laurie Bogle, Brian VanDeMark, and Maochun Yu, eds. *New Interpretations in Naval History.* Annapolis, MD: Naval Institute Press, 2001.

Lüthi, Lorenz M. *The Sino–Soviet Split: Cold War in the Communist World.* Princeton, NJ: Princeton University Press, 2008.

Marolda, Edward J. *The Approaching Storm: Conflict in Asia, 1945–1965.* Washington, DC: Government Printing Office, 2009.

———. *By Sea, Air, and Land: An Illustrated History of the U.S. Navy and the War in Southeast Asia.* Washington, DC: Government Printing Office, 1994.

———. "Confrontation in the Taiwan Straits." In *U.S. Navy: A Complete History*, ed. M. Hill Goodspeed, 578–579. Washington, DC: Naval Historical Foundation, 2003.

———. "Hostilities along the China Coast during the Korean War." In *New Interpretations in Naval History*, edited by Robert W. Love Jr., Laurie Bogle, Brian VanDeMark, and Maochun Yu, 352. Annapolis, MD: Naval Institute Press, 2001.

———. *A New Equation: Chinese Intervention into the Korean War; Proceedings of the Colloquium on Contemporary History.* Washington, DC: Naval Historical Center, 1991.

———. *Ready Sea Power: An Illustrated History of the U.S. Seventh Fleet.* Washington, DC: Naval History and Heritage Command, 2011.

———. "The U.S. Navy and the Chinese Civil War, 1945–1952." PhD diss., The George Washington University, 1990.

Marolda, Edward J., and Oscar P. Fitzgerald. *From Military Assistance to Combat, 1959–1965.* Vol. 2 of *The United States Navy and the Vietnam Conflict.* Washington, DC: Naval Historical Center, 1986.

Ministry of Foreign Affairs of China. "China's Indisputable Sovereignty over the Xisha and Nansha islands," *Beijing Review* 23, no. 7 (February 18, 1980): 15–24.

Muller, David. *China as a Maritime Power.* Boulder, CO: Westview Press, 1983.

Myer, Ramon H., and Jianlin Zhang. *The Struggle across the Taiwan Strait.* Stanford, CA: Hoover Institution Press, 2006.

Newsweek. "Pressure and a Pact." December 13, 1954.

Park, Chang-Kwoun. "Consequences of U.S. Naval Shows of Force, 1946–1989." PhD diss., University of Missouri–Columbia, 1995.

Petina, David. "Unified Germany: Friend or Foe?" *Res Publica* 2, no. 1 (January 1991). http://www.ashbrook.org/publicat/respub/v2n1/petina1.html (accessed on October 27, 2011).

Porch, Douglas. "The Taiwan Strait Crisis of 1996: Strategic Implications for the United States Navy," *Naval War College Review* 52, no. 3 (Summer 1999): 17–48. Original edition downloadable from https://www.usnwc.edu/Publications/Naval-War-College-Review/Archivedissues/1990s/1999-Summer.aspx.

Powell, Ralph L. *The Rise of Chinese Military Power, 1895–1912.* Princeton, NJ: Princeton University Press, 1955.

Rahman, Chris. "Ballistic Missiles in China's Anti-Taiwan Blockade." In *Naval Blockades and Seapower; Strategies and Counter-Strategies, 1805–2005*, edited by Bruce A. Elleman and S. C. M. Paine, 215–223. London: Routledge Press, 2006.

Reardon, Lawrence C. *The Reluctant Dragon: Crisis Cycles in Chinese Foreign Economic Policy.* Seattle: University of Washington Press, 2002.

Ross, Robert S., ed. *After the Cold War: Domestic Factors and U.S.–China Relations.* Armonk, NY: M. E. Sharpe, 1998.

Schell, Orville. *Mandate of Heaven.* New York: Simon and Schuster, 1994.

Schreadley, R. L. *From the Rivers to the Sea: The United States Navy in Vietnam*. Annapolis, MD: Naval Institute Press, 1992.
Shen, James C. H. *The U.S. and Free China: How the U.S. Sold Out Its Ally*. Washington, DC: Acropolis Books, 1983.
Shen, Jianming. "China's Sovereignty over the South China Sea Islands: A Historical Perspective," *Chinese JIL* (2002): 94–157. Available online at http://chinesejil.oxfordjournals.org/content/1/1/94.full.pdf.
Stevens, David, ed. *Maritime Power in the Twentieth Century*. St. Leonards, Australia: Allen and Unwin, 1998.
Swanson, Bruce. *Eighth Voyage of the Dragon: A History of China's Quest for Seapower*. Annapolis, MD: Naval Institute Press, 1982.
Synder, Edwin K., A. James Gregor, and Maria Hsia Chang. *The Taiwan Relations Act and the Defense of the Republic of China*. Berkeley: University of California Press, 1980.
Szonyi, Michael. *Cold War Island: Quemoy on the Front Line*. New York: Cambridge University Press, 2008.
Tai, Wan-chin. "U.S. Intervention in March 1996 Taiwan Strait Crisis: Interpretation from the Model of Coercive Diplomacy," *Tamkang Journal of International Affairs* 2, no. 1 (March 1998): 1–20.
Thomas, John R. "The Limits of Alliance: The Quemoy Crisis of 1958." In *Sino–Soviet Military Relations*, edited by Raymond L. Garthoff, 114–149. New York: Frederick A Praeger, 1966.
Tkacik, John J., Jr. "Strategy Deficit: U.S. Security in the Pacific and the Future of Taiwan." In *Reshaping the Taiwan Strait*, edited by John J. Tkacik Jr., 11–56. Washington, DC: Heritage Foundation, 2007.
Tsai, Shih-Shan Henry. *Maritime Taiwan: Historical Encounters with the East and the West*. Armonk, NY: M. E. Sharpe, 2009.
Tucker, Nancy Bernkopf, "Strategic Ambiguity or Strategic Clarity?" In *Dangerous Strait: The U.S.–Taiwan–China Crisis*, edited by Nancy Bernkopf Tucker, 186–212. New York: Columbia University Press, 2005.
U.S. News and World Report. "China Blockade: How It Works; Ships by the U.S.—Sailors by Chiang Kai-shek." February 20, 1953.
———. "A New Type of Formosa Warfare: Reds Spot British Cargo Ships for Chiang's Bombers." November 18, 1955.
U.S. Office of Naval Intelligence. "Aerial Tactics of the Chinese Communists in Naval Operations." *ONI Review* (February 1955): 85–87.
———. "The Chinese Nationalist Navy," *ONI Review* (January 1955): 29–34.
———. "The Chinese Navy, Past and Present." *ONI Review* (January 1947): 21–29.
———. "Current Trends in the Chinese Communist Navy," *ONI Review* (November 1960): 476–81.
———. "Intelligence Briefs: China." *ONI Review* (January 1949): 39.
———. "Intelligence Briefs: China," *ONI Review* (August 1952): 336.
———. "Intelligence Briefs: Japan." *ONI Review* (October 1946): 47.
———. "The Red Chinese Navy." *ONI Review*, secret supplement (Summer 1956): 5–8.
———. "The Southeast China Coast Today." *ONI Review* (February 1953): 51–60.
———. "The Struggle for the Coastal Islands of China." *ONI Review Supplement* (December 1953): i–ix.
Wang, Gabe T. *China and the Taiwan Issue: Impending War at Taiwan Strait*. Lanham, MD: University Press of America, 2006.
Whiting, Allen. *China Crosses the Yalu: The Decision to Enter the Korean War*. New York: Macmillan, 1960.
Yang, Zhiben. 杨志本, ed. *Zhongguo Haijun Baikequanshu* 中国海军百科全书 [*China Navy Encyclopedia*], vol. 2. Beijing: 海潮出版社 [Sea Tide Press], 1998.
Young, Marilyn B. *The Vietnam Wars, 1945–1990*. New York: HarperCollins, 1991.
Yu, Peter Kien-hong. *The Four Archipelagoes in the South China Sea*. Taipei: Council for Advanced Policy Studies, 1991.

Zhang, Shu Guang. *Economic Cold War: America's Embargo against China and the Sino–Soviet Alliance, 1949–1963.* Stanford, CA: Stanford University Press, 2001.
Zhonghua guochi ditu, zaiban [Map of China's National Humiliation, Reprint]. Shanghai: Zhonghua Shuju, 1927.

INTERNET SOURCES

Abrahamson, Sherman R. "Intelligence for Economic Defense." Central Intelligence Agency. September 18, 1995. Last updated August 3, 2011. https://www.cia.gov/library/center-for-the-study-of-intelligence/kent-csi/vol8no2/html/v08i2a03p_0001.htm.

Bender, Donald E. "The Nike Missile System: A Concise Historical Overview." Last modified May 2, 2004. Accessed December 16, 2010. http://alpha.fdu.edu/~bender/N-view.html.

Bublitz, Bob. "To Speak of Many Things (Part One)." *VQ Association Newsletter* (Winter/Spring 2005): 2–4. http://www.vqassociation.org/Documents/VQ_Newsletter_Winter-Spring_2005-4.pdf.

Bogart, Charles H. "Christmas in the Formosa Straits." Dennis J. Buckley and Other Navy Links. Accessed December 13, 2010. http://djbuckley.com/bogy1.htm.

Claytor, Joe. "USS *Keppler* (DD-765)." Korean War Project. Accessed October 23, 2014, http://www.koreanwar.org/html/units1/navy/uss_keppler.htm.

Commander-in-Chief, U.S. Pacific Command. "CINCPAC Command History, 1974," vol. 1. Accessed October 16, 2014, http://oldsite.nautilus.org/archives/library/security/foia/Japan/CINCPAC74Ip263.PDF.

"Commanding Officers Annual History Reports" (accessed October 16, 2014), http://www.uss-buchanan-ddg14.org/Annual%20History/History77.htm

Current Digest of the Russian Press. "Report by Soviet Sailors of the Tanker *Tuapse*," 10, no. 25 (July 30, 1958). Available online at http://dlib.eastview.com/browse/doc/13821870 (accessed October 23, 2014).

Dictionary of American Naval Fighting Ships. "*Philippine Sea.*" Accessed October 23, 2014. http://www.history.navy.mil/danfs/p6/philippine_sea.htm.

———. "*Taussig.*" Accessed October 23, 2014. http://www.history.navy.mil/danfs/t3/taussig.htm.

Facts and Details. "Population in China." Accessed October 23, 2014. http://factsanddetails.com/china/cat4/sub15/item129.html.

Federation of American Scientists, Space Policy Project: Special Weapons Monitor. "Hawk." Accessed December 20, 2010. http://www.fas.org/spp/starwars/program/hawk.htm.

Freeze, Ken. "Rescue off China; Crash of CG PBM-5G 84738." Check-Six.com. Accessed October 23, 2014. http://www.check-six.com/Coast_Guard/Rescue_off_China.htm.

GlobalSecurity.org. "First Taiwan Strait Crisis: Quemoy and Matsu Islands." Accessed December 14, 2010. http://www.globalsecurity.org/military/ops/quemoy_matsu.htm.

———. "Taiwan Strait: 21 July 1995 to 23 March 1996." Accessed October 23, 2014. http://www.globalsecurity.org/military/ops/taiwan_strait.htm.

Hays, Jeffrey. "Communists Take Over China." Facts and Details. Last updated August 2013. http://factsanddetails.com/china/cat2/sub6/item74.html.

History of the Grey Knights"VP-46: History of VP-46." Accessed October 16, 2014. http://www.vp46.navy.mil/history.html.

Hullnumber.com. "USS *Turner Joy* (DD-951)." Accessed October 16, 2014. http://www.hullnumber.com/DD-951.

Kawashima, Shin. "Soviet-Taiwanese Relations during the Early Cold War." Wilson Center, Cold War International History Project. September 23, 2009. Accessed De-

cember 14, 2010. http://www.wilsoncenter.org/event/soviet-taiwanese-relations-during-the-early-cold-war.
Keng, Robert. "Republic of China F-86's in Battle." Aircraft Resource Center. 2003. Accessed March 22, 2011. http://www.aircraftresourcecenter.com/Stories1/001-100/021_TaiwanF-86_Keng/story021.htm.
Marolda, Edward J. "Invasion Patrol: The Seventh Fleet in Chinese Waters." Naval History and Heritage Command. Accessed December 13, 2010. http://www.history.navy.mil/colloquia/cch3c.htm.
McCurley, Robert. "USS *Fletcher* DDE-445 Chronology 1952." USS *Fletcher* Home Page. Accessed December 13, 2010. http://www.ussfletcher.org/history/1952.html.
The National Association of Destroyer Veterans. "*USS Boyd* DD-544." Accessed October 16, 2014. http://www.destroyers.org/uss-boyd/history/start/43_58_boyd_history.htm.
Naval Historical Center. "Patrol Squadron (VP) Histories; VP-1 to VP-153." Chap. 3 in *Dictionary of American Naval Aviation Squadrons*, vol. 2. Washington, DC: Naval Historical Center, Department of the Navy, 2000. Accessed December 13, 2010. http://www.history.navy.mil/avh-vol2/chap3-1.pdf.
The Nuclear Information Project. "USS *Randolph* and the Nuclear Diplomatic Incident." December 20, 2006. http://www.nukestrat.com/dk/randolph.htm.
Osenton, Jim, ed. "USS *Manatee* (AO-58)." Unofficial USS *Manatee* Homepage. Accessed December 13, 2010. http://www.ussmanatee.org/mohhist.htm.
Schnabel, James F. "The Relief of MacArthur." Chap. 20 in *Policy and Direction: The First Year*. Washington, DC: U.S. Army Center of Military History, 1992. Accessed March 14, 2011. http://www.history.army.mil/books/pd-c-20.htm.
Simonton, Ben. "Leadership in Frustration, a Sea Story." *Gather*. June 3, 2006. Accessed December 13, 2010. http://webcache.googleusercontent.com/search?q=cache:VUwGylXk-J0J:www.gather.com/viewArticle.action%3FarticleId=281474976757231+&cd=2&hl=en&ct=clnk&gl=us&client=firefox-a .
TaiwanAirPower.org. "ROCAF F-104 Retirement." Last updated August 24, 2005. Accessed December 15, 2010. http://www.taiwanairpower.org/history/f104ret.html.
U.S. Navy Patrol Squadrons. "VP-28 History." Accessed December 13, 2010. http://www.vpnavy.com/vp28_history.html.
USS Orleck Association. "*USS Orleck* Chronology." Accessed October 23, 2014. http://www.ussorleck.com/uss-orleck-chronology/.
USSWiltsie.org. "USS *Wiltsie* DD-716." Accessed October 23, 2014. http://www.destroyersonline.com/usndd/dd716/.
Voice of America. "Pentagon Reports Naval Incident in Yellow Sea." May 5, 2009. http://www.voanews.com/content/a-13-2009-05-05-voa24-68787162/359961.html.

Index

28 February Incident, 82, 115

A-bomb, 40, 41, 42, 43. *See also* nuclear weapons
Admiral Hardy, 54
Admiralty, Royal Navy, 17, 90
Aegis Cruisers, 131, 132
Afghanistan, 115, 144
air control, 75, 81
Aleutian Islands, 19
Alfred Holt and Co., 106
Amoy, 76. *See also* Xiamen
amphibious operations, 3, 21, 23, 35, 50, 60, 62, 80, 129
Amur River, 156, 157
Anderson, Admiral George, 37, 79
Anglo–American Relations, 47, 49, 51, 55, 96, 157
Anhui Army, 8
Anhui Province, 15
Annam. *See* Vietnam
Annapolis, 16, 136. *See also* U.S. Naval Academy
Ansel, Rear Admiral Walter (ret.), 77
antiship missiles, 129, 159. *See also* missiles
antisubmarine warfare, 36, 39–40, 62, 65, 79
Armitage, Richard, 136
artillery, 65, 94, 96, 97
artillery barrage, 97
artillery blockade, 94
Association of Southeast Asian Nations (ASEAN), 146
asymmetric warfare, 34, 123
Aurora, 16. *See also* Chongqing
Australia, 19, 66, 150, 154

B-29 Bomber, 40, 41
Barber, James, ix, 43, 109, 110

baseball, 81
Battle Act, 52
Battle, Laurie C., 52
Beijing, 3, 4, 6, 7, 8, 9, 15, 17, 59, 104, 112, 113, 114, 124, 125, 157
Beijing Massacre, 126. *See also* Tiananmen Massacre
Belgium, 79
Bennington (CVA 20), 65
Berlin Wall, 115, 158
Beshany, Vice Admiral Philip, 79, 111, 151
Bhutan, 144
Bien, Admiral Lyle, ix, 132, 159
Blair, Admiral Dennis C., 136
blockade, 8, 16–18, 20, 21, 22, 29, 47, 49–52, 53–55, 59, 61, 62, 63, 68, 75, 76, 89, 90–93, 94, 96–97, 98, 129, 132, 133, 152–153
Bo Hai Gulf, 17, 20, 21, 50
Board of Trade (UK), 106
Bombay, 52
Boxer (CV 21), 62
Boyd (DD 544), 65
Brezhnev, Leonid, 114
British Chamber of Shipping, 106
Brunei, 138, 142–143
Brush (DD 745), 25
Buchanan (DDG 14), 40
Bucklew, Captain Phil, 80
buffer patrol, 10, 13, 29, 60, 133, 149, 151, 158. *See also* trip wire strategy
Burke, Admiral Arleigh 37, 68, 69, 77

C-130 Cargo Plane, 111, 142
C-46 Cargo Plane, 53–54
Cai Xihong, 144
Cairo Agreement, xi
Callaghan (DDF 994), 159
Cambodia, 92

Index

Canada, 79, 99
Canton, 4, 5, 76. *See also* Guangzhou
Cao Bai, 141
Carney, Admiral Robert B., 41, 78
Carpenter (DDE 825), 65
Carter, Jimmy, 112, 114, 150, 157, 158
Central Intelligence Agency (CIA), 53, 80
Changchun, 15
Changsha, 15
Chen Shui-bian, 123, 127, 142, 143
Cheng Ch'eng-kung, xi. *See also* Zheng Chenggong
Cheng Wei-yuan, 143
Chiang Ching-kuo, 65, 103, 122, 123, 127
Chiang Kai-shek, xi, 14, 15, 17, 23, 25, 30, 31, 59, 60, 61, 62, 63, 64, 65, 67, 68, 69, 70, 79, 81, 82, 84, 85, 91, 93, 94, 96, 97, 105, 113, 122, 150, 151, 154
China xi, 13, 14, 15, 17, 19, 20, 21, 22, 23, 29, 30, 34, 35, 36, 41, 42, 43, 48, 49, 50, 51, 54, 55, 56n23, 60, 61, 63, 65, 66, 67, 68, 69, 75, 76, 81, 83, 84, 85, 86, 89, 91, 92, 93, 94, 98, 99, 104, 105, 111, 113, 119, 122, 124, 125, 126, 127, 128, 140, 141, 149, 150, 151, 156, 157 : Civil War, 14, 15, 21, 140, 154, 156 : offshore islands, xi, xii, 2, 4, 13, 14, 16, 18, 20–22, 23, 24, 41, 59, 60, 62, 63, 65, 66–67, 68, 69, 70, 75, 76, 77, 78, 80, 81, 85, 92, 93, 96, 97, 99, 104, 105, 106, 138, 150, 151, 156: opening diplomatic relations with the United States, 10, 93, 94, 103, 104, 111, 112, 114, 115, 130, 135, 137, 157, 158: relations with the Soviet Union, 41, 42, 49, 55, 92, 94, 96, 97, 98, 103, 104, 112, 123, 149, 153, 156 : relations with the United States, 10, 93, 94, 103, 104, 111, 112, 114, 115, 130, 135, 137, 157, 158: strategic embargo, xi, 5, 13, 14, 17, 29, 47, 48, 49, 51, 52, 53, 54, 55, 56n23, 62, 89, 90, 95, 96, 98, 103, 108, 113, 123, 149, 152, 153, 155
China Can Still Say No, 135–136
China Committee (CHINCOM), 52
Chinese Communist (CHINCOM), 113

Chinese Communist Party (CCP), xi, 13, 14, 15, 17, 19, 20, 21, 22, 23, 29, 30, 34, 35, 36, 41, 42, 43, 48, 49, 50, 51, 54, 55, 56n23, 60, 61, 63, 65, 66, 67, 68, 69, 75, 76, 81, 83, 84, 85, 86, 89, 91, 92, 93, 94, 98, 99, 104, 105, 111, 113, 119, 122, 124, 125, 126, 127, 128, 140, 141, 149, 150, 151, 156, 157
Ching Chuan Kang (CCK) Airbase, 111
Chongqing, 15, 16
Christopher, Warren, 132
Chung-Hoon (DDG 93), 137, 146, 159
Churchill, Winston, 66, 67, 81, 84, 85
Civil War in China, 14, 15, 21, 140, 154, 156
Clark, Admiral Joseph J. "Jocko," 63
Clark Air Base, 46n57
Cold War, 3, 13, 19, 23, 25, 68, 98, 111, 119, 129, 145, 150, 157, 158
Combat Information Center (CIC), 43, 109
Commander-in-Chief, 31
Commander in Chief Far Eastern Squadron Afloat, 17
Commander in Chief, U.S. Pacific Command (CinCPac), 41, 63, 77, 112, 131, 136, 137
Commander in Chief, Pacific Fleet (CinCPacFleet), 63
Commander of the Seventh Fleet, 21, 30, 36, 61
Commander U.S. Naval Forces, Far East, 30
Commission on the Limit of the Continental Shelf, 146
convoy operations, 68, 93, 94, 95
Cooke, Admiral Charles M., Jr., 21–22
Coordinating Committee for Multilateral Export Controls (COCOM), 29, 52
Cornell University, 122, 128
corruption, 82, 83, 122, 124
Cowell (DD 547), 31–32
Cross-Straits Economic Cooperation Framework Agreement, 144
Cruise, Rear Admiral Edgar A., 36
Cultural Revolution, 103, 120, 126
Cushing (DD 797), 32
Czechoslovakia, 66

Dachen Islands, 20, 23, 53, 59, 62, 63–66, 68, 69, 70, 84, 85, 132
Dalian, 16, 49, 50
democracy, 1, 10, 19, 82, 83, 86, 119, 120, 121, 122, 123, 124, 125, 126, 127, 128, 130, 141, 160
Deng Xiaoping, 114, 115, 120, 121, 122, 124, 125, 126, 127, 128, 158
Denmark, 79
Dennis J. Buckley (DDR 808), 32
Department of Defense, 80, 157
Department of State, 77, 113, 136, 137, 157
Destroyer Escorts (DE), 16, 113
Destroyer Radar Picket Escort (DER), 32, 109
DF-15 missile, 129
Diaoyu Islands 6, 135, 139, 143, 144. *See also* Senkaku Islands
Dien Bien Phu, 40
Dobrynin, Anatoly, 105
Dongshan Island, 61–62, 129
Doyle, Vice Admiral Austin K., 42
Dulles, John Foster, ix, 23, 41–42, 59, 61, 64, 67, 68–70, 85, 96–97, 98, 99, 151, 153, 157
Dutch, xi, 2, 3, 10, 136, 153
Dutch East Indies 2

EA-6B Prowlers, 37
East Asia, 19, 25, 49, 87, 127, 139, 150, 155, 158, 160
East China Sea, 135
East Germany, 144
East Indies, 2. *See also* Indonesia
Eastern Europe, 48, 55, 115, 149, 153
EC-121 electronic warfare aircraft, 111
economic miracle, 84, 127, 149, 156
Eisenhower, Dwight D., 23, 37, 41, 49, 60, 61, 62, 63, 65, 66, 67, 68, 77, 81, 84, 85, 101n46, 153
embargo. *See* strategic embargo
England. *See* United Kingdom
English Channel, 19
EP-3 Incident, 135, 136–137, 146, 159
EP-3E Airborne Reconnaissance Integrated Electronic System (ARIES), 39
Europe, 4, 5, 7, 49, 51, 55, 97

Exclusive Economic Zone (EEZ), 135

F-100 Fighter, 111
F-104 Fighter, 79
F-5A Fighter, 111
F-5E Fighter, 111
F-84G Fighter, 79
F-86F Fighter, 79
face : losing, 67, 69, 99, 159: giving, 117n42, 113, 137
Far East, 20, 30, 35, 39, 41, 50, 78, 80, 84, 113
Felt, Admiral Harry, 41, 42, 77, 79, 80
First Island Chain, 9, 150
First Lord of the Admiralty, 90
First Opium War, 4, 5
First Sino–Japanese War, xi, 8
First Taiwan Strait Crisis, 10, 41, 43, 55, 67, 69, 75, 86, 89, 90, 132, 150
Five-Antis Campaign, 89
Fleet's Finest, 37. *See also* Patrol Squadron 1
fleet-on-fleet battle, 86
Foochow. *See* Fuzhou
Formosa. *See* Taiwan
Formosa Patrol Force. *See* Taiwan Patrol Force
Formosa Patrol. *See* Taiwan Patrol Force
Formosa Resolution, 66, 70, 85
Formosa Strait Force. *See* Taiwan Patrol Force
Formosa Straits Patrol (UK), 90
Fourth Taiwan Strait Crisis, 10, 120, 128–131, 135
France, 7, 8, 9, 114, 139, 140, 141, 145
Frankel, Rear Admiral Samuel, 63
Franklin, A. E., 47
Freeman, Charles W. "Chas," Jr., 130
Fujian Province, xii, 3, 17, 22, 60, 65, 75, 82, 121, 156
Fuzhou, 8, 23, 54, 60

Gallup Poll, 60, 66
General Agreement on Tariff and Trade (GATT), 155
Germany, 1, 9, 19, 97, 144–145
giving face. *See* face, giving
Gorbachev, Mikhail, 115, 124, 125

Grand Canal, 4, 5, 8
Great Famine, 90, 96, 98, 99, 104
Great Leap Forward, 89–90, 94, 96, 97, 98, 104, 120, 153
Greece, 52
Green Island, 138
Greenwich Time, 109
Grey Knights, 36. *See also* Patrol Squadron, 46
Guangdong Province, xii, 139
Guangzhou, 4, 15, 20, 21, 82. *See also* Canton
Guerrilla Parachute Command, 80
Guerrilla, 20, 51, 53–54, 60, 62, 63, 77

Hainan Island, 20, 21, 25, 39, 76, 110, 135, 137
Hainan Province, 142
Hancock (CVA 19), 65
Harriman, Averell, 40, 105
Hatfield, Doug, ix, 43
"Hawaiian Warriors," 36. *See also* Patrol Squadron 28
Hawk Missile, 105–106, 129
Helena (CA 75), 93
Henrico (APA 45), 64
Hissem (DE 400), 109, 110
Hoi Houw, 52–53
Hokkaido Island, 6, 19
Hong Kong, 5, 6, 8, 20, 32, 47, 48, 49, 50, 51, 52, 53, 54, 55, 81, 85, 90, 104, 108, 113, 121, 123, 124, 130, 152, 153, 155
Hopewell (DD 681), 93
Hoskins, Rear Admiral John M. "Peg-Leg," 36
Hu, Major Shih-Lin, 79
Huaihai Campaign, 15
Hunter-Killer (HUK), 36, 40

Iceland, 52
Impeccable (T-AGOS 23), 135, 137, 138, 146, 159
Imperial Germany, 19. *See also* Germany
Imperial Russia, 4, 96
imperialism, 96, 112
Inchon, 35
India, 48, 59, 62, 116n7, 154
Indian Ocean, 130

Indonesia, 2, 19, 85, 138, 142. *See also* Dutch East Indies
Independence (CV 62), 129, 131, 132, 158–159
Inner Mongolia, 138
Intelligence Division of the Admiralty, 17
Itu Aba, 140, 141, 142, 143

Jacobs-Larkcom, E. H., 83
Japan, xi, xii, 3, 4, 5, 6, 7, 8, 9, 10, 11n3, 14, 16, 19, 20, 30, 36, 41, 43, 44n5, 50, 52, 79, 81, 82, 83, 99, 127–128, 129, 130, 131, 135, 139, 140, 143, 146, 150–151, 154, 155, 156
jet aircraft, 20, 40, 54
Jiangsu Province, 15
Jinmen Island, xi, xii, 2, 21, 22, 23, 41, 59, 60, 61, 62, 63, 67, 68, 69, 76, 84, 85, 90, 92, 93, 94, 95, 96, 97, 99, 104, 128, 130, 131
Jinzhou, 15
Johnson, Secretary of Defense Louis, 30
Joint Chiefs of Staff (JCS), 41, 78
Juneau (CL 119), 30
junk fleet, 21, 22, 34–36, 105

kamikaze pilots, 126
kamikaze winds, xii
Kaohsiung, 25, 31, 32, 33, 40, 108, 130
Kaohsiung Incident, 123
KC-135 Tanker, 111
Keelung, 8, 25, 31, 33, 52, 82, 108, 130
Kennedy, John F., 104, 105
Khan, Kublai, 144
Khan, Yahya, 113
Khrushchev, Nikita, 96
Kilo submarines, 119
Kissinger, Henry, 103, 111, 112, 113
Kohl, Helmut, 145
Korea, 1, 8, 9, 10, 13, 14, 19, 20, 25, 29, 30, 31, 34, 35, 36, 40, 42, 43, 49, 51, 55, 59, 60, 61, 62, 63, 75, 76, 77, 96, 99, 130, 144, 149, 150, 152, 154, 155
Korean armistice, 59, 62, 63, 75
Korean Bay, 50
Korean junks, 35
Korean War, 1, 10, 13, 14, 19, 20, 25, 29, 30, 31, 34, 35, 36, 40, 42, 43, 49, 51,

59, 60, 61, 62, 63, 75, 76, 77, 96, 149, 152, 154
Koxinga, xi, 2–3. *See also* Zheng Chenggong
Kuomintang. *See* Nationalist Party
Kurile Islands, 6
Kuroshio current, xii

Lamock Island Group, 61
land redistribution program, 14–15, 83
Landing Ship, Tank (LST), 16, 64, 93
Lashmore, Commander M. E., 52–53
Lebanon Crisis, 92
Lee Teng-hui, 42, 122, 127, 128
Lema Island, 20
Lesser Orchid Island, 138
Lexington (CVA 16), 65
Li Hongzhang, 7, 9
Liao River, 17
Liaoning, 159
LIGHTNING Operation, 93
Liu Dacai, 140
Liverpool, 106
Lloyd, Selwyn, 20, 97, 157
losing face. *See* face, losing
Lüshun, 16, 39, 49, 50
Luzon, xii
Lynn, Lt. Colonel Frank W., 59

Ma Ying-jeou, 127
Macao, 6, 48, 50, 121
MacArthur, General Douglas, 30–31, 40–41
Macclesfield Bank, 139, 142
Macdonald, General John C., 65
Macmillan, Harold, 42, 157
Maddox (DD 731), 30
Malaya. *See* Malaysia
Malaysia, 19–20, 48, 85, 143
Manchuria, 8, 9, 14, 15, 16, 44n5, 49, 50, 51
Manchu, xi, 1, 2, 3, 4, 5
Mao Zedong, 1, 15, 41, 48, 59, 89, 92, 94, 96, 98, 104, 112, 113, 120, 122, 123, 153, 158
MARKET TIME, 108, 110
Marshall, General George C., 14
Marxism-Leninism, 17

Massachusetts Institute of Technology, 16
Matsu Island. *See* Mazu Island
Mazu Island, xii, 20, 22, 23, 41, 62, 67, 68, 84, 85, 97, 99, 104, 131
McConaughy, Walter P., 35, 113
Medicine, 52, 56n23
Mediterranean moor, 33
Medium Landing Ship (LSM), 16
Meiji Reforms, 9, 121, 156
Mendendorp, Lt. Colonel Alfred, 59
Menzies, Robert, 19, 66
Miao Islands, 17, 20
Micronesia, xii
Midway (CVA 41), 65, 114
MiG-15, 37
MiG-19, 79, 93
Military Assistance Advisory Group (MAAG), 76, 77, 80
Min River, 17
Ming Dynasty, xi, 1, 2–3, 6, 10, 15, 236
missiles, 42, 81, 86, 93, 105, 106, 107, 108, 119, 120, 128, 129, 130, 131–132, 133, 137, 159
Mongol, xii, 2, 4, 144
Mongolia 4, 138, 144
morale, 14, 23, 35, 64, 81, 84, 85, 86, 87, 90, 151
morale-building exercises, 14, 81, 84–86, 87, 90
Moscow, 114, 122
Motor Torpedo Boats (MTB), 39, 93, 108
Mukden, 15
Musick, Lt. Meredith, 111
Mutual Defense Assistance Control Act of 1951, 52. *See also* Battle Act
Mutual Defense Treaty (1954). *See* U.S.–ROC Mutual Defense Treaty (1954)
Myanmar, 144

Naha Air Force Base, 36–37
Nanjing, 14, 15
Nanpeng Island, 61
Nanri Island, 60
napalm, 35
Napoleon, 19
National Land Conference, 15

National People's Congress, 124
National Security Council (NSC), 41
Nationalist Air Force, 21, 35, 36, 54, 62, 80, 81, 86, 91, 93, 105
Nationalist Army, 15, 16, 23, 51, 55, 60, 61, 65, 70, 82, 84, 105, 106, 140, 151
Nationalist Navy, 1, 13, 14, 15, 16, 17, 18, 21, 22, 40, 47, 49, 51, 52, 53, 54, 55, 59, 62, 70, 75, 76, 77, 78, 79, 80, 81, 86, 89, 90, 91, 92, 93, 94, 96, 98, 113, 114, 132, 139, 149, 151, 152, 153
Nationalist Party, xi, 1, 10, 13, 14, 15, 16, 17, 18, 19, 20, 21, 22, 23, 25, 29, 30, 42, 43, 49, 52, 53, 54, 55, 59, 60, 61, 62, 63, 64, 66, 67, 68, 69, 75, 76, 77, 78, 79, 81, 82, 83, 84, 85, 86, 89, 90, 91, 92, 93, 94, 97, 99, 104, 105, 106, 111, 112, 113, 122, 123, 127, 140, 144, 145, 149, 150, 151, 152, 154, 156
NATO, 42, 51, 52, 115, 158
Natuna Islands, 138
natural gas, 139
naval demonstrations, 86, 93, 120
Navy Cross medal, 146
Nazis, 19
Nehru, Jawaharalal, 59, 62
Netherlands, the, 2
neutralization policy, 1, 10, 25, 29, 30, 31, 42, 44n5, 60, 61, 92, 132, 150, 151, 152, 158
New London, 79
New York Times, 40, 130
New Zealand, 61
Nike Hercules missile, 105–106, 129
Nimitz (CVN 68), 130, 131, 132, 158–159
nine-dash map, 140, 146
Nixon, Richard M., 104, 112, 113, 114, 149, 151, 157, 158
nonrecognition policy, 44n5
North Korea, 1, 25, 30, 36, 59, 144
North Sea Fleet, 39
North Vietnam, 103, 141. *See also* Vietnam
nuclear power plant, 154–155
nuclear submarine, 96
nuclear war, 112, 156, 157
nuclear weapons, 40, 41, 42, 43, 46n57, 93, 111, 130

O'Brien (DD 725), 108
O'Brien (DD 975), 132
Office of Naval Intelligence (ONI), 20, 22, 39, 54, 63, 70, 75–76, 81
offshore islands, xi, xii, 2, 4, 13, 14, 16, 18, 20–22, 23, 24, 41, 59, 60, 62, 63, 65, 66–67, 68, 69, 70, 75, 76, 77, 78, 80, 81, 85, 92, 93, 96, 97, 99, 104, 105, 106, 138, 150, 151, 156
Okinawa, 6, 7, 19, 20, 36, 37, 41, 131
Operation KING KONG, 64
Operation TAIWAN, 35
Orchid Island, 138
Outer Mongolia, 138
Oyashio current, xii

P4Y Privateers, 36
Pakistan, 113, 144, 180, 181
Paracel Islands, 139, 140, 141, 142, 143, 144, 146
patrol-bomber mariner (PBM), 36
Patrol Squadron One (VP-1), 37, 45n32
Patrol Squadron 28 (VP-28), 36
Patrol Squadron 46 (VP-46), 36–37
Pearl Harbor, xi
Penghu Islands, xi, xii, 2, 8, 9, 20, 22, 23, 30, 36, 41, 43, 61, 63, 65–66, 70, 80, 99, 113, 128, 138–139
People's Daily, 125
People's Liberation Army (PLA), xiii, 1, 15, 19, 21, 23, 25, 36, 59, 61, 62, 63, 76, 92, 99, 104, 108, 116n7, 125, 126, 128, 129, 143, 152, 157, 159
People's Liberation Army Air Force (PLAAF), 63–64, 79
People's Liberation Army Navy (PLAN), 23, 39, 48, 75, 76, 78, 86, 103, 108, 114, 119, 138, 141, 143, 158, 159
People's Republic of China (PRC). *See* China
Pescadore Islands, xi, 72n44. *See also* Penghu Islands
Petunia, 16
Pham Van Dong, 141, 148n18
Philippines, xii, 19, 46n57, 48, 81, 85, 138, 140, 142, 150, 159
piracy, 54
Poland, 66, 105, 144–145

Political Consultative Conference, 14, 15
Port Arthur, 16. *See also* Lüshun
Portugal, 6, 50
Potsdam Agreement, xi, 129, 130
Powell, Colin L., 136
Pratas Islands, 139, 143, 146
primitivism, 34
Princeton (CVS 37), 65
Pritchett (DD 561), 32
Prueher, Admiral Joseph, 131, 132, 136, 137, 159
Public Law 188, 78
Public Law 512, 16
Pueblo Incident, 110

Qing Dynasty, xi, 1, 2, 3, 4, 5, 6, 7, 8, 9, 21, 139, 155. *See also* Manchu
Qingdao, 17, 39, 50
Qinhuangdao, 17
Qiongzhou Strait, 21, 76, 84
Quemoy Island, xi. *See also* Jinmen Island

Radford, Admiral Arthur W., 63, 67, 68
Rankin, Karl L., 84
RC-135 Rivet Joint, 131
Reagan, Ronald, 115
Red River, 7, 8
Redman, Lon, 53
Republic of China (ROC). *See* Taiwan
Republic of Vietnam. *See* Vietnam
Research-and-Development (R&D), 37
Rest and Recreation (R&R), 81, 86, 108
Robertson, Walter S., 68, 106–107
Romanski, Paul, ix, 46n63
Royal Navy, 39, 52, 90, 92
RT-33, 79
rules of engagement (ROE), 39, 94
Rusk, Dean, 104, 151, 157
Russia, 4, 6, 7, 9, 48, 50–51, 90, 91, 96, 119, 122, 126, 138, 144, 150, 153. *See also* Soviet Union
Ryukyu 6, 7, 8, 9. *See also* Okinawa

Sa Zhenbing, 21, 139
sacrificial anode, 43
Saddle Islands, 20
Saint Paul (CA 73), 31

sanctions, 52, 53, 126, 127. *See also* strategic embargo
Sansha, 142, 144
Screaming Eagles. *See* VP-1
Sea Guerrilla Task Force, 62
Sea Line of Communication (SLOC), 25
Sea of Okhotsk, xii
Search-and-Rescue (SAR), 37
Second Taiwan Strait Crisis, xiii, 10, 42, 86, 87, 89, 90, 92–94, 95, 96, 97, 98, 99, 104, 112
Senate Internal Subcommittee, 91
Senkaku Islands, 6, 9, 135, 143, 144. *See also* Diaoyu Islands
Seventh Fleet, U.S. Navy, 1, 10, 21, 25, 29, 30, 31, 32, 36, 37, 40, 60, 61, 63, 64, 65, 81, 84, 93, 112, 149, 150, 152, 157
Shandong Province, 9
Shanghai, 15, 17, 35, 37, 39, 41, 43, 82
Shanghai Communiqué, 113–114
Shantou, 61, 68, 121
SHARK HUNT Exercises, 40, 114
Shenzhen, 121
Sherman, Admiral Forrest, 50
Shigemitsu, Mamoru, 20
Shih, Captain Bei-Puo, 79
Sidewinder missile, 80–81, 86, 93. *See also* missile
Sihanouk, Norodom, 92
Singapore, 48, 155
Sino–French Convention (1887), 141
Sino–French War (1884–1885), 7–8, 139
Sino–French Relations, xi, 7, 139, 141
Sino–Japanese Relations, xi, 6, 8, 9, 10, 11n3, 139. *See also* First Sino–Japanese War
Sino–Soviet Treaty (1924), 92
Sino–Soviet Agreement (1950), 41
Sino–Soviet Alliance, 42, 49, 97, 98, 149, 153
Sino–Soviet Monolith, 98, 112, 149, 153
Sino–Soviet Split, 55, 94, 96, 97, 98, 103, 104, 112, 123, 125, 149, 153, 156
Sino–Soviet Tensions, 94, 98, 112, 156
Sino–Soviet Trade, 55, 97–98, 149
Sino–U.S. Relations, 10, 93, 94, 103, 104, 111, 112, 114, 115, 130, 135, 137, 157, 158

Smoot, Admiral Roland N., 93, 94, 104
Socialist Transformation, 89
South China Sea, 110, 135, 137, 138, 139, 140, 141, 142, 143, 144, 146, 159
South Korea, 1, 19, 20, 25, 30, 139, 155
South Vietnam, 19, 20, 111, 108, 141. *See also* Vietnam
Southeast Asia, 19, 48, 87, 108, 146
Soviet Union, xi, 4, 6, 7, 9, 13, 14, 16, 17, 25, 39, 41, 42, 43, 48, 49, 50–51, 55, 59, 63, 69, 70, 76, 78, 83, 86, 89, 90, 91, 92, 94, 95, 96, 97, 98, 103, 104, 105, 111, 112, 114, 115, 119, 122, 123, 124, 125, 126, 128, 129, 130, 138, 144, 145, 149, 150, 152, 153, 156, 157, 158, 159: Cold War, 3, 13, 19, 23, 25, 68, 98, 111, 119, 129, 145, 150, 157, 158: fall of Berlin Wall, 115, 158: split with China, 55, 94, 96, 97, 98, 103, 104, 112, 123, 125, 149, 153, 156: trade with China, 55, 97–98, 149: Trans-Siberian Railway, 55, 89, 97, 149
Sovremenny destroyer, 119
Spain, 155
Spratly Islands, 135, 138, 139, 140, 141, 142, 143, 146
Stalin, Joseph, 48, 59, 96, 122, 130
stepping stone strategy, xi, 2, 23, 69, 84
Stevenson, Adlai, 61
strategic embargo, xi, 5, 13, 14, 17, 29, 47, 48, 49, 51, 52, 53, 54, 55, 56n23, 62, 89, 90, 95, 96, 98, 103, 108, 113, 123, 149, 152, 153, 155
Stroop, Admiral Paul D., 80
Struble, Vice Admiral Arthur Dewey, 30, 35
Stuart, John Leighton, 17
submarine, 16, 25, 35, 39, 40, 50, 51, 65, 79, 80, 81, 86, 96, 104, 119, 135, 137, 140, 159
super tanker, 109
Swarthmore College, 16
Swatow, 76. *See also* Shantou
Sweden, 52
Switzerland, 52

T-33, 79

Tachen Defense Command Advisory Team, 65
Taipei, 15, 54, 61, 80, 82, 83, 84, 90, 92, 115, 129, 140, 141, 151
Taiping Island. *See* Itu Aba
Taiwan, xi, xii, xiii, 1, 2, 8, 10, 13, 14, 19, 20, 21, 22, 25, 29, 30, 31, 32, 33, 34, 35, 36, 37, 38, 39, 41, 42, 43, 44n5, 51, 52, 53, 54, 54, 55, 59, 60, 61, 62, 63, 65, 67, 69, 70, 75, 76, 77, 78, 79, 80, 81, 84, 85, 86, 87, 89, 90, 92, 93, 94, 96, 97, 98, 99, 103, 104, 105, 106, 108, 109, 112, 113, 114, 115, 119–120, 127, 128, 129, 130, 131, 132, 133, 135, 136, 137, 138, 141, 143, 146, 149, 150, 151, 152, 154, 156, 157, 158, 159, 160: economic miracle, 84, 127, 149, 156: offshore islands, xi, xii, 2, 4, 13, 14, 16, 18, 20–22, 23, 24, 41, 59, 60, 62, 63, 65, : 66–67, 68, 69, 70, 75, 76, 77, 78, 80, 81, 85, 92, 93, 96, 97, 99, 104, 105, 106, 138, 150, 151, 156 : political reforms, 1, 10, 19, 82, 83, 86, 119, 120, 121, 122, 123, 124, 125, 126, 127, 128, 130, 141, 160, 180
Taiwan Patrol Force, 10, 13, 14, 21, 25, 29, 30, 31, 32, 33, 34, 35, 36, 37, 38, 42, 43, 44n5, 52, 53, 60, 62, 65, 70, 76, 77, 78, 79, 81, 84, 86, 87, 93, 99, 103, 104, 105, 108, 112, 113, 114, 115, 119–120, 130, 131, 132, 133, 136, 138, 149, 150, 151, 152, 156, 157, 158, 160
Taiwan Patrol Surface Force. *See* Taiwan Patrol Force
Taiwan Relations Act, 115, 123, 132
Taiwan Strait, xi, xii, xiii, 1, 2, 8, 10, 13, 14, 19, 21, 20, 22, 25, 29, 30, 31, 32, 33, 34, 35, 36, 37, 38, 39, 41, 42, 43, 51, 52, 53, 55, 59, 60, 62, 63, 65, 67, 69, 70, 75, 77, 80, 85, 86, 89, 90, 92, 93, 96, 97, 98, 103, 104, 105, 106, 108, 109, 112, 114, 119, 120, 128, 129, 130, 131, 132, 133, 135, 137, 138, 149, 150, 151, 152, 156, 157, 158, 159, 160
Taizhong, 111
Tajikistan, 144
Tamsui, 151
Tank Landing Ship. *See* Landing Ship, Tank (LST)

Index

Tannu Tuva. *See Tuva*
Tatan Island, 21
Taussig (DD 746), 62
Ten Major Projects, 154
Thackrey, Rear Admiral Lyman A., 35
Third Field Army, 76
Third Taiwan Strait Crisis, xiii, 10, 103, 104–105, 112, 133n3
Three-Antis Campaign, 89
Tianjin, 17
Tibet, 138
Ticonderoga (CVA 14), 65
Tortuga (LSD 26), 35
Trade and: strategic embargo, xi, 5, 13, 14, 17, 29, 47, 48, 49, 51, 52, 53, 54, 55, 56n23, 62, 89, 90, 95, 96, 98, 103, 108, 113, 123, 149, 152, 153, 155: tensions in Sino–Soviet relations, 94, 98, 112, 156
Trans-Siberian Railway, 55, 89, 97, 149
Treaty of Shimonoseki, xi, 9
trip wire strategy, 10, 29, 149
Truman, Harry S., 1, 14, 23, 25, 30, 31, 40, 65, 152
Tsushima current, xii
Tuapse, 90, 91
Turkey, 52
Tuva, 144
Twining, General Nathan F., 41–42
Two Chinas, 1, 13, 14, 18, 20, 25, 68–69, 149

U.S. Marine Corps, 36, 64
U.S. Maritime Shipping Association, 55
U.S. Naval Academy, 16
U.S. Navy, xiii, 10, 13, 14, 16, 21, 23, 25, 29, 30, 31, 32, 33, 34, 35, 36, 37, 38, 39, 40, 41, 42, 43, 44n5, 49, 51, 52, 53, 55, 59, 60, 62, 64, 65, 68, 70, 75, 76, 77, 78, 79, 80, 81, 84, 86, 87, 90, 93, 94, 96, 98, 99, 103, 104, 105, 108, 109, 110, 112, 113, 114, 115, 117n47, 119–120, 127, 130, 131, 132, 133, 135, 136, 137, 138, 149, 150, 151, 152, 156, 157, 158, 159, 160: blockade, 8, 16–18, 20, 21, 22, 29, 47, 49–52, 53–55, 59, 61, 62, 63, 68, 75, 76, 89, 90–93, 94, 96–97, 98, 129, 132, 133, 152–153: creation of Taiwan Patrol Force, 10, 13, 14, 21, 25, 29, 30, 31, 32, 33, 34, 35, 36, 37, 38, 42, 43, 44n5, 52, 53, 60, 62, 65, 70, 76, 77, 78, 79, 81, 84, 86, 87, 93, 99, 103, 104, 105, 108, 112, 113, 114, 115, 119–120, 130, 131, 132, 133, 136, 138, 149, 150, 151, 152, 156, 157, 158, 160: economic support for Taiwan, 84, 127, 149, 156: morale-building exercises, 14, 81, 84–86, 87, 90: training the Nationalist navy, 14, 16, 40, 55, 59, 62, 70, 75, 76–78, 79, 80, 81, 86, 90, 94, 98, 151: transferring naval equipment, 14, 16, 55, 62, 68, 75, 77, 78–79, 80, 81, 86, 96, 98, 114, 119, 151
U.S.–ROC Mutual Defense Treaty (1954), 66, 70, 75, 85, 105, 114
Union of Soviet Socialist Republics (USSR). *See* Soviet Union
United Kingdom, 2, 6, 16, 19, 20, 25, 44, 47, 48, 49, 51, 52, 55, 66, 92, 97, 100n7, 114, 145, 157
United Nations (UN), 25, 30, 114
United States, xi, xiii, 1, 3, 5, 10, 13, 14, 16, 17, 19, 20, 21, 23, 25, 29, 30, 31, 32, 33, 34, 35, 36, 37, 38, 39, 40, 41, 42, 43, 44n5, 47, 48, 49, 50, 51, 52, 53, 54, 55, 56n23, 59, 60, 61, 62, 63, 64, 65, 66, 67, 68, 70, 75, 76, 77, 78, 79, 80, 81, 82, 83, 84, 85, 86, 87, 89, 90, 91, 92, 93, 94, 95, 96, 97, 98, 99, 103, 104, 105, 108, 110, 111, 112, 113, 114, 115, 119–120, 123, 129, 130, 131, 132, 133, 135, 136, 137, 138, 145, 146, 149, 150, 151, 152, 153, 154, 155, 156, 157, 158, 159, 160: Cold War, 3, 13, 19, 23, 25, 68, 98, 111, 119, 129, 145, 150, 157, 158: creation of Taiwan Patrol Force, 10, 13, 14, 21, 25, 29, 30, 31, 32, 33, 34, 35, 36, 37, 38, 42, 43, 44n5, 52, 53, 60, 62, 65, 70, 76, 77, 78, 79, 81, 84, 86, 87, 93, 99, 103, 104, 105, 108, 112, 113, 114, 115, 119–120, 130, 131, 132, 133, 136, 138, 149, 150, 151, 152, 156, 157, 158, 160: relations with China, 10, 93, 94, 103, 104, 111, 112, 114, 115, 130, 135, 137, 157, 158: strategic embargo, xi, 5, 13, 14, 17, 29, 47, 48, 49, 51, 52, 53, 54, 55,

56n23, 62, 89, 90, 95, 96, 98, 103, 108, 113, 123, 149, 152, 153, 155
United States Taiwan Straits Patrol. *See* Taiwan Patrol Force
Ussuri River, 139, 157

Valley Forge (CV 45), 25, 36, 130
venturi, 32
vernier switch, 131, 150
Victorious (T-AGOS 19), 135, 137–138
Viet Cong, 108
Vietnam, 4, 7–8, 19, 20, 32, 40, 45n35, 99, 108, 110, 111, 123, 135, 138, 139, 141, 142, 143, 154, 157

Wan Shan Islands, 20
Warsaw, 105, 113
Wenchow. *See* Wenzhou
Wenzhou, 17, 68
Western, 1, 4, 5, 6, 7, 19, 48, 66, 92, 115, 121, 122, 126, 155, 157, 160
Western Enterprises, Incorporated (WEI), 53, 77, 80
Western Europe, 55
Western Pacific, 30, 37, 62, 67, 111
White Dog Island, 54
White House, 132
Wiltsie (DD 716), 40, 43
Wing Sang, 54

Wisecup, Admiral James P., ix, 159
Wood, Robert, 137
Woody Island, 144
World Bank, 126
World Trade Organization (WTO), 155
World War II, 1, 14, 16, 19, 35, 82, 114, 140, 114, 142, 146, 152
Wuchiu Island, 108, 131
Wuhan, 15

Xi'an, 15
Xiamen, 23, 92, 121. *See also* Amoy
Xinjiang, 4, 6, 7, 125, 138
Xisha, 141. *See also* Paracel Islands
Xuzhou, 15

Yangzi River, 4, 8, 15, 17, 18, 20, 21, 35, 43, 50
Yeh, George K. C., 68–69, 175
Yellow Sea, 137–138
Yijiangshan Island, 62, 63–64, 69, 70
Yokosuka, 35
Yuan Dynasty, 144
Yulin, 39

Zhejiang Province, xii, 65, 67
Zheng Chenggong, xi, 2
Zhou Enlai, 59, 92, 110n30, 141, 150
Zhoushan Islands, 20, 21

About the Author

Bruce A. Elleman was born on May 10, 1959, in Columbus, Ohio, completed Sanderson High School, in Raleigh, North Carolina (1977), received at UC Berkeley the Bachelor of Arts degree (1982), and completed at Columbia University the Master of Arts and Harriman Institute Certificate (1984), the Master of Philosophy (1987), the East Asian Certificate (1988), and the PhD (1993). In addition, he completed a Master of Sciences at London School of Economics (1985) and a Master of Arts in National Security and Strategic Studies (with distinction) at the US Naval War College (2004).

His publications include articles on the USSR's and China's secret diplomacy surrounding the Chinese Eastern Railway, Outer Mongolia, and the United Front policy, plus numerous books, including *Diplomacy and Deception: The Secret History of Sino–Soviet Diplomatic Relations, 1917–1927* (1997); *Mongolia in the Twentieth Century: Landlocked Cosmopolitan*, edited with Stephen Kotkin (1999); *Modern Chinese Warfare, 1795–1989* (2001); *Wilson and China: A Revised History of the 1919 Shandong Question* (2002); *Naval Mutinies of the Twentieth Century: An International Perspective*, edited with Christopher Bell (2003); *Naval Blockade and Seapower: Strategies and Counter-strategies, 1805–2005*, edited with S. C. M. Paine (2006); *Japanese-American Civilian Prisoner Exchanges and Detention Camps, 1941–45* (2006); *Waves of Hope: The US Navy's Response to the Tsunami in Northern Indonesia*, Newport Paper 28 (2007); *Naval Coalition Warfare: From the Napoleonic War to Operation Iraqi Freedom*, edited with S. C. M. Paine (2008); *Moscow and the Emergence of Communist Power in China, 1925–30: The Nanchang Uprising and the Birth of the Red Army* (2009); *Modern China: Continuity and Change 1644 to the Present*, coauthored with S. C. M. Paine (2010); *Manchurian Railways and the Opening of China: An International History*, edited with Stephen Kotkin (2010); *Piracy and Maritime Crime: Historical and Modern Case Studies*, Newport Paper 35, edited with Andrew Forbes and David Rosenberg (2010); *Nineteen Gun Salute: Case Studies of Operational, Strategic, and Diplomatic Naval Leadership during the 20th and Early 21st Centuries*, edited with John B. Hattendorf (2010); *Naval Power and Expeditionary Warfare: Peripheral Campaigns and New Theatres of Naval Warfare*, edited with S. C. M. Paine (2011); *People's Liberation Army Navy (PLAN) Combat Systems Technology, 1949–2010*, coauthored with James C. Bussert (2011); *High Sea's Buffer: The Taiwan Patrol Force, 1950–1979* (2012); *China as a Sea Power, 1127–1368: A Preliminary Survey of* the *Maritime Expansion and Naval Exploits of the Chinese People during the Southern Sung and Yuan Periods*, unpublished manuscript by Professor Jung-pang Lo, edited and with commentary by Bruce A. Elleman (2012); *Beijing's Power and China's Borders: Twenty Neighbors in Asia*, edited with Stephen Kotkin and Clive Schofield (2013); and *Commerce Raiding: Historical Case Studies, 1755–2009*, edited with S. C. M. Paine (2013).

Several of Dr. Elleman's books have been translated into foreign languages, including a Chinese translation of *Modern Chinese Warfare* as *Jindai Zhongguo de junshi yu zhanzheng* (2002), and a Czech translation of *Naval Mutinies of the Twentieth Century: An International Perspective* as *Námořní vzpoury ve dvacátém století : mezinárodní souvislosti* (2004).

Ongoing book projects related to China's international history include *International Competition in China, 1899–1991: The Rise, Fall, and Restoration of the Open Door Policy* (forthcoming).